MODERN
AMERICAN POETRY

· *1865–1950* ·

Twayne's Critical History of Poetry Series
AMERICAN LITERATURE

.

Kenneth E. Eble, Editor
University of Utah

MODERN AMERICAN POETRY

· 1865–1950 ·

ALAN SHUCARD
University of Wisconsin–Parkside

FRED MORAMARCO
San Diego State University

WILLIAM SULLIVAN
Keene State College

Twayne Publishers · Boston
A Division of G. K. Hall & Co.

Published by Twayne Publishers
A division of G. K. Hall & Co.
70 Lincoln Street
Boston, Massachusetts 02111

Copyediting supervised by Barbara Sutton.
Book design and production by Janet Z. Reynolds.
Typeset by Williams Press, Inc., Albany, New York.

Printed on permanent/durable acid-free paper
and bound in the United States of America.

Library of Congress Cataloging in Publication Data

Shucard, Alan, 1935–
   Modern American poetry, 1865–1950 / Alan Shucard, Fred Moramarco,
William Sullivan.
         p.   cm.—(Twayne's critical history of poetry series.
   American literature)
      Bibliography: p.
      Includes index.
      ISBN 0-8057-8451-9 (alk. paper)
      1. American poetry—20th century—History and criticism.
   2. American poetry—19th century—History and criticism.
   I. Moramarco, Fred S., 1938– . II. Sullivan, William J. (William
John), 1937– . III. Title. IV. Series.
   PS323.S5   1989
   811'.009—dc19
                                                               89-30570
                                                                  CIP

Dedicated to the memory of
KENNETH E. EBLE,
1923–1988

· *Contents* ·

· *Preface* ·

This book is the second in a three-volume study of American poetry. It is the middle leg of a journey of deep affection and curiosity that begins with the Puritans at the outset of volume 1 (*American Poetry: The Puritans through Walt Whitman*, 1988) and will end with a consideration of recent poets at the close of volume 3. *Affection* and *curiosity* are moderate, rational words that hint at our passion for the subject. Researching and writing the three books have taken a great deal of time and energy, but we have all relished the enterprise that has given us the chance to rethink what we know of the subject, to reexamine American poetry not just as an end in itself—though that is an amply worthy endeavor—but also as a reflection of American culture, to come to grips with what we have not realized, and to share our ideas with a wider community than the one provided us by our classes.

Volume 2 covers a long portion of the journey, picking up the trail after the death of Whitman. Obviously, the years 1865 and 1950 that bracket this middle portion in our title are useful but arbitrary, the way such dates usually are. They are not intended as definitive beginnings or endings of a poetic era but are roughly descriptive of the period in which our poetry continued to acquire a number of distinctive characteristics that we have come to recognize as "modern."

Alan Shucard, author of the first volume, maintains continuity, beginning this study with a thorough discussion of Emily Dickinson. He explores the personal and intellectual forces that shaped her determinedly independent work following new scholarship that postulates a clear, and highly personal, center of her poetry that eluded critics until the 1980s. Shucard then goes on to the second chapter, appropriately subtitled "A Tale of Paucity," in which he surveys the barren field of American poetry at the end of the nineteenth century and opening of the twentieth, and sees, but for Stephen Crane, few poets of much interest. The third chapter, also by Shucard, tells a very different story, for it covers

Edwin Arlington Robinson, Robert Frost, and Harlem Renaissance poetry in detail, as well as important women and midwestern poets, as the largely colorless fin-de-siècle poetry gave way to that of a searching, often daring new century.

Fred Moramarco extends the journey into the twentieth century with the next three chapters. His chapter 4 explains the emergence of modern poetry as its main body diverges from nineteenth-century romanticism. He notes the odd classicism of the modern, with its fragmentation and habit of yoking together disparate images, and its links with developments in the visual arts. The chapter stresses the preeminent contributions of women—including Gertrude Stein, Marianne Moore, H.D., and Amy Lowell—in defining that term *modern*. Moramarco goes on in chapter 5 to analyze the work and legacy of Ezra Pound and T. S. Eliot, Pound insisting on the recycling of the literature of the past and attempting in his *Cantos* to "make it new," Eliot redefining "tradition," insisting on impersonal poetry and seeming to write it, giving us the most conspicuous metaphor for modernity—the wasteland. Moramarco in chapter 6 examines the ways in which, while Pound and Eliot were attempting to connect American poetry to European and Oriental traditions, William Carlos Williams and Wallace Stevens undertook a more indigenous struggle for the primacy of the American poetic imagination. Both Stevens and Williams were firmly rooted in the physical world, but Stevens sought to transform that world through the imagination into an exotic "supreme fiction" that would rival the mythology of great religions. Williams, on the other hand, following the course that Walt Whitman had plotted, attempted to recreate "reality" plainly and clearly by imitating the cadences of American speech, the rawness of the American landscape, the unpredictability of American urban life. Moramarco's discussion of *Paterson* underscores Williams's linking of the modern human to the city, and the poet's creation of an epic alternative to Eliot's *The Waste Land* and Pound's fragmented *Cantos*.

The first of the final two chapters of this volume, by William Sullivan, begins with Hart Crane, E. E. Cummings, and Robinson Jeffers, who adopted, to a significant degree, the mystical vision of Whitman and the romantic themes of the nineteenth-century transcendentalists. They are grouped in chapter 7 as "The Visionary Company." In chapter 8, Sullivan examines the classical modernism of the Fugitive poets: John Crowe Ransom, Allen Tate, and Robert Penn Warren. He suggests that objectivists Charles Reznikoff, Louis Zukofsky, George Oppen, Carl Rakosi, and Lorine Niedecker, in their following of Pound's insistence on making it new and in their insistence on "sincerity," represent an interesting and innovative contrast to the Fugitives.

We all have people to thank, separately and together, for help with this volume. Alan Shucard is grateful to two colleagues: Professor William Shurr at the University of Tennessee, Knoxville, for paving the way for the chapter on Emily Dickinson with his important book, *The Marriage of Emily Dickinson*, and Professor Carl Lindner at the University of Wisconsin–Parkside for reading the first three chapters of this volume and making helpful suggestions. For their support, Shucard also thanks the Committee on Research and Creative Activity, the library, and the people at the University of Wisconsin–Parkside responsible for the sabbatical leave used to work on this book; Marcy Ricciardi for processing the manuscript of the first three chapters, and Millie Nutini, Trudy Rivest, and Marge Rowley, who helped with that eyeball-destroying task; and his wife, Maureen, for her intelligent patience.

Fred Moramarco expresses gratitude to Robert Pinsky and the participants in the 1986 National Endowment for the Humanities Summer Seminar on Modernism and Contemporary Poetry at Berkeley (Nell Altizer, Robin Behn, Betty Buchsbaum, Angela Estes, Michael Heller, Michael Novak, Jane Somerville, Jason Sommer, Rob Wilson, Gary Young, and David Zucker) for their stimulating discussions of twentieth-century poetry. They helped to shape some of Moramarco's ideas on the subject, especially in his chapter on Stevens and Williams. Moramarco is also grateful for the influence of work by Bonnie Costello (on Marianne Moore), Robert Hass and Marjorie Perloff (on Gertrude Stein), Janice Robinson (on H.D.), Ronald Bush (on Pound and Eliot), Leon Surette (on Pound), Peter Ackroyd (on Eliot), Paul Mariani, Dickran Tashjian, and Benjamin Sankey (on Williams), and Helen Vendler (on Stevens). He is particularly thankful to Steve Kowit for their many long talks about modern poetry. Finally, he is indebted to his two sons, Stephen and Nick, whose eager curiosity is always a great pleasure.

Preface

William Sullivan thanks the staffs at the Keene State College Library and at the New Poetry Archives at the University of California, San Diego, for their help with the research for the last two chapters and Joan Norcross, Judy Powers, Anne La Point, and his wife, Marilyn, for their help in the preparation of the manuscript.

We all acknowledge the contributions of our students, who, over more years than we care to confess, have listened to and helped to shape our interpretations and evaluations of American poets. In addition, we would all like to thank field editor Ken Eble, who—to the deep sorrow of everyone who knew him—died before the completion of this project, and Liz Traynor at Twayne Publishers for their perceptive editing. We were relieved to find that our writing styles are compatible; still, if no seams show, that happy result is partly due to the suggestions of those two redoubtable editors. For any seams that may show, and for any other flaws that may sully this book, we deserve and take the lumps.

Alan Shucard
University of Wisconsin–Parkside

Fred Moramarco
San Diego State University

William Sullivan
Keene State College

· *Acknowledgments* ·

Grateful acknowledgment is made to the following for permissions to use material as indicated:

Harvard University Press for quotations from Emily Dickinson's poems (J 324, J 303, J 1712, J 70, J 103, J 465, J 234, J 401, J 1703, J 1707, J 466, J 518, J 793, J 210, J 211, J 1591, and J 1129) and letters. Reprinted by permission of the publishers and the Trustees of Amherst College from the *Poems of Emily Dickinson*, ed. Thomas H. Johnson (Cambridge, Mass.: Belknap Press of Harvard University Press). Copyright 1951; ©1955, 1979, 1983 by the President and Fellows of Harvard College. Reprinted by permission of the publishers from *The Letters of Emily Dickinson*, ed. Thomas H. Johnson (Cambridge, Mass.: Belknap Press of Harvard University Press), © 1958, 1986 by the President and Fellows of Harvard College.

Little, Brown & Co. for quotations from Emily Dickinson's poems (J 1082, J 1703, and J 657) from *The Complete Poems of Emily Dickinson*, ed. Thomas H. Johnson. Copyright 1914, 1942 by Martha Dickinson Bianchi. Copyright 1929 by Martha Dickinson Bianchi; © renewed 1957 by Mary L. Hampson. Reprinted by permission of Little, Brown & Co.

Houghton Mifflin Co. for quotations from Emily Dickinson's poems (J 1072 and J 1251), from *The Complete Poems of Emily Dickinson*, ed. Thomas H. Johnson, Copyright 1890, 1891, 1896, by Roberts Brothers. Copyright 1914, 1918, 1919, 1924, 1929, 1930, 1932, 1935, 1937, 1942 by Martha Dickinson Bianchi. Copyright 1951; ©1955 by the President and Fellows of Harvard College. Copyright 1952 by Alfred Leete Hampson. © 1957, 1958, 1960 by Mary L. Hampson. Acknowledged, too, are the following: *Life and Letters of Emily Dickinson* by Martha Dickinson Bianchi. Copyright 1924 by Martha Dickinson Bianchi. Copyright renewed 1952 by Alfred Leete Hampson. Reprinted by permission of Houghton Mifflin Co. And *Emily Dickinson Face to Face* by Martha Dickinson Bianchi. Copyright 1932 by Martha Dickinson Bianchi;

Acknowledgments

© renewed 1960 by Alfred Leete Hampson. Reprinted by permission of Houghton Mifflin Co.

Dodd, Mead & Co. for quotation from *The Complete Poems of Paul Laurence Dunbar* (New York: Dodd, Mead & Co., 1955).

Alfred A. Knopf for quotations from *The Collected Poems of Stephen Crane*, ed. Wilson Follett (New York: Alfred A. Knopf, 1930).

Henry Holt & Co. for quotations from *Complete Poems of Robert Frost* (New York: Holt, Rinehart & Winston, 1964). Copyright 1916, 1921, 1923, 1928, 1930, 1934, 1939, 1943, 1945, 1947, 1949 by Holt, Rinehart & Winston, Copyright 1936, 1942, 1945, 1948 by Robert Frost. Copyright renewed 1944, 1951; ©1956, 1958, 1962 by Robert Frost; © renewed 1964 by Leslie Frost Ballantine.

Alfred A. Knopf for quotation from Langston Hughes's "The Weary Blues" from *The Selected Poems of Langston Hughes* (New York: Alfred A. Knopf, 1969), ©1959.

Alfred A. Knopf for lines from John Crowe Ransom, "Necrological" and "Bells for John Whiteside's Daughter," in John Crowe Ransom, *Selected Poems* (New York: Alfred A. Knopf, 1963).

Ann Ridgeway McDonald for quotations from Robinson Jeffers, "Letter to George West" and "Letter to Mark Van Doren and James Rorty," in *The Selected Letters of Robinson Jeffers*, ed. Ann N. Ridgeway (Baltimore: Johns Hopkins Press, 1968).

Black Sparrow Press for lines from Charles Reznikoff, "Suburban River: Summer." Copyright © by Charles Reznikoff; Reprinted from *Poems 1918–1936* with the permission of Black Sparrow Press: For lines from *Holocaust* © 1975 by Charles Reznikoff; The material here is reprinted with the permission of Black Sparrow Press.

Farrar, Straus & Giroux for excerpts from "Mr. Pope," "Last Days of Alice," "Aeneas at Washington," and "Ode to the Confederate Dead," in Allen Tate, *Collected Poems 1919–1976*. Copyright 1952, 1953; © 1970, 1977 by Allen Tate. Copyright 1931, 1932, 1937, 1948 by Charles Scribner's Sons; © renewed 1959, 1960, 1965 by Allen Tate. Reprinted by permission of Farrar, Straus & Giroux.

Harcourt Brace Jovanovich for lines from E. E. Cummings, "all worlds have halfsight, seeing either with." © 1958 by e. e. cummings, Reprinted from his volume *73 Poems* by permission of Harcourt Brace Jovanovich.

Acknowledgments

The Jargon Society for lines from Lorine Niedecker, "Mother Goose," "My Friend Tree," "We Know Him—Law and Order League," "What Horror to Awake at Night," and "In the Great Showfall Before the Bomb," in Lorine Niedecker, *This Condensary: The Complete Writing of Lorine Niedecker*, ed. Robert J. Bertholf (Winston Salem: The Jargon Society, 1985).

Liveright Publishing Corp. for lines from *Hart Crane, The Complete Poems and Selected Letters and Prose*, ed. Brom Weber (New York: Liveright Publishing Corp., 1966). The lines from "i like my body when it is with your" are reprinted from E. E. Cummings, *Tulips and Chimneys*, ed. George James Firmage. Reprinted by permission of Liveright Publishing Corp. Copyright 1923, 1925; renewed 1951, 1953 by E. E. Cummings. © 1973, 1976 by the Trustees for the E. E. Cummings Trust. © 1973, 1976 by George James Firmage.

The lines from "POEM, OR BEAUTY HURTS MR. VINAL," "next to of course god america i," and "my sweet old etcetera" are reprinted from *Is 5* poems by E. E. Cummings, ed. George James Firmage. Reprinted by permission of Liveright Publishing Corp. © 1985 by E. E. Cummings Trust. Copyright 1926 by Horace Liveright. Copyright 1954 by E. E. Cummings. © 1985 by George James Firmage.

The lines from "i sing of Olaf glad and big" and "if there are any heavens my mother will (all by herself) have" are reprinted from *ViVa*, poems by E. E. Cummings, ed. George James Firmage. Reprinted by permission of Liveright Publishing Corp. Copyright 1931, © 1959 by E. E. Cummings. © 1973, 1979 by the Trustees for the E. E. Cummings Trust. © 1973, 1979 by George James Firmage.

The lines from "kumrads die because they're told)" are reprinted from E. E. Cummings, *No Thanks*, ed. George James Firmage. Reprinted by permission of Liveright Publishing Corp. Copyright 1935 by E. E. Cummings. © 1968 by Marion Morehouse Cummings. © 1973, 1978 by the Trustees for the E. E. Cummings Trust. © 1973, 1978 by George James Firmage.

The lines from Robinson Jeffers, *The Double Axe* in *The Double Axe and Other Poems* (Liveright Publishing Corp., 1977).

New Directions Publishing Corp. for lines from George Oppen, "Drawing," "Psalm," and "Ballad," in *Collected Poems* (New York: New Directions Books, 1975). Copyright 1934 by the Objectivist

Press; © 1960, 1961, 1962, 1963, 1964, 1965, 1967, 1968, 1972, 1974 by George Oppen; © 1975 by George Oppen. Reprinted by permission of New Directions Publishing Corp.

Professor Brom Weber for quotations from *The Letters of Hart Crane*, ed. Brom Weber (Berkeley: University of California Press, 1965). Copyright 1952 by Brom Weber; reprinted with his permission.

Carl Rakosi for lines from "And What Were Poets Doing Then" and "The Street" in *The Collected Poems of Carl Rakosi* (Orono: National Poetry Foundation, 1986).

Random House for lines from Robinson Jeffers, "The Beginning and the End," in *The Beginning and the End and Other Poems* (New York: Random House, 1963), and lines from "Shine Perishing Republic," "The Rock & the Hawk," "Wild Swan," and "Purse-Seine," in *The Selected Poetry* (New York: Random House, 1938); lines from Robert Penn Warren, "Infant Boy at Mid Century" and "Three Darknesses," in *New & Selected Poems: 1923–1985* (New York: Random House, 1985).

W. W. Norton & Co. for lines from Louis Zukofsky, "Poem Beginning The," "To My Wash Stand," and "Mantis," in *All: The Collected Short Poems, 1923–1964* (New York: W. W. Norton & Co., 1971).

H. D. (Hilda Doolittle): Excerpts from *Selected Poems* by Hilda Doolittle, copyright 1925, 1953, © 1957 by Norman Holmes Pearson. Excerpts from *Helen in Egypt* © 1961 by Norman Holmes Pearson. Reprinted by permission of New Directions Publishing Corporation.

T. S. Eliot: Excerpts from *The Love Song of J. Alfred Prufrock* and *The Waste Land* in *Collected Poems 1909–1962* by T. S. Eliot, copyright 1936 by Harcourt Brace Jovanovich, Inc.; © 1963, 1964 by T. S. Eliot. Reprinted by permission of the publisher. Excerpts from "Burnt Norton," "East Coker," "Little Gidding," and "The Dry Salvages" in *Four Quartets*, copyright 1943 by T. S. Eliot; renewed 1971 by Esme Valerie Eliot. Reprinted by permission of Harcourt Brace Jovanovich, Inc.

Amy Lowell: Excerpts from "The Basket" and "Patterns" from *The Complete Poetical Works of Amy Lowell*, © 1955 by Houghton Mifflin Company; renewed 1983 by Houghton Mifflin Company, Brinton P. Roberts, Esquire, and G. D'Andelot Belin, Esquire. Reprinted by permission of Houghton Mifflin Company.

Acknowledgments

Marianne Moore: Excerpts from *The Marianne Moore Reader* © 1959 by Marianne Moore. Reprinted by permission of The Viking Press, Inc.

Ezra Pound: Excerpts from *The Cantos*, copyright 1934, 1937, 1940, 1948 by Ezra Pound. Excerpts from *Personae*, copyright 1926 by Ezra Pound. Reprinted by permission of New Directions Publishing Corporation.

Gertrude Stein: Excerpts from "New" in *Bee Time Vine and Other Pieces by Gertrude Stein*, copyright 1953 by Alice B. Toklas. Reprinted by permission of Yale University Press.

Wallace Stevens: Excerpts from *The Palm at the End of the Mind* by Wallace Stevens, © 1967, 1969, 1971 by Holly Stevens. Reprinted by permission of Alfred A. Knopf, Inc.

William Carlos Williams: Excerpts from *Selected Poems*, copyright 1949 by William Carlos Williams. Excerpts from *Paterson*, copyright by William Carlos Williams. Reprinted by permission of New Directions Publishing Corporation.

· *Chronology* ·

1862 Emily Dickinson writes 366 poems; sends a letter to literary lion Thomas Wentworth Higginson asking if her poems have literary merit.

1895 Stephen Crane, *Black Riders and Other Lines.*

1897 E. A. Robinson, *The Children of the Night.*

1909 Ezra Pound's *Personae* published in London.

1912 *Poetry* Magazine established in Chicago.
Robinson Jeffers, *Flagons and Apples.*

1913 Robert Frost publishes *A Boy's Will* in London.
The Armory Show in New York exhibits new European art.
Ezra Pound and F. S. Flint formulate principles of imagism.

1914 Robert Frost, *North of Boston.*
Gertrude Stein, *Tender Buttons.*

1915 Edgar Lee Masters, *Spoon River Anthology.*

1916 Carl Sandburg, *Chicago Poems.*
Ezra Pound defines vorticism.
E. A. Robinson, *The Man Against the Sky: A Book of Poems.*

1917 Amy Lowell, *Tendencies in American Poetry.*
T. S. Eliot, *Prufrock and Other Observations.*

1918 Charles Reznikoff, *Rhythms.*

1919 T. S. Eliot publishes "Tradition and the Individual Talent," an essay defining the new modern poetry.

1920 Ezra Pound, *Hugh Selwyn Mauberley, Life and Contacts.*

1921 Marianne Moore, *Poems.*

1922 E. A. Robinson, *Collected Poems.*
T. S. Eliot, *The Waste Land.*
The *Fugitive*, a classical modernist literary magazine, published in Nashville.

1923 Jean Toomer, *Cane.*
Wallace Stevens, *Harmonium.*
William Carlos Williams, *Spring and All.*
E. E. Cummings, *Tulips and Chimneys.*

1924 T. E. Hulme, a British poet and critic, publishes the influential essay, "Romanticism and Classicism."
Robinson Jeffers, *Tamar.*

1925 Flowering of the Harlem Renaissance.
Ezra Pound publishes the first book-length section of *The Cantos.*
Robinson Jeffers, *Roan Stallion* and *The Tower beyond Tragedy.*

1926 Langston Hughes, *The Weary Blues.*
Hart Crane, *White Buildings.*
E. E. Cummings, *Is 5*

1927 Countee Cullen, *Caroling Dusk, An Anthology of Verse by Negro Poets.*

1930 Hart Crane, *The Bridge.*
I'll Take My Stand, a literary manifesto of southern writers and critics.

1931 Louis Zukofsky announces the objectivist movement in *Poetry* magazine.

1934 Ezra Pound, *The ABC of Reading.*
William Carlos Williams, *Collected Poems 1921–1931.*
George Oppen, *Discrete Series.*

1936 Wallace Stevens, *Ideas of Order.*

1937 Wallace Stevens, *The Man with the Blue Guitar.*

1938 E. E. Cummings. *Collected Poems.*
Cleanth Brooks and Robert Penn Warren, *Understanding Poetry.*

1941 John Crowe Ransom, *New Criticism.*
Carl Rakosi, *Selected Poems.*

1943 T. S. Eliot, *The Four Quartets.*

1945 Ezra Pound imprisoned in Pisa; writes *The Pisan Cantos.*
Pound taken to St. Elizabeth's Hospital, Washington, D.C., where he is institutionalized for the next twelve years.
John Crowe Ransom, *Selected Poems,* 1945. Revised 1963, 1969.

Chronology

1946 William Carlos Williams publishes first book of *Paterson*.

1948 Robinson Jeffers, *The Double Axe*.

1950 Wallace Stevens, *The Auroras of Autumn*.

1953 Publication of *The Poems of Emily Dickinson*, edited by T. H. Johnson and T. Ward.
E. E. Cummings, *six non lectures*.
Robert Penn Warren, *Brother to Dragons*.

1954 *The Collected Poems of Wallace Stevens*.

1957 Robert Penn Warren, *Promises*.
Wallace Stevens, *Opus Posthumous*.

1959 E. E. Cummings, *95 Poems*.

1960 Robert Frost reads poetry at John F. Kennedy's inauguration.

1961 H.D., *Helen in Egypt*

1962 William Carlos Williams, *Pictures from Brueghel*.

1963 E. E. Cummings, *73 Poems*.
Robinson Jeffers, *The Beginning and the End*.

1965 Louis Zukofsky, *All: The Collected Short Poems*.

1966 *The Collected Earlier Poems of William Carlos Williams*.

1967 Marianne Moore, *Complete Poems*.
The Collected Later Poems of William Carlos Williams.

1969 Robert Penn Warren, *Audubon: a vision*.
The Poetry of Robert Frost.

1970 Alan Tate, *The Swimmers and Other Selected Poems*.
The complete edition of *The Cantos of Ezra Pound*.

1971 Wallace Stevens, *The Palm at the End of the Mind*.

1972 E. E. Cummings, *Complete Poems, 1913–1962*.

1975 Charles Reznikoff, *Holocaust*.

1978 Louis Zukofsky, *A*.

1981 Discovery of Emily Dickinson's manuscript books or fascicles.

1985 Lorine Niedecker, *From this Condensary: The Complete Writings*.

· ONE ·

Emily Dickinson and the
Two Modes of Romanticism:
Repelling Attacks on the Self

Title divine—is mine!
The Wife—without the Sign!
Acute Degree—conferred on me—
Empress of Calvary!

—Emily Dickinson, J 1072[1]

Because consistency can be expected of romantic poets no more than of other human beings, because not just Whitman but all of them were complicated enough to "contain multitudes," the romantics can be categorized only tentatively, only for convenience, and only with proper provisos. That understood, it is possible to postulate two modes of romanticism: a lighter, extroverted one and a gloomier, introverted one[2]—with considerable overlapping of each other, sometimes in a shared mysticism.

The first, more lucent manner is that represented by such figures as Wordsworth in Britain and his spiritual American cousins, Bryant and Emerson, Whitman, and the other Transcendentalists. Their tendency is to resolve positively the age-old tension between internal being and external world (in Christian terms, between the parishioner and God, with the clergy making and enforcing the rules and Christ's sacrifice having made reconciliation with God— that is, the reacquisition of God's grace—possible). For the Transcendentalists, for example, God has become nature (or some equivalent entity with such a name as the Over-Soul), and they conceive of no essential impediment to the individual's reconciliation with that Other once he tunes in to the frequencies of the universe and recognizes that he and it are one. Christ may be useful as a model of human behavior but is unnecessary as an intercessor for the restoration of grace, since the person is and always has been inseparable from the All, though too few people are aware of the joyous oneness. For obvious reasons, priests, too, are unnecessary, even counterproductive, although true poets, who have an understanding of the loving and inextricable relationship between the person and the rest of the cosmos, can serve to lead others to self-reliance and unity with the All.

The gladder romantic poets are not inured to the fear and ravages of death, but, as in Whitman's elegies and "Out of the Cradle Endlessly Rocking," they more than make their peace with it; they light it up with their optimism until it becomes an essential and welcome part of the life cycle. Emerson insists in "Terminus" (1867) that he obeys the same voice in the eve of his life that he heeded in his prime, and that voice tells him, now as always, to "banish fear" of death, for "The port, well worth the cruise, is near, / And every wave is charmed." And Whitman, having been birthed from the sea in the ecstasy of knowledge of death decades before in "Out of the Cradle," at the close of his life, bids good-bye to the companion of his lifetime, his Fancy—the power of creative imagination that obviates the need for Savior and priest among modern men; cavalierly, he implies that if there is an afterlife, it will be of interest to him only if he and his Fancy can remain boon companions there: "If we go anywhere we'll go together to meet what happens, / Maybe we'll be better off and blither, and learn something." Even more, it is even possible that death is the work of Fancy itself: "May-be it is you the mortal knob really undoing, turning." ("Good-Bye My Fancy," 1891).

Emily Dickinson (1830–86) may appear to be that optimistic, even ecstatic kind of romantic. Her intuitive certainty of a divine Other, of God, seems similar enough to Emerson's confident belief in an Over-Soul. Though she has seen neither moor nor sea, she says, she has no doubt of how heather looks or what a wave is, and while no more has she seen God, yet she is just as sure of where He dwells "As if the Checks [railroad tickets or perhaps map coordinates] were given—" (J 1052). She is capable of writing witty little riddle poems that capture with relish the essences of natural or human phenomena—a steam locomotive, for example (J 585), or a garden snake (J 986), or a hummingbird (J 1463), the last verse a whimsical tour de force that represents the hum-mingbird as "a revolving Wheel" flying "A Route of Evanescence," to deliver "The mail from Tunis, probably, / An easy Morning's Ride—." And there are poems that attest to her unorthodox, at times almost transcendental, faith in a personal God who can be approached directly and pertly through nature instead of supplicatingly through rigid churchly rigmarole; when God is thus approachable, she can be certain of her personal salvation. A well-known example is J 324, in which she boasts, "Some keep the Sabbath going to Church—" whereas she keeps her faith "staying at Home— / With a Bobolink for a Chorister— / An Orchard, for a Dome—." In such a church, God, "a noted Clergyman," does not let His sermons get long and thus boring, "So instead of getting to Heaven, at last— / I'm going all along,"[3] she saucily comments. And in one of her most frequently anthologized poems, "I taste a liquor never brewed" (J 214), she manages to strike a note of waggish ecstasy in her affirmation of a highly personal sense of eternity; for her religious inebriation she drinks not alcohol but Creation—the air under the blue sky. And more attuned to nature than bees or butterflies, she drinks until even seraphs and saints come to wonder at the spiritual drunkenness of "the little Tippler / Leaning against the—Sun—."[4]

Dickinson as Dark Romantic

But Emily Dickinson, on closer inspection, is not the blithe romantic at all. Her vision is, finally, more Byronic than Wordsworthian, somber enough to place her spiritually closer to Edgar Allan Poe and Henry Wadsworth Longfellow and still closer to Herman Melville and sometimes even to the naturalist Stephen Crane than to Bryant, Whitman, and the Transcendentalists. Although the scale of her rebellion was microcosmic compared with that of Lord Byron, who relished and suffered the role of Peck's bad boy in the eyes of all Europe, Dickinson's was similar in kind and, on the scale of her life, enormous. If Thoreau traveled far in Concord, she traveled no less far in Amherst. There she would not "beg, with Domains in my Pocket—" (J 1772). Hers was the adamant soul who had to select "her own society" and to "Choose One— / then—close the Values of her attention— / Like Stone—" no matter who entreated her for her attention, even "an Emperor" (J 303). She it was who kept the sabbath in the most intensely personal way, staying at home while all those for whom she cared kept it by going to church. She it was who chided the " 'Heavenly Father' " for making us apologize to Him for His "own duplicity" (J 1461). She it was who berated God—whose existence she never really doubted and whose identity as the formal Christian godhead she could almost never accept—for caring for her prayer "as much as on the Air / A Bird—had stamped her foot—" (J 376). Unable to escape the gravity of New England Puritanism but unable to embrace it, she saw herself, not without some pride and much uneasiness, and quite like Byron, as the spawn of Satan. "I have come from 'to and fro,' and walking up, and down' the same place that Satan hailed from, when God asked him where he'd been," she once wrote, for example, to her friend Abiah Root. She quite saw herself as "the Mutineer / Whose title is 'the Soul' " (J 1617).[5]

And if there is a Byronic tonality in her work, no less is there a Melvillean one and hints at the uncaring universe at which Stephen Crane would shout in horror. Indeed, it is widely believed that Crane wrote his poems after William Dean Howells had introduced him to the newly published poems of Dickinson. Crane's representative man would cry to Creation, "Sir, I exist!" and be told flatly by the universe, "The fact has not created in me a sense of obligation."[6] "Silence is the only voice of our God," Melville wrote in *Pierre*. And in *Moby Dick* the blankness of the overwhelming whale, remorselessly negligent of Ahab's puny yet heroic railings, is irresistible. Though Dickinson had not read *Pierre* and could not know the poems of Crane, yet to be written, she felt all too poignantly the oppressive choice that those two writers understood between a maddeningly heedless God and a maddeningly silent one. "Silence is all we dread," Dickinson knew with respect to both God and beloved humans; "There's Ransom in a Voice— / But Silence is Infinity. / Himself have not a face" (J 1251).[7] The courage that Emily Dickinson's rebellion required in the face of the Calvinist society in which she was born and raised and pressured is scarcely measurable. It is suggested by her acknowledgment of damnation in such a passage as this:

> A Pit—but Heaven over it—
> And Heaven beside, and Heaven abroad;
> And yet a Pit—
> With Heaven over it.

To stir would be to slip—
To look would be to drop—
To dream—to sap the Prop
That holds my chances up.
Ah! Pit! With Heaven over it!

(J 1712)

How fragile and how ultimately tough, this Empress of Calvary, who knew that "the depth [of that pit] is all my thought" and that "I dare not ask my feet" lest the foundation of her intellectual bastion slip and she tumble into the Calvinist's eternal pit of hell (or the quagmire of conventional Calvinism perhaps?). Small wonder that she had moments when she struck a coy pose and tried to win the stern Puritan God over with "babytalk," as in J 70. In that poem she hopes "the Father in the skies / will lift his little girl— / Old fashioned—naughty—everything— / over the stile of 'Pearl.'" She varied the tone, sometimes whistling in the dark. In J 103, she asserts with a kind of childlike bravado, reminiscent of Stephen Crane's later, that she omits "to pray / 'Father, thy will be done' today / for my will goes the other way, / And it were perjury!"[8]

The Objects of Dickinson's Rebellion

Two forces during Emily Dickinson's formative years threatened to overbear her, to stifle her independence, and to press her into the mold of Connecticut Valley conformity. They were her formidable father, the pillar of the Amherst community Edward Dickinson (1803–1874), whose presence sometimes merges with that of "the Father in the skies," and the Congregational church in Amherst. Their siege failed to the extent that they never succeeded in breaching the walls of her autonomy and taking the citadel, but she was never able to raise entirely the siege either, and in critical ways her life and work were reactions to their aggressive presence.

AGAINST THE FATHER. Edward Dickinson's severity and its impact on his poet daughter may be exaggerated by some of her biographers,[9] but that he was a dominating and driven man, demanding, hard working, and extremely stern, is beyond dispute.

He and Amherst were made for each other and knew it; the *Amherst Record* singled him out as the most prominent of the town's leading citizens, acknowledging that he and the Dickinson name were associated with "everything that belongs to Amherst," and a history of Amherst College proclaimed him "one of the finest pillars of society, education, order, morality, and every good cause in our community."[10]

His prodigious energy parted the waters in virtually every segment of local life—law, government, politics, religion (he was largely responsible for the new Congregational church), temperance (which he championed), women's suffrage (which he opposed), education (he was treasurer of Amherst College and had a strong voice in its running), even public safety (he was active in the volunteer fire department) and transportation (he helped to bring the Amherst and Belchertown Railroad to town and was a manager of it). And his will extended beyond local civic matters; a Whig stalwart, he was elected to represent Amherst's views, which were, in the main, his own, in both the Massachusetts legislature and the U.S. Congress.

Emily's mother, Emily Norcross Dickinson, lived much in her husband's shadow, and though not a powerful figure in the household, she was a beloved one for whom the children grieved when she died in 1882. About her mother's passing, the poet wrote in a letter to her friend James D. Clarke, "Her dying feels to me like many kinds of Cold—at times electric, at times benumbing—then a trackless waste." To her friend Mrs. Holland, Emily Dickinson summarized her feelings toward her mother in this way: "We were never intimate Mother and Children while she was our Mother—but Mines in the same Ground meet by tunneling and when she became our Child the Affection came—";[11] and in J 1573 she describes the feeling that set in after her mother's death as being "Homeless at home." Because of Emily Dickinson's special relationship with her father, she might have thought that the comparison that her sister Lavinia (1833–99) made between their dead parents was invidious; nevertheless, Vinnie's remark was apt: "Father believed and mother loved," she said.[12]

It seems fair to say that a good deal of Emily Dickinson's behavior and poetry were, in one way or another, a reaction to her father. There are legends, probably exaggerated, of her fear of that dour gentleman—for example, of her not learning to tell time for years after he thought that he had taught her because she was too frightened to tell him that she did not understand.[13] In any case, he was formidable enough. Certainly, for instance, he tried to censor her reading and reception of guests well into her adulthood. But she was as indomitable in her way as he was in his. With her brother Austin (William Austin, 1829–95), her beloved kindred spirit, she contrived to sneak forbidden romantic books into the house. Reportedly when her father beat a horse to teach it humility, she interceded for the horse with lusty yells. When he controlled his haughtiness to the extent of succumbing to a religious conversion during the 1850 revival at Amherst, she, who had often refused to attend church, resisted and was the last in the family to retain control of her own soul. "I am standing alone in rebellion," she wrote to friend Jane Humphrey at that point.[14]

But mainly she rebelled more subtly against her father by achieving a comedic distance from him. The playfulness that runs through much of her work appears to have resulted from the comic sense that she developed over the years, largely as a strategy to cope with living with her father. She might sit with the family members as they recited their morning prayers and addressed "an Eclipse" they called "Father," as she described the activity in a famous letter to Thomas Wentworth Higginson, but her mind was elsewhere. When Edward Dickinson complained about regularly getting a chipped plate at dinner, daughter Emily took it to the garden and smashed it, in a gesture that he would appreciate, to remind herself not to give it to him again.[15] She evolved a way to poke gentle fun at him, which gave her a means to master him without harm to him or to herself. "Father steps like Cromwell when he gets the kindling," she joked, for example, and when she described his attendance at a concert that Jenny Lind gave in the church that had reverberated to the voice of Jonathan Edwards, she said that it was "as if old Abraham had come to see the show, and thought it was all very well, but a little excess of *Monkey!*"[16] Her bemused and affectionate tolerance for his domineering shines through such comments as this one, made 7 October 1863, at the age of nearly thirty-three, in a letter to her cousins Louise and Frances Norcross:

I got down before father this morning, and spent a few moments profitably with the South Sea Rose [she was a skilled botanist, trained at the Amherst

Academy and encouraged by her parents]. Father detecting me, advised wiser employment, and read at devotions the chapter of the gentleman with one talent. I think he thought my conscience would adjust the gender.[17]

The feeling between father and daughter was unspoken but too deep for the rebellion to shed blood. But her life's blood flowed when Edward Dickinson died in June 1874. Expressing her grief to the same close cousins, she conveyed the emptiness with characteristically brilliant precision: "You might not remember me, dears. I cannot recall myself. I thought I was strongly built, but this stronger [her father's death] has undermined me." She speaks of taking him "the best flowers" and says in despair, "If we only knew he knew, perhaps we could stop crying." Ending the note abruptly, she speaks of being figuratively lost in a way that makes her real loss all the more moving: "I cannot write any more, dears. Though it is many nights, my mind never comes home."[18] To Higginson she wrote, "His heart was pure and terrible, and I think no other like it exists."[19] Seven months after the dread event, she was able to recount to Mrs. Holland, with the old touch of loving bemusement: " 'I say unto you,' Father would read at Prayers, with a militant Accent that would startle one." But the sadness of a poem included in the letter bespeaks the adoration of her father that caused her to choose as the important males in her life almost nothing but replicas of him. While her mother sleeps in the library and Vinnie in the dining room, he is asleep "in the Masked Bed—in the Marl House":

> How soft his Prison is—
> How sweet those sullen Bars—
> No despot—but the King of Down
> Invented that Repose!"

Tellingly, she concludes the letter by referring to passing her father's door at night, "where . . . I used to think was safety."[20] Emily Dickinson never entirely recovered from her father's death; without coming to believe in the gentleness of that death, perhaps she could not have survived for the remaining twelve years of her life.

REVOLUTION AGAINST THE CHURCH. Holding off the domination of a stern father and holding at bay the imperious advances of an overbearing church that would gladly have taken over her life in the name of its own harsh Father were, at the core, two facets of the same act—a tough-minded assertion of self that would have made Walt Whitman smile. She might compromise in small ways for the sake of peacekeeping and kindness, by agreeing to go to church sometimes or by sitting at the family's morning prayers, but in fundamental ways never. To select "her own society" and then "close the Values of her attention— / Stone—" (J 303) to resist terrible social pressure unyieldingly required a grit possessed by few people in her time or any other, and not by members of her own family, whom she loved and respected and all of whom, even her powerful father, eventually went down on their knees to the Calvinist Father and converted.

The 1840s, the second decade of her life, saw one of those recurring New England spiritual perturbations that had boiled up whenever religious conservatives sensed that the grip of Puritanism was coming loose on the throat of the region. The most notorious of those Bible-thumping episodes were the Salem witch trials at the end of the seventeenth century and the Great Awakening of the 1740s, and now during Emily Dickinson's girlhood, another bout of Calvinist fever swept the Connecticut River Valley. A series of revivals in Amherst was particularly virulent, claiming numerous converts. The Mount Holyoke Female Seminary succumbed during the academic year she attended (1847–48); she did not return for a second year. Although she enjoyed her studies, especially in the sciences, she could not abide the school's attempt to stifle her spirit. When the students were asked by the school's founder, Mary Lyon, to stand if they considered converting, she was the only one who remained in her seat. Describing the incident, she said, "They thought it queer I didn't rise—I thought a lie would be queerer."[21] For the rest of her life, she would feel herself the outsider, savoring the lesson that "Revolution is the Pod / Systems rattle from / When the Winds of Will are stirred/Excellent is Bloom" (J 1082).

"Looking Positively"

Having fought off, as a schoolgirl, formal religion's assault on her soul, she fortified herself against the pressure that would continue throughout the rest of her life by building a strong framework of the most personal faith—indeed, strong enough to accommodate doubt and anger at her God. In that, she beat her own recusant tune against Puritan harmony as Anne Hutchinson and Roger Williams had done long ago and Emerson, Thoreau, and other Transcendentalists, and Hawthorne were doing in her time. Her God was really coequal with nature and her ego in a kind of tripartite worldview. Though she did not much question His divinity, she felt quite free to question His treatment of His two partners in the triumvirate—that is, to pit her will against His. If she had been asked the name of her God, she could appropriately have answered "Edward Dickinson."

God was certainly not to her what He was to her orthodox Connecticut Valley contemporaries. They would hover around her deathbed waiting for the stupendous moment of "that last Onset— when the King / Be witnessed—in the Room—," but she imagined that instead at the end she would see "interposed a Fly— / With Blue—uncertain stumbling Buzz / Between the light" and her vision (J 465). She parodies (in J 234) their notion that heavenly reward was only for the likes of them, that it would follow their smug lives as surely as profits follow a clever business deal: "You're right—'the way *is* narrow'— / And 'difficult the Gate'—" she chided. There is "the 'Discount' of the *Grave*— / Termed by the *Brokers*—'Death'! / And after *that*—there's Heaven— / The *Good* Man's—'*Dividend*.'" She whimsically concludes, in case the italicized expressions have not carried the satire all the way to the bulls eye, "And *Bad* Men—'go to Jail'— / I guess—." Elsewhere she derides the sanctimoniousness of the "Soft—Cherubic Creatures" of her churchly society, the "Gentlewomen" with their "Dimity Convictions— / A Horror so refined / Of freckled Human Nature— / Of Deity—ashamed—"; the poet identifies with the naturalness, the "freckled," the imperfect but human "Human Nature" that the "Gentlewomen" spurn. In the end such a democratic conviction will be vindicated: "Redemption—Brittle Lady— / Be so—ashamed of Thee" (J 401).

Dickinson well knew her own apostasy. With Emerson she rejected the divinity of Jesus and therefore the holiness of any but her own self, world, and God. "When Jesus tells us about his Father, we distrust him. When he shows us his Home, we turn away, but when he confides to us that he is 'acquainted with

Grief,' we listen, for that is also an Acquaintance of our own,"
she observed to Charles Wadsworth, who, like Jesus, seemed to
her the Man of Sorrows. How in tune she was to sorrow and
suffering: "The loveliest sermon I ever heard was the disappoint-
ment of Jesus in Judas. It was told like a mortal story of intimate
young men."[22] Christianity touched her, that is to say, only where
it reflected "freckled Human Nature." It may be too much to say
that hers was the ancient struggle of the rational mind over
superstition, but complacent superstition surely rankled her. Not
for her either was the romantic escape from pain to the spectral
sphere of an Edgar Allan Poe (though she shared his dark affinity
for pain) or its Calvinist variation. She lived much in a realm of
suffering and deprivation in which "a look of Agony" was desirable
because it could not mislead (J 241), but her survival techniques
were not just highly idiosyncratic but human. She might take to
wearing white and entertaining from a room apart, but she would
love people devotedly and thoughtfully—family, friends, townspeople, Irish workmen and their families. Even in her distance
there was great intimacy. Others could find their salvation in
ghosts and doctrines: "I find myself still softly searching / For my
Delinquent Palaces—," she declared:

> And a Suspicion like a Finger
> Touches my Forehead now and then
> That I am looking oppositely
> For the site of the Kingdom of Heaven—
> (J 959)

Emily Dickinson's rebellion did not entail a definitive denial of
Christian afterlife; rather it involved a fluctuating doubt of it and
a tendency to reject the Calvinistic requirements to attain it. The
implications of damnation and salvation were like remnants of
old chewed gum that she could not quite scrape off her soles—
or if she could rub them off for a time, she could not avoid
stepping in another wad. When the Reverend Dr. W. A. Stearns
was installed as pastor of Amherst's College Church, he preached
a sermon on "death and judgment," which, according to a local
paper "well pleased" the congregation. In the audience, Emily
Dickinson was not at all "well pleased" by the homily about
"what would become of those, meaning Austin and me, who

behaved improperly—and somehow the sermon scared me, and father and Vinnie looked very solemn as if the whole was true. . . . I did'nt [sic] much think I should see you again until the Judgment Day," she continued in a letter to Mrs. Holland, "and then you would not speak to me, according to his story. The subject of perdition seemed to please him, somehow. It seemed very solemn to me." The mixture of levity, skepticism, and fear— which clearly implies a degree of acceptance—with which she wrote of the experience at nearly twenty-four years of age resonates with the same ambivalent combination of attitudes that lasted through her lifetime.[23] In the same letter, she wrote of a dream in which she and Mrs. Holland were picking flowers together but were never able to fill the basket. Good, Dickinson, thought: "God grant the baskets fill not, till, with hands purer and whiter, we gather flowers of gold in baskets made of pearl; higher—higher!"[24] The flowers of gold and baskets of pearl are a loving metaphor for the joy that she will feel when she and Mrs. Holland are reunited, but the hint is sure that she believed in a nondoctrinaire and rather childlike brand of immortality.

Her personal faith was tested whenever she suffered the anguish of a loved one's death. When her father died, she assured Mrs. Holland that he was reposing in the care of "the King of Down," but first she questioned " 'what kind' he had become" and whispered, "Where is he? Emily will find him!"[25] When the Reverend Wadsworth died in 1882, she asked, "Lives he in any other world / My faith cannot reply,"[26] and when her mother died later that year, she said plaintively, "We don't know where she is, though so many tell us." When friend James Clarke died the following year, she asked, "Are you certain there is another life? When overwhelmed to know, I feel that few are sure," and upon the death of her nephew Gilbert, whom she adored, she uttered doubtfully, " 'Open the Door, open the Door, they are waiting for me,' was Gilbert's sweet command in delirium. *Who* were waiting for him, all we possess we should give to know."[27] Even when her dog Carlo died in 1866, she wrote emptily to Higginson, "Carlo died. . . . Would you instruct me now?"[28]

Too committed to earth to let go of it and too attached to a heavenly Father to relinquish hope for His heaven, she paced the distance between with a sensitivity, intensity, and wit that exceeded such exploration by any other American poet. In the end, she

seems to have departed the earth with the secure hesitation of a
child ordered in for dinner: "Called back," she wrote simply and
with the feather touch of her humor to her Norcross cousins from
her deathbed. But her reluctance was expressed in another of her
wonderfully human dying poems:

> T'was comfort in her Dying Room
> To hear the living Clock
> A short relief to have the wind
> Walk boldly up and knock
> Diversion from the Dying Theme
> To hear the children play
> But wrong the more
> That these could live
> And this of ours must *die*.
>
> (J 1703)

With her absence of certainty amid plenty of it in Amherst and
with her hypersensitivity to deprivation and pain, the splendid
isolate also explored destitution. "Winter under cultivation / Is as
arable as Spring," she concluded. No one else has husbanded lack
as Emily Dickinson did, knowing that "Success is counted sweetest /
By those who ne'er succeed" (J 67), that wanting clarifies value
more than having.[29] " 'Tis little—I could care for Pearls— / Who
own the ample sea—" (J 466), she understood about herself. The
"sea" that she "owned" was her poetic imagination, which, though
wiry while Whitman's was brawny, was nonetheless limitless.
With it she bowled over the distinctions between heaven and
earth, the dead and the quick, spiritual and physical love. "I dwell
in Possibility—" she proclaimed, choosing poetry because it was
"A fairer House than Prose." Living there, all she needed "To
gather Paradise—" was "The spreading wide my narrow Hands"
(J 657).

A New Understanding of Dickinson's Poetry

Until the publication of R. W. Franklin's *The Manuscript Books
of Emily Dickinson* in 1981 proved to be a kind of Rosetta Stone
for the comprehension of Emily Dickinson's poetry and William
H. Shurr's *The Marriage of Emily Dickinson*[30] appeared in 1983 as

a compelling interpretation of the Stone, her poetry was widely seen as a collection of discrete, brilliant flashes of natural and spiritual insight; witty word play in which she lightly bends a heavily Calvinistic diction to her own ends;[31] often whimsical humor[32] and a sense of tragedy. True, those are all qualities that weave through her work, but even the best of her critics,—for example, Richard B. Sewall in *The Life of Emily Dickinson*—rightly found "her vision—dispersed and fragmented."[33]

The fascicles, or bound booklets, that R. W. Franklin carefully reconstructed changed that. Between 1858 and 1863, a period of great turbulence for her and the time when she seriously turned to writing poetry, she carefully secured her poems in packets according to some arrangement that had an intensely private meaning for her. It was her own form of personal publication for a sequestered audience of one. The fascicles were disassembled by the editors of her poems in the 1890s, and so, for close to a century, until Franklin's facsimile edition, the significance of their patterning was irretrievable. In *The Marriage of Emily Dickinson*, Shurr retrieved it.

The principle by which Emily Dickinson arranged the poems into forty fascicles was not clustering by "recipients: there is no Higginson fascicle, no Helen Hunt Jackson grouping," and so on. Nor are there "gatherings according to single events or subjects, for there are no flower or sky . . . , no death or nature . . . , no romantic attachment fascicles. Neither are they organized according to emotions or feelings, for ironic . . . , happy, sad, wistful and gay poems all mingle in a single fascicle."[34] Ruled out too as informing principles are "theme, imagery, narrative and dramatic movement, or similar pursuit."[35]

What, then, is the organizational principle? It must have something to do with a particular person, distinct from the reader, for while the reader may find himself in the "you" of, say, "I'll tell you how the Sun rose" (J 318), by Shurr's count he is excluded from the "you" of 125 of the fascicle poems (e.g., "You constituted Time" for me [J 765] and " 'Why do I love' You, Sir?" [J 480]). Moreover, in a number of those poems and some others, Dickinson variously calls her addressee "Sweet," "Dear," "King," "Sovereign," her "Lord," "Lover," "Signor," "Sir," and "Sire." Shurr inescapably concludes "that about 150 of the 814 fascicle poems are love poems addressed to a specific individual," one with whom she shared certain covert activities (for example, the reference in J 616 to her cheering her "fainting Prince") and with whom she had held private conversation, reflected, for example, in the dialogue poem "I cannot live with you" (J 640) and in "It was a quiet way— / He asked if I was his" (J 1053).[36] These and other bits of evidence, both internal and physical (for example, some of the fascicle sheets were folded as if for posting, and one bears the obliterated name of an addressee), lead to the conclusion that Dickinson's work had a center of some shared experience and feeling with an addressee whose identity she was at great pains— by the obliquity of her diction, by her refusal to publish any but the smallest handful, and by her instructions to Vinnie to destroy the manuscripts after her death—to conceal.

The object of Dickinson's love and addressee of her fascicle poems may never be shown beyond contention. She had loving relationships with numerous women, including her sister Vinnie; her sister-in-law Susan Gilbert Dickinson; Mrs. Elizabeth Holland; Kate Scott Turner Anthon; Helen Hunt Jackson; her "Little Cousins" Louise and Frances Norcross; and the much younger inamorata of brother Austin, Mabel Loomis Todd—all of whom she is known to have sent poems. That the addressee might have been a homosexual lover, however, is not supported by internal evidence of the fascicle poems. The only real challenge to that assertion is J 518, in which the speaker reflects on "Her sweet Weight on my Heart a Night," but even that poem can be read as a dream—"If 'twas a Dream"—or, with perhaps more authority, as a representation of the mind of the male lover.[37] At the end, the speaker would

> With Him remain—who unto Me—
> Gave—even as to All—
> A Fiction superseding Faith—
> By so much—as 'twas real—

Enter Wadsworth, Praying

If not a woman, then who was the male addressee-lover of the packets that Emily Dickinson collected, arranged, and bound for herself from 1858 to 1863? As a young lady, she had close and supportive male friends, among them her father's law clerk Benjamin F. Newton and, during the early 1850s, Amherst College student Henry Vaughan Emmons. Later she chose figures very much in the image of her father: Samuel Bowles, editor of the *Springfield Daily Republican*, who published her few public poems; Charles Wadsworth, ranked "perhaps . . . first," by Bowles, "among the 'orthodox' preachers"; in 1862, thus too late to be the mystery man of the fascicles, Thomas Wentworth Higginson, a Boston literary lion, whom she chose as her poetic "preceptor" perhaps because he represented mainstream literary opinion and whose advice to regularize her verse (mainly to perfect her carefully calculated imperfect rhyme and smooth out her roughened four-three hymnal rhythm) she then proceeded to ignore for precisely the same reason;[38] later Judge Otis P. Lord, with whom, after the death of his wife in 1877, she toyed (but probably only toyed) with the idea of marriage. The identity of the phantom of the fascicles, defined by requirements of the dates; the internal clues of the poems; and correlation with outside materials, powerfully suggest only one man, Charles Wadsworth, long known by biographers to have been of profound emotional importance to her.

The family seems to have called upon the well-known Philadelphia clergyman in the mid-1850s to help Emily through an emotional crisis with religious, as well as psychological, dimensions. She had apparently heard him preach on a visit there, and her friend Mrs. Flynt sent her a copy of one of his homilies. At first they corresponded. He wrote, sounding professional, that he stood ready to help, but she was drawn more and more into infatuation with him. In the early spring of 1858, she sent Wadsworth the first of her highly emotional "Master" letters. By then she was mailing him fascicles of poems as well. The letter not only called him "Master" but professed her love and told him, when she had learned that he was ill, "How strong when weak to recollect, and easy, quite, to love. Will you please tell me, please to tell me, soon as you are well."[39] The breathlessness comes through the written words: "If it had been God's will that I might breathe where you breathed,"[40] she wished. She later asked Mr. and Mrs. Bowles and still later the Hollands to be intermediaries, handling letters to keep the correspondence secret. After all, her position as an Amherst Dickinson was delicate, and Wadsworth's, as a married and respectable clergyman in Philadelphia, was even more so.[41] Unlike her daughterly and religious uprisings, her third rebellion, against sexual mores, was to be kept secret from all but a few most trusted confidants. In her work, it could be treated only cryptically.

Numerous references to and imagery drawn from the function and terminology of the clergy throughout the forty fascicles of poems make it clear that the lover in the poems was indeed a clergyman. Though Wadsworth's letters appear not to have encouraged her love, he visited her at Amherst in the spring of 1860, and there is evidence in the fascicle poems that their relationship was, at least on one occasion, consummated. The poems suggest a sense of guilt (e.g., "Best Grief is Tongueless—before He'll tell— / Burn him in the Public Square" [J 793]. Moreover, in letters to Higginson and Bowles, she revealed a "terror—since September [1861]—I could tell to none," implying that she might have been pregnant or feared that she was.[42] When she wrote a "Master" letter to Wadsworth in the summer of 1861 complaining that he was doing nothing for her despite his knowing of her plight, he seems to have shrugged off responsibility. She wrote again, this time with sarcasm: "I don't know what you can do about it—thank you."[43]

Another letter, though, attests to her undying love and devotion. And so does her behavior for the rest of her days: her marriage poems, her wearing of white, her continuing correspondence with him over the years, her renewed relationship with him when he returned to Amherst in 1880, nearly twenty years after an intimacy that she would henceforth regard as nothing less than a marriage. She had never been naive. Indeed, the public perception in her own time and since of Emily Dickinson as a sexless white-clad spinster flitting among the shrubs is inaccurate. That fact is suggested by the sexual awareness in such a simile as this: "The thought beneath so slight a film— / Is more distinctly seen— / *As laces just reveal the surge*— / Or Mists the Appenine—"(J 210; my italics). She was well aware of what "bees" were after too; the one in J 211, for example, hums round the chamber of a flower, then "Counts his nectars— / Enters—and is lost in Balms."

In fragments of an uncompleted poem (J 1591) dated from after Wadsworth's death in 1882, she revealed much of her conception of her "husband" by that time: "The Bobolink is gone—the Rowdy of the Meadow— / And no one swaggers now but me," she sadly wrote. "He recognized his maker—overturned the Decalogue," she said, thinking of his violation of his own moral strictures. Then she experimented on the worksheet: "He swung upon the Decalogue / And shouted Let us pray," and finally, "He gurgled— Let us pray— / bubbled."

Emily Dickinson discontinued her binding of fascicles in 1863 and instead took to gathering much larger numbers of poems in unbound groupings called *sets*. But she had already provided in the fascicles a tool for scholars well more than a hundred years later to find the biographical center of her poetic sensibility and so better understand the work of the American poet who best learned how to "Tell all the Truth but tell it slant," knowing that her private as well as artistic "Success in Circuit lies" (J 1129).

Along with Poe and Whitman one of the three great poets of the nineteenth century, in doing that she unwittingly assured herself a place at the center of the corpus of American poetry. When Thomas H. Johnson's work permitted her discovery in the twentieth century, her poetry rose phoenix-like into a world that was ready to admire its great wit; its flashes of insight; its oblique confessional quality; its brittle, nervous strength; and its prosodic flexibility. And it is a world better prepared than her own to ratify her singularly tough assertion of female self against its suppression by male authority. No wonder that this woman—as heroic in her fight against domestic, spiritual, and artistic male domination as Hester Prynne was in her way—has been enormously important to contemporary feminist writers such as Adrienne Rich, Alicia Ostriker, Sandra Gilbert, and Suzanne Juhasz.

· TWO ·

The Late Nineteenth and Early Twentieth Century: A Tale of Paucity

> You tell me this is God?
> I tell you this is a printed list,
> A Burning candle and an ass.
>
> —Stephen Crane, *War is kind*, "*85*"

In 1896 Edwin Arlington Robinson declared in his sonnet "Credo" that he was lost in the emptiness of a universe with "No star / In all the shrouded heavens anywhere" and with "not a whisper in the air / Of any living voice," except for one so oppressively distant that he could detect "it only as a bar / Of lost imperial music." The poem ends with the wishful affirmation that "through it all—above, beyond it all" there is a "far-sent message of the years" that permits the speaker to "feel the coming glory of the Light," but the sense of drifting through dark immensity is much more convincing than the halfhearted, wistful avowal of the conclusion.

There was much to cause Robinson anguish at the close of the nineteenth century in the United States. The social Darwinism of Herbert Spencer and others and the jungle mores of the Gilded Age had been widely substituted for the old morality—or pretense of it—since mid-century. Particularly since the rampant industrialization during and after the Civil War, skepticism had by and large replaced the spiritual certainties. As Woody Allen was to express the doubt in *Without Feathers*, three-quarters of a century later: "If only God would give me some clear sign! Like making a large deposit in my name at a Swiss bank." Manifest Destiny was broadly popular, but it was offensive to many sensitive people who inclined toward some loftier motivation for human beings than territoriality. Now, in the late 1890s, with the continent conquered from sea to shining sea, America was on the skids, greased by jingoism, toward the Spanish-American War, the second imperialist war in its short history. The Civil War had settled the issue of the unity of America's body, but the American soul seemed uncomfortable in its body, and the literature that expressed it seemed adrift when it was not smug. The popularly rejected Whitman, and generally unknown Emily Dickinson, both now dead, had decades to wait to become admired, and, with the fires of American Renaissance banked, the American cultural scene was truly a wasteland. When such expatriate writers as Henry James, Ezra Pound, and T. S. Eliot in one way or other described it as that, they were being more than just snobbish. They were quite right.

To serious American poets and novelists at the end of the nineteenth century and into the first years of the twentieth, the "future glory of America" seemed to have come and gone—or, if it was arriving, it was far from glorious. The prophetic poets—Emerson, to the extent that he had the capacity to be one, and Whitman—had worked on the naive theory that to name was to awaken and transform, to cause the individual and the nation of nations to fulfill their godly potential. American poetry had long been an expression of American mythology, of the millennial vision and advertising that the Puritans had introduced and believed. Now with the soot and row houses of industrialization and the unrestrained greed of industrialists shattering the vision and regulating the rhythms of American life, American literature generally degenerated into effete mannerism or was lost in the smoke groping for new direction, or was sent into exile. As Roy Harvey Pearce puts it, "American culture, its destiny no longer simply and clearly manifest, was being torn asunder by its own increasingly depersonalized, mechanized, bureaucratized power to move men and mountains. . . . [The American poet] was in the position of the first Adam, cast out of his new world. But he had no Raphael to give him a vision of the ultimate rightness of his fall from his natural state."[1] He had, essentially, the choices that the heroes of contemporary fiction had in their disenchantment. He could "light out for the Territory" like Huck Finn and avoid being "sivilized" American style. A number of Western bards, such as Hamlin Garland and Eugene Field, advocated just that. Field, for example, advocated building one's nest "on top of a carmine hill," leaving eastern and European civilization behind and going to the open spaces where "I have no master but the wind, / My only liege the sun."² Ironically, by the time those lines were published in 1893, the frontier, which, according to Frederic Jackson Turner, had a purgative quality that was nothing short of mythical, was already closed. Certainly, by 1890, 44.8 percent of the population in the West lived in cities.³

Another choice for the poet was to pack up his ideals and take them to Europe like a Jamesian hero or heroine to test them in a society that was at once more sophisticated and more jaded and corrupt than the one back home. Or he could remain at home and, like Stephen Crane, bay at the universe and listen to the echo of his own voice. Or he could affect the pinched voice of a Victorian, perhaps the delicate intricacy of an Oscar Wilde. Almost everyone chose the alternatives of Victorian complacency or preciosity or both.

Any list of active poets of the late nineteenth and turn of the century is dispiriting: Thomas Bailey Aldrich, Ambrose Bierce, George H. Baker, Madison Cawein, Paul Laurence Dunbar, Eugene Field, Hamlin Garland, Louise Imogen Guiney, Richard Hovey, Lloyd Mifflin, William Vaughan Moody, Louise Chandler Moulton, Lizette Woodworth Reese, George Santayana, Edmund Clarence Stedman, Trumbull Stickney, Elizabeth Stoddard, Richard Henry Stoddard, and Bayard Taylor.⁴ The New York group—Stoddard, Taylor, Stedman, and Baker—was spent by the end of the century and had never had much poetic power. The gentility of the city poets seemed even more affected than it was in the face of such local-color versifiers as Bret Harte and James Whitcomb Riley with their studied roughness and Joaquin Miller with his overwrought application of pre-Raphaelitism to the American West.

Indeed, typical of most other periods of cultural upheaval and now in the wake of the passing of America's respected nineteenth-century poets—Bryant, Emerson, Longfellow, Lowell, Whittier, even the controversial but highly visible Whitman—the literary scene in the United States toward the end of the century divided itself between conservatives and liberals. The conservatives, vested in such traditional poets as Thomas Bailey Aldrich, saw themselves manning the trenches of immutable, sacrosanct, and romantic American culture against the dangerous forces of realists, naturalists, free-verse poets, and other such radicals represented by the likes of Emily Dickinson and Stephen Crane. Aldrich, predicting oblivion for Dickinson, rewrote some of her lines in the *Atlantic Monthly* to bring order out of her "poetical chaos." But those who saw change as building on tradition and extending it were gaining influence. Dickinson's work was reviewed favorably by such important journals as the *Critic*, *Harper's Magazine*, and the *Nation*, and sales of the posthumous volumes of her poems were healthy (with sixteen editions of the 1890 *Poems* in eight years, and five reprintings of the 1891 *Poems, Second Series* in two years). Though naturalist Stephen Crane's first collection of his verse, *Black Riders and Other Lines* (1895), looked as little like poetry to conservative critics as Whitman's and was about as offensive in its substance, it was reprinted five times in its first year. Edwin Arlington Robinson's two volumes published in the last years of the century used orthodox prosody but rejected the old shopworn poetic diction of the past in favor of new natural language with which to express the spirit of his day accurately and movingly.

Three Prometheans: Moody, Lodge, and Stickney

Three end-of-the-century conservative poets who looked back to the classics, and especially to the myth of Prometheus, to attempt to express the malaise of contemporary American society were William Vaughan Moody, George Cabot Lodge, and Trumbull Stickney.

Moody, (1869–1910), an early example of the twentieth-century American poet who commonly supports himself through membership on a university faculty, could not, and did not particularly wish to, escape the strong influences of the great poets he taught in his English literature classes—Keats, Shelley, and others, and mainly Milton. More obviously than many other poets, he anchored himself in a particular time through his work, which reflects a strong Victorian moralist streak and disapproval of American imperialism and the results of industrialization. Less clearly did he tie himself to a specific place. He was born in Spencer, Indiana, in 1869, and he taught at the University of Chicago. In those respects he added his weight to the shift in the cultural center of gravity from the East Coast westward that had been established by Mark Twain. But he had been educated at Harvard and in Europe and was not inclined to glorify the "husky, brawling, City of the Big Shoulders" or the industrial ethos the way Carl Sandburg and the other Chicago poets, Edgar Lee Masters and Vachel Lindsay, were. The very title of such a poem as "The Brute" (1900) conveys his view of machinery and its effect. Some of the city's vitality did osmose into his poetry to enliven it, though ultimately not enough to air out the stuffiness entirely.

Moody is best recalled for two essentially political poems, "Gloucester Moors" (*Poems*, 1901), which he began during a summer holiday at Cape Ann, Massachusetts, in 1900, and "Ode in a Time of Hesitation," first published in the *Atlantic Monthly* in May 1900. The disillusionment that characterized much American literature toward the turn of the century, and was to remain a major theme, resounds in both pieces. The former, in its fine description of the Gloucester seashore, looks backward to such romantic nature poets as William Cullen Bryant. But in his use of nature as a background against which human foibles harshly stand out, rather than as a book in which to read either God or the human relationship to God, Moody also looks forward to such twentieth-century "nature" poets as Robert Frost. His use of a sailing vessel as a metaphor for the earth or the state anticipates William Carlos Williams's "The Yachts" (1935). Moody condemns the haves, the selfish "haggard ruthless few" in command of the have-nots, who are represented by "the many broken souls of men" who "Fester down in the slaver's pen." Unfortunately, Moody's descriptive passages, particularly of the local flora, are more attractive than the convoluted imagery of his social commentary is effective.

The same sort of unevenness diminishes the quality of his 227-line "Ode in a Time of Hesitation," published to protest the United States's annexation of the Philippines in the Spanish-American War and the crushing of the movement for Philippine independence led by Emilio Aguinaldo. At the outset, Moody conjures a strong enough sense of America's traditional high political ideals as exemplified by Colonel Robert Gould Shaw, the commander of the first black enlisted regiment, the Fifty-fourth Massachusetts, who was martyred in battle in 1863 and commemorated in the famous Saint-Gaudens statue on Boston Common. But the poem, which appears with James Russell Lowell's "For the Union Dead," marches too far into rhetoric as it rehearses the ignoble veering of national policy from aiding the oppressed who call out for help to oppressing them in the name of America's own imperialism. It is not too late for honor, Moody instructs at the end, warning America's leaders to "Take heed! / Blindness we may forgive, but baseness we will smite." Moody was a poet of some ability—his imagery is sometimes sufficient, and he could loosen up patterns of rhyme and rhythm for effect—but his most ambitious poems bear the imprint of the speech-maker, and his lesser ones (for example, "The Bracelet of Grass," 1901) of a rather tiresome end-of-the-century ennui.

Yet Moody did not entirely relinquish his American idealism. If by the close of Darwin's century and the century of the robber barons he could no longer entrust it to God or the helmsmen of the American ship of state, he could still bank on more generalized human potential. Thus he composed two plays in verse (*The Masque of Judgment*, 1900, and *The Fire-Bringer*, 1904), which, with a third such drama (to be called *The Death of Eve*, incomplete at his death in 1910 and published posthumously in 1912), dealt with the questions of the relationship between humanity and the deity. Based on the Greek legend of Prometheus, with some good lyrical passages, *The Fire-Bringer* proved to be among Moody's best and most optimistic works, accentuating the hero's exemplary self-lessness as the basis of hope for the future in the absence of the old theological certainty. This did not stop the cultural reactionaries from attacking *The Fire-Bringer* for reflecting the changing times, however. Moody had a good reputation as a poet generally, but he could not win at either extreme. He was attacked by the cultural Turks for evading the issue and spirit of the times.

The Prometheus legend, involving estrangement between gods and mortals, seemed apt at the turn of the century. At least two members of the self-named Laodician group of poets at Harvard (a more classically oriented lot than the Victorian-romantic New York poets), George Cabot Lodge (1873–1909) and Trumbull Stickney (1874–1904) were, along with Moody, also attracted to the Prometheus story. Indeed Moody's *The Fire-Bringer* and Lodge's verse plays *Cain, a Drama* (1904) and *Herakles* (1908) were all at least loosely based on Stickney's verse drama *Prometheus Pyrphoros* (1900), a much more pessimistic version of the story than Moody's. Stickney found much less hope than Moody that without a strength beyond and greater than its own humankind could succeed. The world was too much with Stickney in his pessimistic lyric poems as well, and Lodge's dramas reflect the same sort of Weltschmerz.

Lazarus, Guiney, and Reese

Of the women poets of the late nineteenth century, Emma Lazarus (1849–87), won the praise of Emerson and later wrote some strong, if insufficiently controlled poems, about the situation of Jews (*Songs of a Semite*, 1882). Her sonnet "The New Colossus" (1883), enshrined at the base of the Statue of Liberty, and the kind of poem that is more effective in bronze than in ink, is not untypical of her work.

Louise Imogen Guiney (1861–1920), who emigrated from New England to old England, where she wrote some interesting pieces evoking the Cavalier past (for example, in *A Roadside Harp*, 1893; *England and Yesterday*, 1898; *The Martyr's Idyl*, 1899; and *Happy Ending*, 1909), is a competent but rather repetitive curiosity.

But Lizette Woodward Reese (1856–1935) is among the best poets of her time—a qualification not intended to denigrate this truly underrated poet. She was a Baltimore teacher whose lapidary lyrics contain quick flashes of insight reminiscent of Emily Dickinson's. Like Dickinson, she rejoiced in common, often botanical, things. For instance, she thanks the Lord, in "In Praise of Common Things," for "Stock and stone / For grass and pool; for quince tree blown / A virginal white in spring."[5] The first section of *The Selected Poems*, which uses the same title as this poem, uses as an epigram the lines from Blake, "To see a World in a grain of sand / and a Heaven in the wild flower." She also often reflected the same kind of personal touch-and-go relationship with God that Dickinson did. In "Lord, Oft I Come," for example, she recognizes her own apostasy and prays to be cured of it; meanwhile, however, she claims to do the opposite of what God commands as she approaches yet turns away from Him: "Lord, oft I come unto Thy door, / But when Thou openest it to me, / Back to the dark I shrink once more, / Away from light and Thee." The variation on basic hymnal rhythm, as well as the naughty-girl tone of the piece, recalls Dickinson, though Reese's prosody, in its regularity, lacks the deliberate prosodic roughness that Dickinson used to underscore her meaning and that is part of Dickinson's genius.

Another striking similarity between the two poets is their affinity for the subjects of death and deficiency. Reese's poem "The Dust," for instance, but for its orthodox form could almost be mistaken for a Dickinson poem. Watching the dust blow through the town, the speaker muses, "What cloudy shapes do fleet / Along the parchéed street; / Clerks, bishops, kings go by— / Tomorrow so shall I!" And in "After Disaster," Reese contemplates what remains after great pain: "Lovely, secure, unhastening things / Fast-kept for this, grip as of yore;— / The drowsy traffic of the bees; / The scarlet haws behind a door." In a way, it is unfortunate that her poetry is good enough and similar enough to invite comparison with Dickinson's, for that is an unwitting competition that she would not come close to winning. She simply did not have Dickinson's whimsical wit, original and synthesizing intelligence, emotional resonance, and control of language and form, but then, who did?

Paul Laurence Dunbar

More successful and more talented than other end-of-the-century black American poets—James Edwin Campbell, Daniel Webster Davis, and J. Mord Allen—Paul Laurence Dunbar (1872–1906) demonstrates the force that American racism could exert to crack a sensitive soul in the decades following the Civil War. Born in Dayton, Ohio, of former slaves, Dunbar was popular as the only black student in his high school class. Indeed, he was popular enough to obtain a job as an elevator operator in Dayton after his graduation—about as lofty a situation as a black could hope for in those many years after Emancipation. Yet he felt a vocation to write and struggled through two privately published volumes of poems (*Oak and Ivy*, 1893, and *Majors and Minors*, 1924). William Dean Howells was told of him and wrote the introduction to Dunbar's third collection, *Lyrics of Lowly Life*, in 1896. Although Howells's bigotry was unintentional, by praising Dunbar's most lightweight, humorous verses, the facile dialect pieces written in a contrived composite black dialect that was never heard anywhere on earth but sounded sufficiently authentic to please the ears of whites, Howells both made Dunbar instantaneously famous and condemned him to be a poet who could never be taken seriously. For the remainder of his short life (he died of tuberculosis in 1906 after years of illness), Dunbar was assured an audience for his poems and novels but primarily for his work in the "plantation tradition," which, like the stories of Thomas Nelson Page, romanticized antebellum southern plantation life to the point where it not only seemed humane but desirable. Dunbar did not even know the contemporary South very well, much less the South of half a century earlier, but it was attractive to him for a reason other than merely to curry the favor of white readers. He felt oppressed by the present, not only by racism, but by urban conditions generally. The dirt and noise of burgeoning industrial centers offended his health and sensibility, and that is, partly, why his characters long for, and often return to, the bucolic South, even the old slave plantation. Thus the ex-slave in "To the Eastern Shore" thinks nostalgically (in his spurious dialect), "My sandy roads is gleamin' w'ile de city ways is black," and "Possum Trot" bears a typical indictment of the urban scene as contrasted with the rural South: "The circuses don't come that way, they ain't no railroad line. / It ain't no great big city, where the schemers plan and plot."[6]

Since his death, and with the changes in the racial climate in America, Dunbar has come to be generally admired as a poet with a considerable lyric gift who wrote with sympathy for black Americans but with a sentimental prevarication that was forced upon him. The serious Dunbar, who watched the necessarily compliant side of his nature with resentment, burst into speech in standard English in poems that are now seen as his best and most telling. "We Wear the Mask" intimates the violent tension that roiled under "the grins and lies," and "The Poet" is his own bitter assessment of the career that America permitted him:

> He sang of life, serenely sweet.
> With, now and then, a deeper note.
> From some high peak, nigh yet remote,
> He voiced the world's absorbing beat.
> He sang of love when earth was young,
> And Love itself was in his lays.
> But ah, the world, it turned praise
> A jingle in a broken tongue.

Stephen Crane

The two fin-de-siècle poets who speak most congenially to a modern audience are undoubtedly Stephen Crane and Edwin

Arlington Robinson. Crane, (1871–1900), born in Newark, New Jersey, was two years younger than Robinson but ought to be considered first because, unlike Robinson, who died in 1935 and continued to publish until then, Crane lived only until the first year of the new century, by which time he had published both of his slim volumes of poems. *The Black Riders and Other Lines* appeared in 1895, the same year as his magnum opus, *The Red Badge of Courage*, and two years after his other novel, the controversial *Maggie: A Girl of the Streets*. The second small collection of poems, *War Is Kind*, came out in 1899.

By modern standards, Crane did well as a poet for a man who did not think of himself as one. It is no small compliment to him to acknowledge that there are some broad similarities between Crane's poems and Emily Dickinson's that make him attractive: both have a terse, gnomic, highly symbolic style used in the service of rebellion.[7] But while there is a lovely, sensuous surface to her work, a brilliant play of wit shimmering through her language, a fascinating complexity of thought, his work tends to be far more bluntly and simply symbolic and merely curt. Crane certainly expresses himself cleverly in his poems, and clever style is appealing, but the cleverness often seems to express a pervasive petulance.

That Crane knew Dickinson's work from William Dean Howells's reading it to him in 1893 (from Mabel Loomis Todd and Thomas Wentworth Higginson's editions of 1890 or 1891 or both) is sure. There is a contemporary report of it,[8] and one of Crane's poems from *The Black Riders* is unquestionably based on her "Two Swimmers Wrestled on the Spar" (J 201). It is possible that Dickinson's poetry moved him to write some of his own. But clearly there were other influences on his work. His sharp irony, for instance, which appeared in the earlier *Maggie*, was partly invoked by the fiction of Ambrose Bierce, which he greatly admired.

The fourteenth and final child of a charitable and rather unworldly Methodist minister, Crane had to face the narrower Methodist militancy on his mother's side of the family and in the church at large from the age of ten, when his father died. With that contrast in his life between the relative gentleness of his father's example and the fear of damnation that was the cornerstone of his mother's faith and that of her pietistic family, the rebellion in his poems against their conception of a tyrannical, capricious, and peremptory God was almost predictable. That became the foremost theme of his verse, along with its concomitants: a kind of limited earthly salvation, or at least surcease from the wicked God through kinship with other humans and the exercise, however futile, of one's individual will, and an insensitivity on the part of worshippers to God's cruel arbitrariness. Poem after poem of *The Black Riders* fits the model. In "A god in wrath" (*BR* 19),[9] the deity is bullying and beating a man who does all a sovereign human being can do in such a hopeless circumstance. He bites "madly at the feet of the god," while the people cry out against the valiant man and call the brutal god "redoubtable." "I saw a man pursuing the horizon"(*BR* 24) suggests that in a world ruled by a savage deity, insanity is admirable; when the persona remarks that going around and around in pursuit of an ever-receding horizon is futile, the pursuer cries, "You lie," and continues his absurd search. And yet there is something existentially magnificent in the madman's relentless quest for his own grail.

The truth, to Crane, is that people have invented the wrong God and look for Him in the wrong places, in the misconceived places of their own mythology. Thus in "Two or three angels" (*BR* 32), the angels, presumably not encumbered with the same theological baggage as mortals, on seeing "black streams of people" flowing into and out of a "fat church," are "puzzled / To know why the people went thus, / And why they stayed so long within." "I can't buy of your patterns of God, / The little gods you may rightly prefer," the first-person narrator declares to purveyors of their own images of God, in "I stood upon a highway" (*BR* 34). Crane wishes neither to foist his own notion of God on others nor accept theirs. In a world of absurdity, the only hope—even if it is remote—is through love and will. To him, the courageous individual devises his own pattern in his own way and must live with that one and no other. But the individual as Crane sees him is generally too absorbed with the new American materialism to find courage. "If you seek the attention of men," he wryly admonishes in "If you would seek a friend among men" (*BR* 122), one of his posthumously published poems, "Remember: / Help them or hinder them as they cry their wares."

War Is Kind, published in 1899, the year before Crane's premature death, solidifies the modern apocalyptic vision suggested by *The Black Riders* and does so in essentially the same style. The vehicle of his socioreligious rebellion is, for his time, a revolutionary form closely akin to the French *vers libre* of the period, though he may well have come to the same open form independently. The poems in both volumes are much more narrative than lyric, often containing two or more voices, one of which tends to seem more trustworthy, although Crane claimed that he deliberately presented the competing points of view without prejudice and left the reader to decide where his or her sympathies lay. The influence of the parables of his Christian training is unmistakable. In "The trees in the garden rained flowers" (*WIK* 102), which attacks social Darwinism with biting irony, a "little spindling tutor" runs to a father (the Father?) to cry against "this unjust thing in your garden!" "This thing" is that the more powerful children have grabbed "great heaps" of flowers for themselves until "only chance blossoms / Remained for the feeble." The father looks, all right, but he admonishes the tutor not to suppose that there is anything unnatural or unfair about the piggishness:

> "Not so small sage!
> This thing is just.
> For, look you,
> Are not they who possess the flowers
> Stronger, bolder, shrewder
> Than they who have none?
> Why should the strong—
> —The beautiful strong—
> Why should they not have the flowers?

The tutor, crushed, "Upon reflection, . . . bowed to the ground"; with savage irony, Crane has him venerate the infallible Father: " 'My Lord,' he said, / 'The stars are misplaced / By this towering wisdom.' "

Arguably, Stephen Crane's finest work was his fiction, especially the unerring verbal brush strokes of *The Red Badge of Courage* and some of his short stories, in which he managed to combine his fundamentally naturalistic, deterministic view of a godless world with a hope that man could survive spiritually by finding kinship with others of his kind. He did not think of himself as a poet, and in fact he denigrated his poems by insisting on referring to them as "lines." The "plots" of his poems were sometimes twined with incidents in the fiction.[10] Yet by adding his weight to Whitman's in the process of legitimizing free verse, by further exploring that misty area between prose and traditional poetry, by contriving an appropriate and effective parable format in which to express the religious and social anger and uncertainty of much of end-of-the-century America, and by bringing journalistic concision to his expression of the American milieu, Crane contributed more to the foundations of modern American poetry than he could perhaps realize. In the brevity and freedom of his diction; in his open, organic form; in his unflinching choice of subject and direct treatment of it, he helped to pave the way for imagism and beyond. He struck a chord close to the essential pitch of modern literature, and few others have sustained it in their work as he did. Daniel G. Hoffman observes, "Only Poe and Hemingway have neared Crane's lonely outpost from which in his verse he views, and makes us feel, the reality of a universe where force is law, where love is doom, where God is cold, where man's lot is fated misery, where hope is narrowed to the possibility of courage, and the reward of courage is self-sacrifice."[11]

· THREE ·

On to the Twentieth Century: Edwin Arlington Robinson, Robert Frost, the Midwestern Poets, and the Harlem Renaissance

> They cannot scare me with their empty spaces
> Between stars—on stars where no human race is.
> I have it in me so much nearer home
> To scare myself with my own desert places.
>
> —Robert Frost, "Desert Places"

At first glance, Stephen Crane seems far more modern than either of America's two outstanding poets of the beginning of the twentieth century, Edwin Arlington Robinson (1869–1935) and, one of America's most distinguished poets of any time, Robert Frost (1874–1963). With his conspicuously irregular free-verse lines and skeptical, even angry, stance, Crane's poetry bears the stamp of modernism, whereas, with their traditional rhyme schemes and prosodic patterns, Robinson and Frost conceal the stamp subtly in the tenor of their work. They are no less modern, however— at least in viewpoint and in the unadorned, direct use of language— than Crane or the three most outstanding poetic innovators of the period from the Midwest, Edgar Lee Masters (1869–1950), Carl Sandburg (1878–1967), and Vachel Lindsay (1879–1931).

Edwin Arlington Robinson

Edwin Arlington Robinson was born 22 December, 1869 in Head Tide, Maine, but it was Gardiner, Maine, where he moved in his first year and lived for the next twenty-seven, that he filtered through his imagination and transformed into the "Tilbury Town" of many of his best poems.[1] He articulated the world from behind the eyes of his Tilbury Town denizens—sad romantics, defeated men driven to drink or suicide, failures of many differing stripes. The models were close enough to home. One of his elder brothers succumbed to an addiction to alcohol, the other to morphine; his father was a bankrupt whose death during Robinson's two-year stint at Harvard contributed to his son's financial plight. Robinson was adroit at using the forms of his optimistic romantic predecessors, including Whittier, Holmes, Longfellow, and Bryant. However, his personal experience and laconic nature, combined with the historical play of Darwinism, industrialization, unfettered greed, and jingoistic expansionism—all of which were having an excellent run in his day—turned those traditional forms in his work into vehicles for the expression of pessimism and confusion. Influenced by a doctor friend in Gardiner, Alanson T. Shumann, who wrote verse of his own that sometimes regretted the inane warbling of contemporary poetasters, the young Robinson committed himself to being a poet.

Robinson published two collections of poems in the 1890s when he was in his late twenties: the small privately published *The Torrent and the Night Before* in 1896 and *The Children of the Night: A Book of Poems* the following year. From the first, in such sonnets as "George Crabbe" and "Credo" (both from the 1896 chapbook), he gave traditional forms, especially the poor faded sonnet, the transfusion that they sorely needed at the *fin de siècle*. He pays tribute to the English poet George Crabbe (1754–1832) because blood flowed vigorously through Crabbe's vivid poems of English country life in a way that it was not flowing through most late nineteenth-century American poetry. Robinson condemns "the Shame / And emptiness of what our souls reveal" by comparison. So awed have we become by shadows that "we kneel / To consecrate the flicker, not the flame." In his idealism, however, Robinson shows himself to be no mere complainer: ultimately, there is something like an Emersonian optimist *trying* to light a lamp in him. True, he challenges the overweening materialism of America in his work because he sees it as a terrible impediment to awareness of the self and of a benign and intelligently ordered cosmos. In "Credo" he speaks of "The black and awful chaos of the night"; he is adrift, unable to find his way with "no star / In all the shrouded heavens anywhere." Yet for all of that despondency, there is a voice of hope, so remote that he "can hear it only as a bar / Of lost, imperial music," but it is "the far-sent message of the years," nothing less than "the coming glory of the Light." Even the frequently anthologized "Luke Havergal," from *The Torrent and the Night Before*, which seems to suggest a bereaved lover's contemplation of suicide (the *western* gate is death, and that is where Havergal must go to be reunited with his love; there he can find "the dark [that] will end the dark, if anything"), can be read as a struggle between light and dark, which light can win when the dark dissolves itself.[2] Whatever one's reading of "Luke Havergal," Robinson seldom lost for very long the fundamental optimism that was at the core of his doubt; his incredulity mainly involved the foibles of his fellow humans, not some cosmic force greater than they. Indeed, his characters are frequently wont to fail when they lose that force.

He sometimes resorted to bare abstraction in the 1896 publication, rather less in *The Children of the Night*, but his achievement in both collections was of great importance. One critic rightly lauds the 1897 volume as "one of the hinges upon which American poetry was able to turn from the sentimentality of the nineties toward modern veracity and psychological truth."[3] Those attributes were suffused through the honest skepticism that he expressed in refreshingly accurate representations of the New England speech of his characters—the folks of his Tilbury Town.

In 1897, even before *The Children of the Night* was published, Robinson moved to New York, which he came to regard as his home. He began work on a number of longer pieces intended to avoid the didacticism for which his earlier work had been criticized, including *Captain Craig*, published in 1903, and "Aunt Imogen." It was an extremely difficult time for him. He had William Vaughan Moody, his exact contemporary and now at the zenith of his success as a poet, as an acquaintance and yardstick against which to measure his own success. Robinson was sharply aware of the vast differences between his own work and Moody's public protest poems and *The Masque of Judgment*, not the least of which was that Moody was widely published and popular. But to his credit, Robinson continued to develop his own voice and message.

He had considerable trouble finding a publishing house for *Captain Craig;* Houghton Mifflin ultimately agreed to handle the book in 1902 but only on condition that its costs be backed by friends of Robinson. Robinson himself had money troubles. He had had to return to Maine for most of 1898, and he had taken a job that he loathed at Harvard—secretary to President Charles W. Eliot—for the first half of 1899. Returning to New York, he continued to have a hard time supporting himself. He found work in 1903 as a time checker during the building of the subway system. Working in the gasses and dampness of the tunnels so depressed him mentally and physically that he became an alcoholic. Eventually he dried himself out, but in the process, he discovered how much easier it is to contract the disease than overcome it.

Friends continued to help Robinson, and in 1905 his luck changed because of both old and new ones. His old friend William E. Butler brought him to Boston to work in the advertising department of Butler's store and—of paramount importance to Robinson—to have time to write. That year another friend, Henry Richards (whose family, through Laura E. Richards, had helped to underwrite the publication of *Captain Craig*), a teacher at the Groton School, showed *The Children of the Night* to a student who liked the poems well enough to bring them to the attention of his father. The student was Kermit Roosevelt, whose father, President Theodore Roosevelt, wrote enthusiastically to Robinson and saw to it that a sinecure was found for him as a special treasury agent in the U.S. Customs Service in New York. The president also took the trouble to write a critique for *The Outlook* that did Robinson's reputation no harm; it was an era when some presidents still took an interest in literary matters. With good reason, Robinson saw Teddy Roosevelt as his personal and artistic savior; years later he wrote to Kermit that his father had "fished me out of hell by the hair of the head."[4]

Robinson was not out of the financial woods for good, but 1905 was the turning point. *Captain Craig* was neither critically acclaimed nor popular, but his job afforded him the chance to work on a new and better collection of poems, *The Town Down the River*, published in 1910, and on some plays—*Van Zorn* (originally *Ferguson's Ivory Tower*), the one-act *Terra Firma*, and *The Porcupine*—none of which brought him the recognition that he wished for. His job, with which he supported himself and assisted the family of his brother Herman, disappeared with Theodore Roosevelt's presidency in 1909, a setback that caused him to redouble his efforts in the more lucrative field of drama. In March 1913, however, he admitted that his attempts at drama that would please the public resulted in "the damndest rubbish that you ever heard of," and he resolved to return to writing poetry.[5]

Gradually, by 1917, his financial woes were resolved permanently. He had been spending summers at a writers' retreat, the MacDowell Colony in Peterborough, New Hampshire, since 1911, a wonderfully creative habit that he continued for the rest of his life. A modest bequest from a friend in 1914, a trust fund anonymously established in 1917 by other friends, and free lodging given to him by friends in New York permitted him to live a kind of ideal life for a poet until his death from pancreatic cancer in 1935.

THE CHRONICLER OF FAILURE. The reasons that Edwin Arlington Robinson chose failure for his major theme—or that it chose him—can only be surmised. Presumably they have to do with his sensitivity to the plight of his addict brothers, his bankrupt father, his own alcoholism, and his monetary struggles through nearly the first half-century of his life. Moreover, there seems to have been something in his nature that made him more cerebral than physical in his response to the world. He was spiritual in his insistence upon a mystical being in the universe outside of humanity and greater than it; that much he had in common with Emerson and Whitman, both of whom he admired. But he could be only about half a Transcendentalist, unable to find the exuberance, the *joie de vivre*, that was given to them by their confidence in humanity's capacity to discover that stupendous entity and merge with it.

Robinson's fascinating characters typically are perplexed, unfulfilled, and disgruntled in various proportions. Sometimes that is because they do not quite know what hollowness plagues them or because they do not know where to search for truth or because they have searched but have been stymied in the quest. Of Robinson's famous title characters, the romantic failure Miniver Cheevy (in *The Town Down the River*) lives in a past that never really was, curses the fate that landed him in the reality of the present, and drinks as a substitute for controlling his life. Bewick

Finzer (also in *The Town Down the River*) invested so much of himself in money that when the money went, his selfhood went with it. Now, "Familiar as an old mistake, / And futile as regret," he haunts the townspeople, who help him because they recognize enough of themselves in him. Pathetic old Eben Flood (in *Avon's Harvest*, 1921) has no internal resources and has outlived all of his friends but for the jug, from which he is inseparable. Robinson's sense of humor plays through many of these and other poems (for example, though Cheevy never saw a Medici, "He would have sinned incessantly / Could he have been one"), but there is more sardonic wit than mirth in the laughter. He may have esteemed Emerson, but Robinson is often as condemnatory of the human race as Melville. The wife in "Eros Turannos" (in *The Man Against the Sky: A Book of Poems*, 1916) cannot leave her Judas of a husband because she is too proud and too afraid of loneliness, and so she lives in a home "where passion lived and died." The narrator of "Karma" (in *Dionysus in Doubt: A Book of Poems*, 1925) tells of a moral bankrupt who has wrecked a friend in a business venture and atones by giving a sidewalk Santa "from the fullness of his heart . . . / A dime for Jesus who had died for men." Robinson's Cassandra (in *The Man Against the Sky*) sums up one of the human sins: she inveighs against the exchange of material sin for spiritual values and self-esteem in human affairs:

> "Your Dollar, Dove and Eagle make
> A Trinity that even you
> Rate higher than you rate yourselves;
> It pays, it flatters and it's new.

The home-grown prophetess is as well received as the classical Cassandra. The crowd laughs; "None heeded, and few heard." The multitudes who pray to the new Trinity do so at their dire peril, Robinson held. Even when such an apparent success as Richard Cory (in *The Children of the Night*, 1897) seems to have all that modern people wish for, there is such emptiness at the core that, inexplicably to all who envy him and subscribe to his values, Cory chooses a "calm summer night" to go "home and put a bullet through his head." Sometimes the weight of the world bore so heavily upon Robinson that death looked attractive. In

"How Annandale Went Out" (in *The Town Down the River*), the solution, haltingly spoken by a distraught physician, is euthanasia.

THE ARTHURIAN TRILOGY. There was much Miniver Cheevy in Robinson, both in the drinking problem and, more consequentially for his work, in the sense of romance that he shared with his character. Beginning with *Merlin: A Poem* (1917), the poet revealed his own compulsion to retreat to the past, to the world of gallantry and courtly love. But when he got there, he did not find it as wondrous as the Cheevy in him must have hoped. There is love in his conjured world of King Arthur, but, composing during the period of World War I, Robinson could not avoid linking the legendary material with the misery of modern warfare. "Arthur and his empire serve as an object lesson to coming generations that nothing can stand on a rotten foundation," Robinson wrote.[6] And a vivid object lesson he presented indeed, with Merlin having an apocalyptic vision that serves as a warning, even to atomic warriors, of "a crumbling sky / Of black and crimson, with a crimson cloud / . . . . And there was nothing but a crimson cloud / That crumbled into nothing." The physical description at the close of *Merlin* is grim and icy: "Colder blew the wind / Across the world, and on it heavier lay / The shadow and the burden of the night; / And there was darkness over Camelot," the poem concludes. *Lancelot* is no cheerier. Merlin's fiery vision comes to pass, and in the end, Lancelot rides through dark despair. "There was nothing," the narrator declares in the third line before the end. In the poem's final line, Robinson says of the lonely darkness in which Lancelot lives, "and in the darkness came the Light." But here as elsewhere in Robinson, the darkness is far more convincing than that mystical "Light" of his, which almost always comes as the superimposition of an afterthought, a puff of wish breathed against a gale of despondency. In fact, the "Light" does come to the trilogy at the end as Isolt of Brittany, mourning the loss of her beloved husband Tristram to Isolt of Ireland and death, but the comfort that she discovers in the transcendence of her love is not especially persuasive. Looking out over the sea for her Tristram, now forever lost, she sees "white birds flying, / Flying, and always flying, and still flying, / And the white sunlight flashing on the sea." The lines are lovely, as are many others in the trilogy, but the white light she sees is much like the light that comes to the mystic who has stared into the sun.

For a modern reader, Robinson's philosophy does not ring truer in his famous "Man against the Sky" (1916), a 314-line contemplation of life that he composed against the—unspoken—background of World War I and the period's deepening loss of faith, than it does in his Arthurian trilogy. The poem uses a description of a man seen climbing a hill and silhouetted against a sunset sky, "before the chaos and the fare / As if he were the last god going home / Unto his last desire," to trigger a reverie on the nature of mankind in relation to the universe. Robinson postulates five human philosophical stances in order of religious acceptance, ranging from "a faith unshaken" down through "easy trust assumed of easy trials," then "sick negation born of weak denials," still less, to "crazed abhorrence of an old condition," to the very bottom of Robinson's philosophical scale, "blind attention of a brief ambition," or self-indulgent materialism. The descent of faith has apparently been progressive and has lately been abetted by "infant Science," which "makes a pleasant face / And waves again that hollow toy, the Race." Use of such biblical allusions as Nahum's grasshoppers serves to emphasize the contrast between the age of faith and Robinson's own age of skepticism: modern scientific man may be "so great / That satraps would have shivered at his frown," but, Robinson admonishes the complacent doubters, "Nahum's great grasshoppers were such as these, / Sun-scattered and soon lost." Nahum 3:17 contains the prophet's forecast of a destruction of Nineveh.

"Man against the Sky" is no exception to the rule that Robinson was at his best in his character sketches, often suggesting ontological insights that went well beyond the immediate limits of those poems, and at his weakest in the prolixity of his deliberately philosophical poems and passages. Indeed, his discursiveness was remarkable in a man as notoriously laconic as Calvin Coolidge. What he gets around to saying at the end of "Man against the Sky" is that even in the absence of belief in the old verities, such as heaven and hell, humans have no choice but to believe in something greater than themselves and the mockery of death: "If after all that we have lived and thought, / All comes to Nought,— If there be nothing after Now, / And we be nothing anyhow, / And we know that,—why live?" Perhaps existentialists and some modern theologians have done better with the conundrum than Robinson; such argumentation is better suited to tract than poem anyway. His later, longer poems are even less attractive, because they are more hortatory and lacking in structure, than "Man against the Sky."

But none of this criticism is to denigrate Edwin Arlington Robinson's importance as an accurate prophet among early twentieth-century American poets. *Transition figure* is an overused term but in relation to Robinson, it is accurate. He did loosen up traditional forms (for example, the dominant measure of "Man against the Sky" is iambic pentameter, but many lines and rhymes break the pattern to reflect the crisis in belief that is the sense of the work). But he was, fundamentally, a traditionalist in form, whose conservative prosody, chiefly English blank verse, was used to convey—best in those taut sketches of his—the essence of the new, modern person, struggling with a flimsy match to get a fire lit in the dark on a windy mountain top before there comes what Emily Dickinson called "the letting go."

Robert Frost

When Edwin Arlington Robinson's *King Jasper: A Poem* (a highly symbolic treatment of the dissolution of society) was published posthumously in 1935, Robert Frost, who often displayed an irrational jealously toward his fellow poets,[7] contributed a preface with a generous and correct assessment of the "rival" Robinson:

Robinson stayed content with the old-fashioned way to be new. . . . His theme was unhappiness itself, but his skill was as happy as it was playful. There is that comforting thought for those who suffered to see him suffer. . . . The style is the man. Rather say the style is the way the man takes himself. . . . If it is with outer seriousness, it must be with inner humor. If it is with outer humor, it must be with inner seriousness.[8]

Frost's observation is fascinating because his accurate picture of Robinson is an equally accurate self-portrait. Like Robinson, he "stayed content with the old-fashioned way to be new." Though he was wisely regarded as a white-haired grandfatherly figure with twinkling eyes, Lionel Trilling was correct in calling him a "terrifying" poet.[9] The twinkle in his eye was the glow from a hellish flame.

Like Robinson, Frost was often misconceived as a regional poet, an easy enough mistake to make because both of them (and Frost far more than Robinson) used the down-home speech of the rural Yankee. The error was made by the many who did not or could not listen through the voices to hear their torment and warning. With Robinson, the misconception was not so common because he produced a good deal of verse that overtly announced his fear of crumbling civilization and substitution of material for spiritual values. But Frost's playfulness, which could sometimes be spiteful in personal relationships, frequently made him elusively dark in his poetry as he used it to disguise his vitriol and pain. He could smile and smile and still suggest villainy. Like Emily Dickinson, whom he discovered as a young man and greatly admired, he preferred to "Tell all the Truth but tell it slant"—to play the benign New England nature poet while really talking about what Trilling calls "a disintegration and sloughing off of the old consciousness."[10] Frost remained conservative about some things all of his life: generally about patriotism (in his essay "On Emerson," he confessed that, though he was not "a shriner," he was never unmoved at seeing the lines from Emerson's "Concord Hymn" inscribed in stone).[11]

A stalwart traditionalist in matters of form, he pointed out in his preface to *King Jasper* that he and Robinson believed that poems are written in spite of theory. As for content, Frost argued in that essay that propaganda is inadmissible in his poetry. "But for me, I don't like grievances," he said. "I find I gently let them alone wherever published. What I like is griefs, and I like them Robinsonianly profound." If prose would accept grievances, that was where they should be, "leaving poetry free to go its way in tears. . . . Let weasels suck eggs. I know better where to look for melancholy," he added with characteristic acerbity.

THE ROOTS OF MELANCHOLY. Frost knew where to look for melancholy because the ravaging personal tragedies of his life, as well as what seems to have been an innate, family disposition toward despondency, always left it in his plain sight. His work may have been his coping mechanism, but he did not escape to neverland the way Poe did. Frost, like Emily Dickinson and others before him, saw too "New Englandly" for that, but by the time he yielded to cancer and other ailments in 1963, just short of age eighty-nine, his personal disasters recalled those of the soap opera life of Poe.

Born in San Francisco in 1874, Frost lost his father there eleven years later. His mother, Isabel Moodie Frost, took her husband's body, young Robert, and his little sister, Jeanie, to Lawrence, Massachusetts, home of the boy's paternal grandparents, but with minimal help from them, Frost's family regularly had money problems as he was growing up in eastern Massachusetts and New Hampshire. His sister walked the line between hypersensitivity and insanity for many years, and eventually she had to be institutionalized. His mother was intelligent and well intentioned, but she was unable to control children very well and thus had a spotty income as a teacher. Frost did not visit her much in the sanitorium where she died of cancer in 1900, but he saw enough of her wasting away to be profoundly affected.

He married Elinor White, his high school co-valedictorian, in 1895, and they had six children. Elliott, the first born, died at the age of four. Lesley, the second child, grew up as close to normal as any of the other children, but she too suffered from the Frost instability and could, as on the occasion of her mother's death, attack her father for his selfish willfulness as intensely as at other times she could love him.[12] The third, son Carol, practiced at self-destruction assiduously for years before his rehearsals finally culminated in suicide in 1940. Irma, the fourth child, came to harbor the irrational fears of her Aunt Jeanie. The fifth, Marjorie, died in 1934 of an infection that followed the birth of her child; she had recently recovered from a life-threatening bout with tuberculosis. Elinor Bettina, the sixth, died in infancy. Each blow to his children struck Frost profoundly, for though he could seem aloof and self-absorbed, he invested all that he could of his affection and time in them, and to the end, he remained bound up in their lives and deaths.

When Elinor Frost died in 1938, Lesley berated her father, and there was some truth in her indictment. He knew it. He blamed his selfishness for his wife's having to bear five more children after the birth of the first had nearly killed her and doctors had warned that her heart had been so weakened by the experience that she must have no more children.[13] His sense of guilt was heightened by the refusal of his vexed wife and factotum of forty-three years to admit him to the side of her deathbed. His contrition at the time of Elinor's death did not stop him, however, from attempting later that year to tear apart the lives of two of his closest friends and benefactors, Kay and Theodore Morrison (he the poet, professor at Harvard, and director of the Bread Loaf Writers' Conference), when Frost asked the happily married woman to marry him. She was kind enough, honorable enough, and astute enough to rebuff Frost yet remain his loyal friend and helper.[14]

There is an episode that, among many, bears repeating for the light that it sheds on the petty side of Frost's complex personality. After Elinor's death in Gainsville, Florida, his friend Stanley King, president of Amherst College, where Frost had a faculty post that afforded him maximum freedom to write, travel, read, and lecture, took the trouble to travel all the way from Massachusetts to offer his assistance, particularly to help arrange a memorial service at Amherst. When Frost returned to Amherst, he was at loose ends over his loss and was engaged in a campaign among his friends to secure a position at Harvard. Frost resigned against the advice of King and refused to change his mind despite the opportunity that King gave him to reverse what was entirely his own decision. Yet in accounting for his departure from Amherst, the poet, at first by innuendo and soon by outright misrepresentation, transformed King into a villain who had forced him out. Within a year, Frost believed his own invention.[15] He sometimes liked to see that he was more bad than good.

Certainly the words on his penchant for vengeance that he uttered as a young man applied to the rest of his life: "I take a long time to wreak vengeance, when I've been wronged, but I never forget, and I never forgive a wrong"—real or imagined, he might have added.

THE PLAYFUL MASK. Given the chain of catastrophes in Frost's life, those that the fates obviously wove for him and those they more ambiguously caused him to manufacture himself by dint of his personality, there was an inevitability about the terrifying quality of his poetry. He was something of a classical protagonist whose virtues were artistic genius and single-minded dedication, fortitude, and wit, whose flaw, when it displayed itself, was an amalgam of jealousy, pettiness, willfulness, and cruelty. His uncanny ability to mask his dark weakness in his work by indirection and playfulness accounts for his having been easily the most popular poet in America since Longfellow. The remarkable affection of the American public for him at a time when the general appetite for poetry was in precipitous decline was based on the contrived grandfatherly and waggish impression that he was able to project of himself.

The fears and tensions of Frost's life governed much of his work from the start. As a young family man on a farm in Derry, New Hampshire, angered over his inability to find much of an audience for his poems (though he had had considerable high school success and did manage to place some poems afterward) and working diligently to perfect his craft, he began to infuse his experiences and his feelings into his poems. They were the basis of his truth. As he would write years later in one of his most often anthologized prose dicta, "The Figure a Poem Makes" (1939), "No tears in the writer, no tears in the reader. No surprise for the writer, no surprise for the reader. For me the initial delight is in the surprise of remembering something I didn't know I knew."[16] For that, he had to rummage in his own memory and psyche. But he also knew that experience and feeling must not be articulated outright. They had to be filtered through the creative imagination, controlled and disguised. The appropriate metaphor—what T. S. Eliot called the "objective correlative"—had to convey them to the reader; without the metaphor, there could be no poem worthy of the name: "Every poem is a new metaphor inside or it is nothing." No one has ever said it better than Frost: metaphor, he declared in *the Atlantic Monthly* in October 1946, in the essay "The Constant Symbol," "saying one thing and meaning another, saying one thing in terms of another, the pleasure of ulteriority. Poetry is simply made of metaphor."[17] And in a particularly Frostian observation, he said, "Every poem is an epitome of the great predicament; a figure of the will braving alien entanglements." Perhaps no other twentieth-century poet in English has had such a monumental will as he had to deal with predicaments and to brave entanglements.

In 1912 the determined Frost took his family with him to England into artistic exile. For his career as a poet, the move was a turning point. He was a thirty-eight-year-old aspiring unknown when he sailed; he returned three years later as the established author of two volumes of poems, both published in London by David Nutt and Company, a firm clearly more sensitive to his talents than the American publishing establishment had been. The first, *A Boy's Will*, appeared in 1913, and it was highly touted by Ezra Pound, whom Frost met in London, although the book was at first not generally received well by critics. Nevertheless, through his friend Harriet Monroe, editor of *Poetry* in Chicago, Pound helped Frost get a foot firmly in the door of the American market. Nutt came out with the second collection, *North of Boston*, in 1914, the year before Frost returned to the United States after at last finding an American publisher, Henry Holt and Company, of New York, which would print the two books there. *North of Boston* was widely acclaimed in England. At that point, the career as a poet that Frost had doggedly pursued for many years was assured, though he would never be secure enough in himself to stop promoting himself and fighting phantom enemies.

In fact, many of the poems that went into the two volumes in England and attracted his first audience there were pieces that he had brought with him from New Hampshire. The best of those—as would be true for the rest of the poems that he would write in his long lifetime—drew most directly from his own personal physical and psychic experiences and sublimated them—the poems in which, to paraphrase him, he said something else but meant those experiences. "Reluctance" for example, which appeared in *A Boy's Will*, had been composed before he was married, when he was still living with his mother and sister in Lawrence. It captures the despondency that he felt when, in a fit of jealousy, he visited Elinor at her school, St. Lawrence University in Canton, New York. To get even with her for apparently rejecting him there, he toyed with suicide by losing himself in the Dismal Swamp of Virginia.[18] The experience is reconstituted in the poem in terms of dead leaves, the passing of "the last lone aster," and the withering of witch hazel flowers, but at the end, with renewed courage (or Frostian bravado), the speaker resolves not to go "with the drift of things," not to accept the end / Of a love or a season," for to do so would be treasonous to the independent "heart of man." "Storm Fear," also from the first volume, offers another example.[19] Among the several fears that lurked in Frost's mind beyond rationality and caused him to keep a loaded revolver at the farm in Derry was terror of the dark and a dread of tramps (the latter he would express later in "The Hill Wife" [*CP* 160–162], in which he speculates that a tramp's smile "never came of being gay" and imagines the tramp "watching from the woods as like as not"). "Storm Fear" deals with the trepidation that storms raised in him. In it, he images the wind as a brute calling the speaker out of the house in which, when he counts his strength, he can find but "Two and a child"; the speaker doubts that he and his family can, "unaided," survive until daylight. "A Tuft of Flowers" (*CP* 31–32), from *A Boy's Will* too, is based on personal experience, in this case one that Frost had while making hay for a farmer at Gobbetts Pond, New Hampshire, in 1891.[20] The magnanimous side of Frost was able to find a symbol of universal kinship in the flowers the mower had left.

"Home Burial" (*CP* 73), from the *North of Boston* collection, was written in England in 1912 or 1913 and quite clearly reflects the terrible sense of loss that Robert and Elinor Frost suffered at the death of their first child, Elliott, a dozen years before—as well as, inevitably, the palpable tension that often crystallized between them.[21] As usual, Frost worked his magic, in this poem transforming the raw material of personal grief into something far more refined. Fundamentally, the poem, which seems to be about the loss of a child, really explores the dark failure of human understanding and communication. The rural husband is superficially less sensitive than the town wife, but ultimately, by achieving a fine dramatic irony, Frost wins more sympathy for him than for her. The reader comes to perceive what the wife cannot: that the husband's sorrow is as great as hers; it is merely externalized differently. She has not the power, or perhaps the will, to comprehend his rue or even that he feels any; he has not the power, or perhaps sufficient will, to articulate it to her.

Frost loved the kind of misdirection that careful reading reveals in "Home Burial." It is a serious kind of playfulness, and it is at work in many of even his best-known poems, which, because of his deceptions, are often partially misread. "The Road Not Taken" (*CP* 131), from *Mountain Interval*, for instance, is almost always read as advocating the seeking of adventure, the testing of oneself by breaking new ground, the way Frost did when he chose for himself (and for his family) the most difficult of the paths that life presented to him—becoming, exclusively, a poet. This is a fair enough interpretation, but readers are likely to lose track of what the poem actually has said by the time they reach the end, with the narrator's crowing over his having taken, of two possible roads, "the one less traveled by, / And that has made all the difference." He is proud to have taken the one with "the better claim, / Because it was grassy and wanted wear." Ah, but the narrator forgets, and so leads the reader to forget, what he noticed earlier: that "the passing there / Had worn them really about the same." Unable to take both roads, the narrator is later compelled to make a virtue of the one he actually chose *quite arbitrarily*, since, as far as he could see at the time, it was really identical to its alternative. The poem is less about trailblazing than it is about a basic human necessity: rationalization, justifying to oneself the wisdom of a decision that was more a matter of chance or instinct than anything else.

Similarly, even many of Frost's seemingly uncomplicated down-home vignettes—"Mending Wall" (*CP* 47–48), for example, from *North of Boston*, a poem he composed in England when he was depressed by the initial reaction to *A Boy's Will* and was feeling keenly nostalgic about New England—call for an alert reader. It is dangerous to stop at the obvious in Frost. Yes, the narrator mocks the "old stone savage" neighbor, who likes to repeat, " 'Good fences make good neighbors,' " as the two repair the stone fence between their properties, not for any useful purpose but out of blind obedience to custom. Frost's case is not closed, however; there is a further dimension, that playfulness to consider, for it is not the Neanderthal neighbor but the narrator himself who, first of all, calls on the neighbor to play the stupid game with him in the spring and then the narrator who equally fails to voice any misgivings about it as they walk the line. The poem is about being enslaved by tradition, but it is also about smugness and self-isolation, the hazard of cutting the lines to another human being.

THE RELIGIOUS POET. Considered from another perspective, "Mending Wall" begins to suggest another facet of Frost's poetry that is frequently overlooked. Even when he was being darkly playful, he did not stop posing the kinds of questions that had been at the heart of the poetry of his Puritan forebears and his nineteenth-century New England predecessors, notably Emerson and Dickinson: cosmic questions of first cause and governance of the universe, of a human being's relationship to a cosmic force and, in the light of that, to other human beings. Frost had a cruel and petty side to his personality, but he was, in his late-nineteenth, twentieth-century way, a poet with his roots as deep as any other in the rocky religious soil of New England, though not always obviously. The " 'Something there is' " in "Mending Wall," " 'that doesn't love a wall, / That wants it down,' " the mystical entity that the narrator would like to call " 'Elves' " to his stone-age neighbor to keep the idea simple, sounds very much like the Swedenborgian religious force that subtly signifies its presence by working surreptitiously through nature.

Although Frost would not always acknowledge the religiosity of his work or his mother's strong Swedenborgian influence on him from his boyhood and youth, occasionally, and increasingly as he got older, he would. "I was brought up a Swedenborgian," he declared in an interview. "I am not a Swedenborgian now. But there's a good deal of it that's left with me. I am a mystic. I believe in symbols."[22] A number of Frost's poems suggest the Swedenborgian influence in addition to "Mending Wall"—"Two Look at Two" (*CP* 47–48), for instance, in which some spiritual force brings insight to the two deer and two humans as they stand looking at each other in a magic moment, "As if the earth in one unlooked-for favor / Had made them certain earth returned their love." "For Once, Then, Something" (*CP* 276) provides the questor-narrator with an insight into something like cosmic truth in a white object he spies at the bottom of a well, down through the self-absorbed surface image of himself wreathed godlike in ferns; then, before he quite has it, as if to conceal such truth from a mere mortal, a drop of water is made to disturb the still surface and so hide the truth from the mortal. "Design" (*CP* 396) hints of some force that brings three objects together—a white heal-all (normally a blue flower), a white moth, and a white spider—in extraordinary conjunction in a blanched pattern of doom. The choice that the assemblage calls to the attention of the narrator is a very modern one: either there is a cosmic maker of such a deadly design or the phenomenon is merely random, both extremely disturbing possibilities. But the point is that the possibility of Swedenborg's mystical force is clear in the poem and that although the poem is spiritually discomfiting, Frost is preoccupied with a spiritual quest.

Although such poems as "Neither Out Far Nor in Deep" (*CP* 394), "Desert Places" (*CP* 386), "Acquainted with the Night" (*CP* 324), "Fire and Ice" (*CP* 268), and many others certainly justify Trilling's formulation of Frost as "terrifying," with their view of humanity as disconnected, alone, and incompetent to find the answers, on balance Frost found at least much of the spiritual stamina that he searched for to comfort him in his own "desert places." Fascinated by science and often oppressed by its effect on spiritual certainties, he had his regrets about both, as in "The Lesson for Today" (*CP* 471–76). "Space ails us moderns: we are sick with space," he understands in that poem, noting that "science and religion really meet." He adds that he is treating "universals, not confined / To any one time, place, or human kind. / We're either nothing or a God's regret." But he is not vanquished. He has never stopped questing through all the trials of his life and, as a poet at least, loving. In the poem, he summarizes his resolution of the questions, in the absence of real answers to them, with his oft-repeated self-insight: "I had a lover's quarrel with the world." The interstellar spaces of external and internal space can be so forbidding that death can be enticing, as in "Stopping by Woods on a Snowy Evening" (*CP* 275), but he never really altered the view he expressed in the early poem "The Trial by Existence" (*CP* 28–30) that God presides over human life of bitter testing and that, in the end, "are we wholly stripped of pride / In the pain that has but one close, / Bearing it crushed and mystified." Frost is the Job of his *A Masque of Reason* (*CP* 587–606) who learns ultimately that God has punished him, put him on trial, to show Satan that Job could withstand the cruelly unjust treatment. God, in effect, has brutalized Job in order to be able to boast of the constancy of humans who believe in Him.

The existential commitment to be as tough as those New England progenitors, as tough as death, as tough as it takes to absorb any punishment God could deliver—the existential commitment to accede to the harness bells and honor the "miles to go before I sleep"—never deserted Frost. Unable to read the dour but just God of his Puritan ancestors in nature and unable to intuit there the romantic and progressive God of Emerson and the Transcendentalists, he found in nature the doubtful modern God and no way to make much sense of His cruel testing but to look Him in the eye, absorb the punishment, and maintain the balance of his mind by making lyrical and sometimes dramatic poetry of it. He learned too the lessons—the wiles that nature taught for that kind of endurance. Like the drumlin woodchuck in the poem of that name (*CP* 265-66), he was cocky in the knowledge that he would survive: "though small / As measured against the All," he knew, "I have been so instinctively thorough / About my crevice and burrow."

So well did Robert Frost build, in fact, that at the end of his long life, he was celebrated by two presidents, Eisenhower and Kennedy, even reading his poem "The Gift Outright" at Kennedy's inauguration ceremony and briefly serving that president as goodwill ambassador to the Soviet Union. He built not just with brittle self-promotion, though he was even better at that than Walt Whitman himself; he built a shelter of pain against pain, but he made it sound so homey with the misleading simplicity of what seemed traditional verse, [23] and with a convincing use of rural American idiom and sense of place, that he came closer to becoming a national poet than anyone else since Henry Wadsworth Longfellow a century before.

The Midwestern Poets

Five other early twentieth-century poets—Carl Sandburg, Edgar Lee Masters, Vachel Lindsay, Edna St. Vincent Millay, and Sara Teasdale—merit consideration. The first three were from Illinois (though Masters was a transplant from Kansas), and Sandburg and Lindsay were associated with Harriet Monroe's influential Chicago magazine *Poetry*. Like Twain, Moody, Garland, Dunbar, and others, the three of them contributed to the westward movement of the American cultural fulcrum.

CARL SANDBURG. Sandburg, born in Galesburg, managed to excite something like the popular attention accorded to Robert Frost, but as a self-proclaimed poet of the masses self-consciously in the mold of Walt Whitman, Sandburg always missed the critical interest and acclaim that Frost relished while standing in the public limelight. Moreover, unlike Frost, who once having decided that poetry was his vocation devoted himself single-mindedly to it, Sandburg divided his energies. He learned America by roaming through it, supporting himself with a variety of temporary jobs, including newspaper reporting. He joined the staff of the *Chicago Daily News* in 1912 and began writing *Chicago Poems*, nine of which Harriet Monroe printed in *Poetry* in 1914, before Sandburg was able to publish the collection in 1916. He published a number of volumes of poems over the next couple of decades but spent much of the 1920s and 1930s working on a substantial six-volume biography of Abraham Lincoln, published in two groups as *The Prairie Years* and *The War Years*, that established him as a popular expert on Lincoln and won Sandburg the 1940 Pulitzer Prize for history.

Sandburg used the long-line cadences and repetition of Walt Whitman to express his own version of love for the great democratic experiment and the great En Masse. His poetry, beginning with *Chicago Poems*, anticipates the proletarian novels of John Steinbeck and John Dos Passos in the 1920s and during the Great Depression. His famous "Chicago" (*Chicago Poems*, 1916) established his chief mode: celebrating in free verse the defiant, laughing toughness of working-class America and its cities. "Happiness," from the same collection, is typical of his poems. Having asked professors and business executives to explain the meaning of happiness, to no avail, the narrator finds the answer to his question on Sunday afternoon along the Desplaines River among "a crowd of Hungarians under the trees with their women and children and a keg of beer and an accordion." Rare indeed has been the intellectual who could discover truth in accordion music. Twenty years later, in the title poem of *The People, Yes*, (1936), Sandburg was still finding fundamental inspiration in the raw power of the proletariat. "The fireborn are at home in fire," he said of the working people in that poem. "Man is a long time coming. / Man will yet win," he chanted.

Curiously perhaps, the other influence on Sandburg's poetry in addition to the maximalist influence of Walt Whitman, was the spreading minimalist influence of Pound and the other imagist poets, which was well known in Chicago and throughout the rest of America through appearances of imagist poems in the magazine *Poetry*. Sandburg's imagistic six-line poem "Fog" (1916), a small jewel in Sandburg's sprawl, is an obvious and renowned example, with its clear metaphor of fog as a transient cat that pussyfoots into the city, lingers awhile, and then goes on its way. That treatment of the fog anticipates T. S. Eliot's in "The Love Song of J. Alfred Prufrock," published the following year.

MASTER'S *SPOON RIVER ANTHOLOGY*. Edgar Lee Masters grew from the composer of undistinguished traditional lyric poetry fraught with classical allusion to the poet of the free-verse *Spoon River Anthology* (1915). His artistic development was fundamentally arrested at that volume, though he later published numerous other books of poetry and biographical studies (one of them a vitriolic study of Vachel Lindsay). *Spoon River Anthology* is a compilation of pieces, first published in the *St. Louis Mirror*, based on Master's observations mainly as a small-town lawyer in Petersburg and Lewistown, Illinois. By and large, the poems of the anthology have the effect of attacking the idealization of small-town life in America and so were precursors of the fiction of Sinclair Lewis and Sherwood Anderson.

The brief poems of the *Anthology* after the prologue called "The Hill" are each narrated by one of the townsfolk buried in the imaginary little town's hilltop graveyard. Each poem is named for its narrator. In free verse of uneven quality, each of the ghosts—many of whom have such bizarre or capricious names as Roscoe Rockapile, Petit the Poet, Percy Bysshe Shelley (the town's ne'er-do-well), and Voltaire Johnson—tells a story of his or her relations with others in Spoon River before death. The stories often reflect Master's sympathy for the strength of many of the characters—Anne Rutledge, for example, married to Abraham Lincoln "not through union, / But through separation," or Lucinda Matlock, who lived a hard, nurturing life for ninety-six years and had no patience for "Degenerated sons and daughters" for whom life is too strong. But the stories are laced with anger, greed, hypocrisy, betrayal, frustration, and failure. Petit the Poet, for instance, tells of the dead poet's having missed the human drama, composing instead trivial "Triolets, villanelles, rondels, rondeaus, / Seeds in a dry pod, tick, tick, tick / . . . what little iambics, / While Homer and Whitman roared in the pines!" Masters might well have been thinking in part of his own early technical exercises before Whitman's work got to him. In another example, the notorious Daisy Fraser, object of the town's disdain, recalls that she was never hailed before the judge "Without contributing ten dollars and costs / To the school fund of Spoon River!" while the pillars of the community—Editor Whedon, who took graft from politicians, the canning factory, and the bank for his support or his suppression of unfavorable news; the Circuit Judge, who was in the pocket of the "Q" railroad and the bankers; the local clergymen Peet and Sibley, who earned their salaries "by keeping still / Or speaking out as the leaders wished them to do"—hogged everything and gave nothing to the town. At times mention of stories or characters threads through several of the poems in a way that gives *Spoon River Anthology* something of the narrative quality of a novel. That quality, the sensational aspect of the townspeople's secrets, and the sensitivity of Masters's characterizations helped to establish the considerable popularity of the collection in Masters's time and since.

VACHEL LINDSAY. Vachel Lindsay had a big following, too, in the teens and 1920s, though he is rather a poetic curiosity now. Combining, as he did, a keen sense of showmanship with debts to such disparate sources as Edgar Allan Poe, Swinburne, Whitman (for a while), vaudeville, minstrel shows, and even college cheers, it could scarcely have been otherwise.

Lindsay was born in Springfield, Illinois, and took in some schooling at Hiram College in Ohio, the Art Institute in Chicago, and the New York School of Art before he undertook the first of a series of walking tours across stretches of the United States (from Florida to Tennessee in 1906, for example). The purposes of his perambulations were to recite and distribute printed copies of his poems in exchange for bed and board, and, incidentally, to learn first hand about his nation. The peripatetic poet came to the attention of Harriet Monroe in Chicago, and she published his "General William Booth [founder of the Salvation Army] Enters into Heaven" in 1913. That poem caught the public eye, got Lindsay on the lecture circuit, and made him forgetful about his allegiance to poverty. Some of his most effective poems ("The Congo" in 1914, "The Santa Fe Trail" in 1914, and "John L. Sullivan" and "Bryan, Bryan, Bryan, Bryan" in 1919) were written and performed during the rest of the decade and held his audience.

The word *performed* is used advisedly here. His verse was intended to be read aloud and his appearances to be entertainment. Lindsay was nothing if not theatrical in his sometimes whispered chanting of his poems, some of which, as in the cases of the

General Booth piece and "Simon Legree:—A Negro Sermon," were published with stage directions. What attracted Poe to him was Poe's musical pyrotechnics. Lindsay tried a good deal of his own, as in the "boomlay-boom" drumbeats of "The Congo."

To an extent, Lindsay anticipated the staginess of the Beat poets of the 1950s—Allen Ginsberg and Lawrence Ferlinghetti, for example. But America did not need the transparent, stereotypical racism of such poems as "The Congo," to which he gave the subtitle "A Study of the Negro Race" and in which he included sections on "Their Basic Savagery" and "Their Irrepressible High Spirits." Many a schoolchild, when it was popular for decades to have students memorize that hypnotic poem, was burdened with the bigotry that it taught. The question of whether Lindsay cleaned the slate by helping to get the fine Afro-American poet Langston Hughes published in the 1920s is moot. Lindsay's suicide in 1931 might have been caused by remorse, but it was not; poverty stricken, ill, and aware of his limitations as a poet, he gave up.

EDNA ST. VINCENT MILLAY, SARA TEASDALE, AND ELINOR WYLIE. Edna St. Vincent Millay (1892–1950) and Sara Teasdale (1884–1933) were also among the poets for whom Harriet Monroe found an audience in *Poetry*, which, under her editorship, sought a readership for conservative and avant-garde poets alike. Millay, like E. A. Robinson, was a native of Maine, and like Poe and Bryant, she made her mark early. Her most famous poem was "Renascence," a lyrically promising but somewhat gushy Wordsworthian romantic meditation that she composed at seventeen, published at twenty, and made the title poem of *Renascence and Other Poems* in 1917. She won a Pulitzer Prize in 1923 and a prize from *Poetry* in 1931 but never seemed to develop her potential as a gifted singer. There tended to be a kind of breathlessness in her love poems. She was disappointed in her reception as the decades passed, and when she turned to propaganda poetry in the 1940s (for example, "Poem and Prayer for an Invading Army" celebrating D-Day in 1944), she became as disappointed in herself as those who had noted her early promise were disappointed.

Sara Teasdale was probably the most self-conscious aesthete of these three, a poet who was deeply sincere but seemed to strike an artificial the-world-is-too-much-with-us pose in her work— partly because she too frequently described her feeling rather than showed it through potent imagery. She cried, for example, in "Sun of the Earth" that "with my singing I can make / A refuge for my spirit's sake, / A house of shining words to be / My fragile immortality."[24] The preciousness of her English romantic stance, her insistence that beauty is all there is to use as a shield against the woefulness of life, but that beauty itself brings its own woe to the sensitive—increasingly the sense that solace lies only in the direction of death—palls through much of her eight volumes of poetry.

On balance probably a better poet than Millay and Teasdale was the New Jersey–born Elinor Wylie (1885–1925), who was sometimes as fond as the other two of glittering surface but was capable of sure, concentrated imagery that the others could seldom manage. There was a perceptible progression in her poetry from a strong Shelleyan influence toward John Donne and the metaphysicals, evident in the use of conceits in such poems as "Address to My Soul" in the 1928 volume *Trivial Breath*.[25] Indeed, the potential that Millay lost somewhere along the way Elinor Wylie was fulfilling increasingly at the end of her short life.

The Harlem Renaissance

Among the most exciting intellectual events to occur in the United States in the early twentieth century was the Harlem Renaissance of the 1920s. The movement, also called the New Negro Renaissance after the essay published by black American sociologist Alain Locke in 1925, derived its name from the great flowering of Afro-American arts centered in Harlem.[26] In his essay, Locke asserted the cultural maturity of Afro-Americans and observed that black race consciousness was coming to fruition in Harlem for the first time in America.

Locke was quite right. Under the most difficult of circumstances, the poetry of such black poets as Phyllis Wheatley, Jupiter Hammon, George Moses Horton, and, more recently, Paul Laurence Dunbar had found its way into print, but slavery and racism had made certain that such voices were rarely heard. By the 1920s, civil rights for black people in America were yet to be won, racism would not succumb to decency or reason, and publishing was still a white industry. Nevertheless, conditions had changed for black artists.

It took a world war to change them. World War I cut off the supply of cheap white European immigrant labor for American industries, and, as the war machine cranked up and managers found white workers were enlisting, large numbers of blacks migrated from the rural South to fill the vacant jobs in factories in such urban areas as Detroit, Chicago, and New York. In less than a decade between America's deepening involvement in the war, even before the country formally entered it, and the publication of Locke's essay, the essential sense of black community, the critical mass of Afro-American urban consciousness necessary for a flowering of Afro-American arts, developed. Moreover, in the decade following World War I, there was sufficient affluence among whites in cities like New York to indulge an interest in black American culture. The 1920s were the first moment in American history when an Afro-American renaissance could have taken place, and that is when it happened.

Under the leadership of such intellectuals as W. E. B. Du Bois, James Weldon Johnson, and Locke, a racial pride welled up and took expression in political action, in music, painting, sculpture, literature, and all other forms of outlet for strong human emotional and intellectual ferment. Marcus Garvey's back-to-Africa organization, the Universal Negro Improvement Association (UNIA), was, for all its fancy uniforms and comic opera trappings, a serious reflection of black American feeling and had the support of hundreds of thousands of blacks in Harlem and beyond. Indeed, it became a serious enough matter to white authorities to cause them, finally, to look for and find dubious grounds on which to prosecute Garvey and put UNIA out of business.

CLAUDE MCKAY. Claude McKay (1889–1948)—with Jean Toomer, Langston Hughes, and Countee Cullen the outstanding poets of the Harlem Renaissance—was born in Jamaica and published two volumes of verse (*Constab Ballads* and *Song from Jamaica*, both in London in 1912) before coming to the United States for further education. He arrived with a vigorous racial pride that his Jamaican peasant parents had inculcated and with a hatred for racial injustice that he acquired as an observer of the British colonial system when he was a constable (hence the title of his first volume) in Kingston. Thus sensitized, he was appalled by the racial conditions he discovered in the United States, and he became the most militant poet of the Harlem Renaissance, indeed, perhaps the most militant Afro-American poet to confront American racism before the black power movement of the 1960s.

He set the tone for his crusade in two of his early American poems. In *Pearson's Magazine* in 1917, he drew his line in the sand in one of his most frequently reprinted poems, "To the White Fiends," warning white lynchers that he, too, can be "fiend and savage" and can "shoot down ten of you for every one / Of my black brothers murdered." Two years later he published in the *Liberator* his well-known sonnet "If We Must Die," another powerful reaction to lynching—this time to the multiple murder of blacks during what came to be called the "bloody summer" of 1919. "If we must die, let it not be like hogs," he exhorted black Americans in that poem. He was enraged by the racial violence he had witnessed for years as he moved around the country working at odd jobs in kitchens and as a Pullman car waiter, when he and his colleagues found it necessary to carry weapons for protection. Better not to be butchered obsequiously, he declared, but to die, if necessary, "Like men . . . / Pressed to the wall, dying, but fighting back!"

In 1922 Harcourt published what may be McKay's best volume of poems, *Harlem Shadows*, a collection that excoriated violence perpetrated against black Americans ("The Lynching"), gave vent to his own hatred as a response to racism ("Baptism" and "The White City"), and served notice (in "America") that the United States would perish without racial reform. Though he continued to write and publish poems, *Harlem Shadows* was the last volume of his verse that he published before his death in 1948. His literary energy after 1922 was largely expended in writing novels (*Home to Harlem*, 1928; *Banjo*, 1929; and *Banana Bottom*, 1933), an autobiography (*A Long Way from Home*, 1937), and an impressionistic view of Harlem (*Harlem: Negro Metropolis*, 1940). *Harlem Shadows*, though, was strong enough and technically adroit enough in its use of the sonnet form and its lyricism to earn Claude McKay a place not only in the pantheon of the Harlem Renaissance but at least a small niche in the poetic pantheon of a nation still struggling to live up to its ideals.

JEAN TOOMER.   Jean Toomer (1894–1967), born in Washington, D.C., produced but a single book during his lifetime that attracted much public notice, but what a book! Probably more because it defies classification than for any other reason—and perhaps, alas, for racial reasons—it has enjoyed some critical acclaim but has not widely been acknowledged as what it is. *Cane*, published by Boni and Liveright in 1923, is one of America's most distinguished literary accomplishments of the twentieth century.

Critics are generally uncomfortable when they cannot name things, as if, in some way, to name were to control. Because they have not been able to label Toomer's magnum opus, have not known how to get hold of it, they have tended to handle it gingerly or to ignore it. How should one approach and take hold of a book that is at once a collection of poems, a volume of short stories and sketches, a novella, and a drama?

Toomer came to write *Cane* as a result of a fortuitous event in his life in 1921. Filled with a sense of unease over what he took to be failed attempts to write poetry and pieces of prose fiction and nonfiction in New York for a couple of years and with the conviction that his failure emanated from an inner disharmony (a condition that he spent much of his life seeking to cure), Toomer, on a visit from New York to his grandparents in Washington, D.C., met the principal of a small country school for blacks in Sparta, Georgia, who invited him south to run the school temporarily. Glad for a chance to see the South and get out of his rut, Toomer accepted. Living alone in a poor shanty in the Georgia countryside, he was moved by the spiritual dignity of the rural blacks—often as expressed in their music—and by the economic, political, social, and human oppression to which the dominant white society subjected them. He began to give controlled utterance in poetry and poetic prose to the emotions that welled up inside; he was giving birth to *Cane*.

Toomer arranged the elements of the volume in three sections. The first is a beautifully sensuous and lyrical grouping of poems and sketches portraying seven rural Georgia women, all downtrodden sexually and socially—even the one white woman among the seven who reflects the awful damage that racism wreaks on the oppressor race as well as the oppressed in the South. She, crazy Becky, "was the white woman who had two Negro sons," and all the family was cast out. In the portraits of the black women—Karintha, Carma, Fern, Cloine, Louisa, Esther—there are strength, pathos, powerful sensuality, earthiness, and lovely music, but the blood of violence never runs far beneath the surface. At the end of the first section, a black man is forced to kill a white rival for Louisa's attention and is lynched. Louisa gives in to the madness that racism produces, as Becky does earlier in the section, and she is left in the moonlight singing, "Red nigger moon. Sinner! / Blood-burning moon. Sinner! / Come out that fact'ry door."

Section 2 comprises five poems and seven sketches in lyrical prose. Together they record the movement of black Americans into the cities, in this case, Washington, D.C., and Chicago, with all the disillusionment and determination that accompanied the migration. Section 3 is a return to rural Georgia through the experience of Ralph Kabnis, a northern black teacher and poet, clearly in part a fictional manifestation of Toomer himself, who works through his oppressive experiences towards a sense of self—and black identity.

The poems of *Cane*, which relate tonally and spiritually to the prose segments, are occasionally regular in form, at times reflective of the music of Afro-American folk culture. The best of them, however, may be the free-verse lyrics that were clearly influenced by the imagist poetry and tenets of the previous decade. For instance, in the middle section of the book, immediately following the sketch "Theater," which deals with the frustrated emotions of a dancer called Dorris, Toomer places an exquisitely evocative little imagistic poem, "Her Lips Are Copper Wire," to reinforce the passion of Dorris and those who want her. The speaker urges her to breathe on him so that her breath is "like bright beads on yellow globes"—globes of streetlights that gleam and seem to move in the fog "like bootleg licker drinkers" (*Cane* 54).

Jean Toomer lived until 1967, and he did publish poetry after *Cane*. "Blue Meridian," for example, a long visionary poem on America's potential, influenced by Walt Whitman and Hart Crane, appeared in an anthology in 1936, but the touch, except occasionally for some lyrical lines, was essentially gone.[27] Searching for a means to secure that spiritual harmony that he believed he lacked, soon after *Cane* Toomer discovered in the work of the mystic G. I. Gurdjieff a system to integrate the intellectual, emotional, and spiritual self, and he very largely gave himself to it for the rest of his life. It tended to flavor everything he did, and its artistic effect was not, overall, salutary. "Blue Meridian" tends to be too mystically rhetorical, a Gurdjieffian essay in poetic camouflage. But what Gurdjieff did for him was personally more important. Like Countee Cullen, another poet of the Harlem Renaissance, Toomer, a cosmopolite and the product of a predominantly white education, resisted being categorized as black or as anything else other than human. Gurdjieff gave him the intellectual basis on which to free himself from labels and integrate himself with all human experience.

COUNTEE CULLEN. Countee Cullen (1903–1946) is probably as representative of the Harlem Renaissance as any of the other poets associated with it; certainly, he embodied the ideas of its intellectual leaders—W. E. B. Du Bois, Alain Locke, and James Weldon Johnson—and his work resounds with the paradoxes of the movement: its romantic quality yet its urbanity; its search for black roots in the soil of Africa yet its expression of twentieth-century American urban life; its fury at racial injustice in America yet the dream that America could learn to act civilly; its strident racial protest yet its intention to show whites what black intellectuals could produce and to bring the races together through art. Du Bois declared that "it is a fine and praiseworthy act for Mr. Cullen to show through the interpretation of his own subjectivity the inner workings of the Negro soul and mind."[28] While black critics of a later generation would criticize Cullen because he refused to categorize himself or be pigeonholed by others as a racial poet, that was precisely what the intellectual leaders wanted. As Johnson said, "Cullen himself has declared that, in the sense of wishing for consideration or allowances on account of race or recognizing for himself any limitation of 'racial' themes, he had no desire or intention of being a Negro poet. In this, he is not only within his right; he is right."[29]

It was natural for Cullen to regard his poetry, and art in general, as a bridge between the races, for he was brought up and educated with one foot in the black culture and the other in the white. As the adopted son of the pastor of the largest congregation in Harlem, whose rectory was close to the heart of activities undertaken to ameliorate the condition of Afro-Americans, Cullen was sharply aware of the injustice and struggle. But he was educated at a predominantly white high school in New York; then at New York University, where he took his bachelor's degree; and at Harvard, where he went on for his M.A. He excelled in all of those institutions, seeing his poems in print and winning prizes for some of them. He won not only the approbation of the white community but, with four books of his poems published by 1929, an anthology of Afro-American poetry, columns in both the NAACP and Urban League organs, and a two-year marriage to the daughter of Du Bois (1928–30), he was one of Harlem's darlings too.

He died from uremic poisoning at the beginning of 1943, before his forty-third birthday, and long before that he would write less and less poetry as the 1920s gave way to the 1930s, as the white audience and publishing industry needed to sustain the Harlem Renaissance had their attention diverted by the unhappy economic realities of the Great Depression, and as praise for Cullen's poetry became muted. He would become a teacher, flirt with fiction, drama, and children's literature, and publish but a single book of poems after the 1920s (but for his posthumous volume of self-selected poems *On These I Stand*, which contained only a half-dozen previously unpublished pieces, in 1947). But in the 1920s, Countee Cullen was a young poetic star glittering in the sky over Harlem.

Cullen, because of his belief in the integrative force of art, criticized Langston Hughes's first volume of poems, *The Weary Blues* (1926), for being too Negro in its jazz rhythms. When Cullen brought out his anthology of Afro-American poetry, *Caroling Dusk*, in 1927, he carefully subtitled it *An Anthology of Verse by Negro Poets* and explained in the introduction that the expression was intended to convey the idea that while there was surely poetry written by Negroes, he denied any such classification as Negro poetry that could be defined by the characteristics of the poetry itself. Yet if Negro—or what came to be called black or Afro-American—poetry is taken to mean poetry written out of the black American experience that can scarcely be written by anyone who has not had that experience, then Cullen himself wrote Afro-American poetry almost exclusively. His models—Shelley, A. E. Housman, and especially Keats—came from his conservative education, and he continued to use their traditional English verse forms, but the stuff of his poems was his life as a black man in America. Even the titles of four of the five books of his poems published during his lifetime—*Color* (1925), *The Ballad of the Brown Girl: An Old Ballad Retold* (1927), *Copper Sun* (1927), and *The Black Christ and Other Poems* (1929)—intimate his racial absorption.

Furthermore, he could theorize about the bridge of art all he wished, but in those quiet moments when he listened to the voice within, he heard the cry of outrage and could only echo it. More than half of his poems are quite direct protest poems, many of them powerful outcries, even if lacking the violence or threat of violence that characterizes Claude McKay's poetry.

Among Cullen's best-known poems are three from his first volume, *Color.* In "Yet Do I Marvel," the narrator can accept all of God's hurtful jokes, such as making moles blind, except the most painful trick of all: "To make a poet black, and bid him sing!" "Incident" tells the bitter story of the narrator's visit to Baltimore as a boy of eight when he was called "nigger" by another boy on a bus; of everything that he saw in Baltimore, that racial slur is all that he can remember. "Heritage" (along with "Atlantic City Waiter," "Fruit of the Flower," and "A Song of Praise" in the same collection) reflects the Negritude theme— the yearning for a romanticized Africa—that runs through Harlem Renaissance literature and art. The speaker is an urban black who feels the atavistic pull of Africa competing in his blood with the civilization in which he finds himself. Alien that he is made to be in his own land, he concludes, *"Not yet has my heart or head / In the least way realized / They and I are civilized."*

Unlike Jean Toomer, Cullen kept his work well insulated from the influence of such influential moderns as Ezra Pound, Amy Lowell, and the imagists (treated in detail in Chapter 4) though he knew the poetry of such people and commented on it favorably in his critical writing. He stayed with his conventional models, using his lyrical gift to advantage, but failing to build on his strengths, so that by the end of the Harlem Renaissance, the effete quality of his poetry and its lack of growth were becoming clear to critics; he was a fading star. But he was also sensitive to the nonliterary basis for some of the adverse criticism both in his own time and that was to come later, and so in *On These I Stand* he left this testament in the poem "To Certain Critics": observing, "No racial option narrows grief," he declared "I'll bear your censure as your praise, / For never shall the clan / Confine my singing to its ways / Beyond the ways of man."

LANGSTON HUGHES. Langston Hughes (1902–67), born in Joplin, Missouri, remained closest to the folk of all the poets of the Harlem Renaissance. He became the most popular poet of the group and quite probably the most popular black poet in America to date. He lived long enough both to absorb and lead the changes in the attitudes of black Americans in the 1960s, and so he never lost touch with his large audience. Like one of the other black artistic leaders of the 1920s, James Weldon Johnson, who adapted dialect, sermons, and folklore to his own poetry, Hughes also mined the rich vein of Afro-American folk materials for his work, most notably musical forms—jazz, blues, and work songs.

Vachel Lindsay called Hughes to public attention in 1924 when Hughes, then a busboy in a New York restaurant, showed Lindsay some of his poems. By 1926 Hughes had his first collection of poems, *The Weary Blues*, in print. Its music, which suggested a sense of superficiality of American whites, while capturing the rhythms of Harlem at night, the ache of black life, and the attempts to assuage it, made the book exciting. The title poem seems to bear the weight of all the oppression of urban blacks in the description of a blues tune played from "a black man's soul." The man sings and the piano moans:

> 'I got the Weary Blues.
> And I can't be satisfied.
> Got the Weary Blues
> And can't be satisfied—
> I ain't happy no mo'
> And I wish that I had died.'

The blues singer croons that tune so far into the night that "The stars went out and so did the moon"; finally, he goes to bed with the echo of those "Weary Blues," and "He slept like a rock or a man that's dead." No one who had lived or was familiar with black American life could fail to apprehend the accuracy of that world-weariness. And no less acurate than his representations of black feelings were his uses of common black speech—a feat all the more remarkable considering the erudition of Hughes's own language.

Though Countee Cullen was uncomfortable with Hughes's assertion of race, both were writing poetry from much the same perspective, though the verses of each sounded different from those of the other. (Cullen was among the few who had reservations about *The Weary Blues*, which was widely applauded, and even Cullen, a friend of Hughes, was generally encouraging.) Both were writing from the outrages of their experience to protest racial conditions in America, and Hughes, like Cullen, was sometimes caught up in the romantic, escapist yearning for mother Africa. Hughes's best-known poem associated with the Negritude theme is "A Negro Speaks of Rivers," also in *The Weary Blues* volume, which came to him quite spontaneously as he crossed the Mississippi by train on his way to Mexico to visit his father, who had emigrated there when Hughes was a boy to avoid further racial injustice in the United States. In the poem, which manages in its cadence to mimic the slow, rich flow of a large river, the speaker merges with blacks and other oppressed peoples beside the great rivers of history—the Euphrates, the Congo, the Nile, the Mississippi. He has become one with time and the flow of the river: "I've known rivers: / Ancient, dusky rivers, / My soul has grown deep like the rivers."

Hughes was more than a poet. He was a translator (of García Lorca and Gabriela Mistral, among others); a writer of fiction, long and short; the creator of the character Simple, the most offhandedly telling character and still the most popular in Afro-American fiction; as well as a journalist, dramatist, and world traveler. But his posterity rests mainly on his poetry. Indeed, he is known as the poet laureate of black America, and if anyone has claim to that title, he probably has. Perhaps what this gentle, sardonic poet was most essentially about is to be found in his poem "Theme for English B," from his 1951 *Montage of a Dream Deferred*. In it, the speaker faces an assignment for his English class; he is to write a page, "And let that page come out of [him]" so that "it will be true." He does not find the task easy, but he understands much about that page. He wonders whether it will be "colored"; he knows that "Being me, it will not be white." And he has a little secret to share with America:

> . . . it will be
> a part of you, instructor.
> You are white—
> yet a part of me, as I am a part of you.

White instructor and black student learn from each other, although the instructor is "older—and white- - / and somewhat more free," the speaker observes in a tart understatement. Implied is the simple truth that they had better learn from each other.

· FOUR ·

The Emergence of the Modern: Amy Lowell, H.D., Gertrude Stein, Marianne Moore, and the Imagists

> It may be said that the self-conscious awareness of a break with the past may be felt in two main ways: as emancipation, a joyful release from the dead hand of convention, from stale pieties and restrictions; or as a disinheritance, a loss of tradition, belief and meaning.
>
> —Monroe Spears, *Dionysus and the City*

When "the modern" happened, no one is quite sure. Literary historians have argued that the "transition from Romantic and Victorian to 'modern' modes of poetry is one of the fundamental shifts in all the history of art."[1] That transition involved a major shift in the consciousness of Western civilization. From the idea that the poetic expression of human experience required the order of traditional verbal forms like the sonnet, the iambic pentameter line, the rhymed quatrain, the balanced and purposeful stanza, there emerged a counteridea that gathered force throughout the nineteenth century and exploded in the early twentieth century, its fallout affecting all the major art forms. That counter-idea asserted that traditional formal values were too restrictive and were no longer viable in the vast, complex, chaotic, urban world of modernity.

Some of the key changes in modern thought can be traced to the ideas of Darwin, Marx, Freud, and Einstein, who were reassessing the relationship of human beings to the world around them and the worlds within them. From Darwin came the idea that the emergence of human forms was a natural, not supernatural, event that occurred over millions of years, the result of random forces and natural selection. Chance, not divine will, seemed the governing principle of what appeared to be an increasingly accidental universe. From Marx came a view of human society as perpetually engaged in class struggle. In Freud's work the inner world of humanity was depicted as dominated by unconscious drives and motives, accessible only through dreams and deep exploratory analysis. And from Einstein came the revolutionary principle that time and space, the psychic and physical environment of humanity, were relative, not absolute, entities, subject to continuing alteration and redefinition as the mysteries of the cosmos unfolded.

In American poetry these radical reconceptions of the inner and outer worlds of humanity emerged in strikingly different ways in the work of the poets who began searching for new modes of verbal expression that would set their work apart from the literary traditions they inherited. Modern poetry was necessarily a difficult and complex poetry, reflecting the difficulties and complexities of life in the twentieth century. Yet modern poets were acutely aware of a sense of loss and lack of certitude that this separation from the past implied. To compensate, some early twentieth-century writers sought to revive classical and religious myths in new formal configurations. Others sought "to purify the language of the tribe," as Ezra Pound put it—to use words as exactly as the terms of a mathematical equation. Put another way,

The modernists have been as much imbued with a feeling for their historical role, their relation to the past, as with a feeling of historical discontinuity. . . . Modern writers, working often without established models and bent on originality, have at the same time been classicists, custodians of language, communicators, traditionalists in their fashion.[2]

This paradoxical quality of modernism—its simultaneous assertion and rejection of literary and historical traditions—appears in the work of nearly all the avant-garde American poets of the early twentieth century. Amy Lowell, Hilda Doolittle (H.D.), Gertrude Stein, Marianne Moore, T.S. Eliot, and Ezra Pound are the major figures of this period, and all of them redefined poetic values. Although they were aesthetic revolutionaries—that is, appreciation of their work required a radical change in literary values—they were also, for the most part, classicists in the sense defined by British poet and critic T. E. Hulme.

The Reaction to Romanticism

The theoretical "speculations" (as his most important book was titled) of T. E. Hulme helped to define the new international dimensions of twentieth-century American poetry and the new emphasis on visual rather than purely literary values: "A man cannot write without seeing at the same time a visual signification before his eyes. It is this image which precedes the writing and makes it firm."[3] In his famous essay, "Romanticism and Classicism," published in 1924 but written at least a dozen years earlier, Hulme defined what he saw as a newly emerging classicism in poetry, a counter to the romantic excesses of the nineteenth century. For Hulme the terms *romantic* and *classical* applied not merely to particular periods of literary history but rather to ways of seeing the world, to philosophical concepts that alternated in various epochs of human history. The root of all romanticism, he argued, was the idea "that man, the individual, is an infinite reservoir of possibilities; and if you can so rearrange society by the destruction of oppressive order, then these possibilities will have a chance and you will get Progress."[4] Romantic poetry for Hulme was inherently political; it regarded human potential as nearly unlimited if only the prevailing social order could be changed.

The classical he defined as "quite clearly the exact opposite to this. Man is an extra-ordinarily fixed and limited animal whose nature is absolutely constant. It is only by *tradition* and *organization* that anything decent can be gotten out of him" (Hulme, 116). For Hulme, as well for Pound, Eliot, H.D., and others of their generation, the modern meant a reassertion of tradition and a discovery of the modern poet's relation to it. Poetry did not emerge from the privacy of an individual soul; it was an art form that had evolved over centuries, and modern poets needed to become students of the literary past in order to express their modernity. This idea was developed to its fullest by T. S. Eliot in his seminal essay of modernism, "Tradition and the Individual Talent" (see chapter 5), but for Hulme it meant primarily a jettisoning of the excesses of a highly personalized romantic poetry that he felt was characterized by poets' "moaning and whining" rather than concentrating on the art of poetry as well as its craft. "I object," he wrote, "to even the best of the romantics. . . . I object to the sloppiness which doesn't consider a poem is a poem unless it is moaning or whining about something or other. I always think in this connection of the last line of a poem of John Webster's which ends with a request I cordially endorse: 'End your moan and come away' " (Hulme, 126). Modern art, in all of its generic manifestations, was to involve a basic change in the terminology by which we express appreciation for aesthetic achievement. "Instead of epithets like graceful, beautiful, etc., you get epithets like austere, mechanical, clear cut, and bare, used to express admiration" (Hulme, 96).

These same terms could well be used to describe much of the new visual art that was beginning to alter modern consciousness of the physical world. Poets particularly were cognizant of developments in other art forms, especially the visual arts, and they attempted, however covertly, to find parallels for the radical experiments of the impressionists, the cubists, the surrealists, and the futurists in their poetry. To understand modern American poetry, it is important at least to glance at the changing view of the modern world as it was being depicted by artists, in both America and abroad.

Developments in the Visual Arts

Artists, said Ezra Pound, are the "antennae of the race," and although the work of Darwin, Marx, Freud, and Einstein crystallized and epitomized the newly emerging worldview of the twentieth century, writers and visual artists of the late nineteenth century had already begun to revise the cultural expression of the modern world. In the visual arts, these changes became manifest in the remarkable canvases of the French impressionists where the previously static and orthodox landscape is shattered into a fluid array of dots, colors, and vigorous brush strokes that create a sense of the transitory and shifting environment of the modern world. Claude Monet's *Sunrise, An Impression* (1872), the painting that named the movement, renders its physical scene not as landscape but as "the sensation produced by a landscape."[5]

Even more pertinent is Vincent Van Gogh's famous *Starry Night*, a canvas of swirling, electrified colors and textures conveying the humility of the human world in relation to the immense energy of the cosmos. The dazzling night sky nearly overwhelms the little town, which only softly asserts its fragile presence into the mystery above it. The dominant feature of the earthly world is a tall, swirling tree, which assumes a much more central and significant position in relation to marvelous and mysterious sky than the puny human landscape around it.

In the United States, these developments in the arts appeared in the work of the New York realists of the turn of the century— a group of painters who came to be known as the Ashcan School because of their affinity for offbeat, urban subjects and their concentration on the less picturesque aspects of American life. This group included Robert Henri, John Sloan, William Glackens, Everett Shinn, and George Luks, and their work is perhaps best epitomized by Sloan's *The Wake of the Ferry* (1907), a rough, off-center canvas depicting a lone, shadowy figure on the back deck of a ferry bobbing in the waters of the New York Harbor. Here is an image of humanity isolated, caught off-balance, and set adrift in the dark, dense, impenetrable atmosphere of modern urban life.

The visual manifestations of the modern did not take root in America until 1913, the year of an exhibition of international art in New York organized by the Association of American Painters and Sculptors. The Armory Show, so called because it was mounted at the Sixty-ninth Infantry Regiment Armory in New York, linked developments in American art to the vigorous and experimental continental scene where innovative movements were flourishing. The cubist and expressionistic painters of the early twentieth century—Picasso, Braque, and Kandinsky, for example—were displayed along with the even more avant-garde work of Francis Picabia and Marcel Duchamp. Duchamp's *Nude Descending a Staircase* (1912) became the symbol of the exhibit.

At the opening of the exhibit, John Quinn, an American lawyer and patron of the arts (Quinn was to become T. S. Eliot's primary financial backer) announced that "this exhibition will be epoch-making in the history of American art. . . . Tonight will be the red-letter night in the history not only of American, *but of all modern art*" (Dunlop, 163). In retrospect, few would disagree; the Armory Show created a sense of an international community of artists who shared an awareness of the revolutionary and distinctive newness of twentieth-century life and culture. The parochialism of nationality and regionalism was superseded by images of the rapidly changing urban, industrial, and fragmented twentieth-century world. This world could be expressed only in radically new images that departed from the formally structured, natural or supernatural images of the art of previous times. The new art was an art of motion, speed, urbanity, machinery, and the accelerated pace of life. Duchamp's *Nude* was an appropriately representative piece for the exhibit because it presented the human form as a succession of lines and planes in motion, a quintessential expression of the wedding of human and machine.

The Imagist Movement

Although there is a long history of related developments in the visual and verbal arts, the congruence of American poetry and painting established itself clearly in that most "painterly" of literary movements, imagism, the dominant trend in American poetry in the second decade of the century. Its main practitioners—Ezra Pound, Amy Lowell, Hilda Doolittle, and William Carlos Williams—though differing in many of the particulars of their aesthetic views, were agreed on the importance of finding a verbal equivalent to the transformations of the visual image occurring in painting. They sought also to imitate the exactness of science in rendering their interpretations of the physical world. The imagist movement had a relatively short life, but it is important because of the attention it directed to the sensuous qualities of poetry. It emphasized the fact that language, when used precisely, should appeal to the senses of readers and evoke a response as close as possible to the response generated by whatever is being described.

In March 1913 Ezra Pound and F. S. Flint enunciated the principles of imagism in *Poetry* magazine. Flint observed that the imagists were concerned with conveying in poetry a "direct treatment of the 'thing' whether subjective or objective." He emphasized their concern for precision: "To use absolutely no word that did not contribute to the presentation." And he stressed their interest in metrical innovation: "As regarding rhythm: to compose in sequence of the musical phrase, not in the sequence of a metronome" (Coffman, 9). Pound further defined an image as the new school was to use the term: "An 'Image' is that which presents an intellectual and emotional complex in an instant of time" (Coffman, 9). Here is the crux of the new conception of imagery as it is to be used in much modern poetry: images are not merely physical description but containers for ideas and feelings.

This definition of the image is well illustrated by Pound's best-known imagist poem, a tight, compact lyric of two lines called "At a Station in the Metro." Pound had been thinking about this poem for over a year after he saw in the "jostle" of the Paris underground "a beautiful face, and then turning suddenly, another and another, and then a beautiful child's face, and then another beautiful face." For days and weeks afterward he tried to make a poem from the experience but could "get nothing but spots of colour. . . . If I had been a painter I might have started a wholly new school of painting."[6] After many attempts to convert the experience into words, it occurred to him "that in Japan, where a work of art is not estimated by its acreage and where sixteen syllables are counted enough for a poem if you arrange and punctuate them properly, one might make a very little poem which would be translated as follows":

> The apparition of these faces in the crowd;
> Petals on a wet, black bough.

> (Stock, 136)

Here are two contrasting images that can be explicated intellectually as an implied metaphor comparing the appearance of a mass of faces in the Paris subway to something far removed from it: the fragility of petals on a wet branch. Human life is as tenuous as that of leaf or flower. But the poem resists paraphrase, though its images are haunting and carry something of the force of a painting of the same objects. The language is used as exactly as brush strokes. Though Pound's association with the imagist movement was short-lived, his continuing association with painters and sculptors underscored his contention that "one's *contemporaries* in the full sense of the term, are nearly always artists who use some other medium" (Coffman, 18).

Amy Lowell

In 1913, the year of the Armory Show, news of experimentation and innovation in the international art world permeated the poetry scene as well. Harriet Monroe's recently established *Poetry* magazine (founded in Chicago in 1912) had just published the Pound–F. S. Flint imagist doctrine in its March issue, and Pound was busy in London promoting the new movement and collecting material for *Des Imagistes: An Anthology*, which was to be the first gathering of the new poetry.

Amy Lowell (1874–1925), a New Englander from the illustrious Lowell clan, had just completed her first book of poems, a rather conventional collection called *A Dome of Many-Coloured Glass*, and was anxious to take her poetry in new directions, to infuse it with the modernity of distinctively twentieth-century forms and techniques. She arrived in London with a letter from Harriet Monroe introducing her to Pound, and although their initial contacts were amiable and stimulating, it was not long before their clash of egos made it impossible for them to remain friends. As Louis Untermeyer put it, "Amy Lowell 'invaded' England, met Pound head on, convinced his conferes that she was an even more pugnacious dictator than Pound, and 'captured' the group—with the obvious exception of Pound."[7] Lowell returned to the United States to disseminate the ideas of the imagists on this side of the Atlantic, and the announcement for her second book of poems, *Sword Blades and Poppy Seed*, described her as "the foremost member of the 'Imagists,'" a designation that made Pound so angry he threatened a libel suit (Coffman, 26).

In her own anthology of imagist poets, published in 1915, Lowell included a list of six "rules" that attempted to redefine the principles by which the imagist poets wrote:

1. To use the language of common speech and employ always the *exact* word which fits the description.
2. To create new rhythms in poetry. We do not insist upon free verse, but we believe that a poet's individuality is better expressed in this form.
3. To allow absolute freedom in the choice of subject.
4. To present an "image" (hence the name: Imagist). Poetry should render particulars exactly and not deal in vague generalities. We oppose the "cosmic poet" who shirks the real difficulty of his art.
5. To produce poetry that is hard and clear, never blurred nor indefinite.
6. Concentration is the essence of poetry.
   (Coffman, 28–29)

This emphasis on exactness, conciseness, free inquiry, and opposition to vague generalities and cosmic expansiveness echoed

Hulme and mirrored the precision of the scientific method. It also rejected the dominant voice in nineteenth-century American poetry, Walt Whitman, America's poet of the "Kosmos." The new poetry was to be "hard and clear," as Lowell put it, "never blurred or indefinite." These principles were not at variance with Pound's earlier definition, but so alienated had Pound become from Lowell's assertive leadership of the movement in America that "he dissociated himself from the American publications of the Imagists and always referred to the group as the 'Amygist' movement" (Untermeyer, xxiii).

Lowell herself became impatient with the rigid confines of almost any poetic doctrine. In her lifetime, she published eleven volumes of poetry, including over 650 poems in a vast array of genres, forms, techniques, styles, and voices. She wrote poetry with a fiery intensity unmatched by that of any of her peers. "I do not suppose," she ventured, "that anyone not a poet can realize the agony of creating a poem. Every nerve, even every muscle, seems strained to the breaking point. The poem will not be denied; the refusal to write it would be a greater torture. It tears its way out of the brain, splintering and breaking its passage, and leaves that organ in the state of a jellyfish when the task is done" (Untermeyer, xxviii). She was a relentless experimenter and an indefatigable ambassador for poetry. Eliot referred to her as the "demon saleswoman of poetry." It is easy to imagine her hefty physical presence (she was just under five feet and weighed over 200 pounds for much of her adult life) intimidating rooms filled with poetasters, as she smoked one cigar after another and read what were then shockingly suggestive poems.

One of her unique innovations was the development of what she called polyphonic prose, essentially a precursor of the contemporary prose poem, which ignores traditional line breaks but utilizes other poetic elements, such as metaphor, alliteration, repetitive sound patterns, and particularly striking images, often creating a surrealistic effect. "The Basket," a long poem in five polyphonic prose sections, is an excellent example of this form. It begins

The inkstand is full of ink, and the paper lies white and unspotted, in the round light thrown by a candle. Puffs of darkness sweep into the

corners, and keep rolling through the room behind the chair. The air is silver and pearl, for the night is liquid with moonlight.
See how the roof glitters like ice! (Untermeyer, 58)

The poet's vision in "The Basket" materializes from the "white and unspotted" paper that begins the poem into a drama of lovers, Peter and Annette, drawn inextricably toward one another, surrounded by the recurrent imagery of a silver-blue moon, geraniums, an ice-covered roof, and bellying clouds. Each section of this increasingly passionate poem concludes with a variation of this pattern of images framing the dialogue and lovemaking of Peter and Annette until it nearly literally explodes in the irrepressible passion of the fourth section:

How hot the sheets are! His skin is tormented with pricks, and over him sticks, and never moves, an eye. It lights the sky with blood, and drips blood. And the drops sizzle on his bare skin, and he smells them burning in, and branding his body with the name "Annette."
The blood-red sky is outside his window now. Is it blood or fire? Merciful God! Fire! And his heart wrenches and pounds "Annette!"
The lead of the roof is scorching, he ricochets, gets to the edge, bounces over and disappears.
The bellying clouds are red as they swing over the housetops. (Untermeyer, 59)

The poem's final section is a denouement following the expense of passion in a gathering of the recurrent images that are now transformed to convey a sense of emptiness and loss. The house aflame has become a remote and unapproachable "palace of ice":

The air is of silver and pearl, for the night is liquid with moonlight. How the ruin glistens, like a palace of ice! Only two black holes swallow the brilliance of the moon. Deflowered windows, sockets without sight.
A man stands before the house. He sees the silver-blue moonlight, and set in it, over his head, staring and flickering, eyes of geranium red.

Annette! (Untermeyer, 59–60)

"The Basket" shows how effectively Lowell makes use of patterns of imagery to convey emotional states. It is not surprising that her most famous poem is called "Patterns." It contrasts the "stiff brocaded gown" worn by the narrator with the soft, passionate womanhood that flows beneath it. "For my passion / Wars against the stiff brocade," she writes, and "Underneath my stiffened gown / Is the softness of a woman bathing in a marble basin" (Untermeyer, 75). This aristocratic young woman is strolling along the garden paths of a vast estate thinking about her lover, Lord Hartwell, who is apparently about to return from war to marry her. She is daydreaming about the future patterns of their life together when the reader is startled to learn she has just received a letter informing her that Lord Hartwell has been killed in battle. The patterns of her life rigidify, epitomized by the stiffness of the brocaded gown she wears, and she can now contemplate only a life of perpetual grief and formalized mourning:

> I shall go
> Up and down,
> In my gown.
> Gorgeously arrayed,
> Boned and stayed.
> And the softness of my body will be guarded from embrace
> By each button, hook, and lace.
> For the man who should loose me is dead,
> Fighting with the Duke in Flanders,
> In a pattern called war.
> Christ! What are patterns for?

> (Untermeyer, 76)

The final couplet converts what could be a sentimental, almost maudlin expression of personal loss into a tough-minded political expression of the futility of war, the most destructive of human patterns because it shatters all others.

No discussion of Amy Lowell's work would be complete without some mention of her importance as a critic of poetry. Her first biographer correctly observes that her book *Tendencies in American Poetry* (1917) "was the most important critical work produced in the United States for many years. It gave a structure and a meaning to our modern poetry, which hitherto had been aimless and confused in the minds of the public."[8] In it, Lowell divided the new directions in American poetry into three groups: evolutionists, revolutionists, and imagists. She chose two of her contemporaries to represent each group. Edwin Arlington Robinson and Robert Frost, with their roots in nineteenth-century metrics and poetic forms, were evolutionists in the sense that they were adapting those forms to the new realities of twentieth-century life and language. Edgar Lee Masters and Carl Sandburg she described as revolutionists, primarily because of their liberation from the metrical constraints of their precursors and their focus on both the urban and rural dimensions of modern life. Hilda Doolittle and John Gould Fletcher represented the imagists, the most avant-garde tendency and the model for future directions in American verse. Notably missing in her assessment was any consideration of Pound and Eliot—Pound because of the imagist-Amygist controversy and Eliot because his most important work had not yet appeared. However, in "A Critical Fable," a long satirical poem modeled after her distant relative James Russell Lowell's famous "A Fable for Critics," she made her views on the two most influential poets of the modern period abundantly clear. She ultimately thought Eliot a more important writer than Pound but had little use for either:

> Eliot's mind is fixed and alert;
> Pound goes off anywhere, anyhow, like a squirt.
> Pound believes he's a thinker, but he's far too romantic;
> Eliot's sure he's a poet when he's only pedantic.
> But Eliot has raised pedantry to a pitch,
> While Pound has upset romance into a ditch.
>
> (Untermeyer, 430)

The invective continues for dozens of lines—more than enough to make Amy Lowell's position in relation to what she regarded as the pedantic and academic thrust of Eliot's work and the pretentious intellectualism of Pound an unequivocal one. While literary history has not concurred in her judgment and the work of Pound and Eliot has been far more influential than her own, it seems equally clear that her contribution to the development of American poetry has been largely undervalued and is in need of reassessment.

Lowell was a pioneer in the development of the prose poem, in the startling and innovative use of surrealistic imagery, in evaluating the major new tendencies in twentieth-century poetry, and, like Pound, in bringing concepts derived from her close study of Oriental poetry into the poetry of the English language. (Two of her books, *Pictures of the Floating World* and *Fir-Flower Tablets*, are loose adaptations rather than translations of Chinese verse.) One other distinction is worth noting: on 8 September 1922, on radio station WGI she read her poems on the air to an estimated audience of 50,000 listeners, probably the first broadcasting of free verse in America (Damon, 615). Louis Untermeyer called her "not only a disturber but an awakener. Her exhilarating differences invigorated the old forms while affecting the new techniques. Her pioneering energy cleared the field of flabby accumulations and helped establish the fresh and free-searching poetry of our day" (Untermeyer, xxix).

H.D.

When Hilda Doolittle (1886–1961), who signed her poetry with the initials H.D., published a book of poems with Oxford University Press in 1944, an author's note on the page proofs described her as "at one time well known to all lovers of verse as one of the earliest 'Imagists.' " On the corrected proofs returned to the publisher, she crossed out "at one time" and replaced it with a bold "IS."[9] This incident illustrates her continuing identification with a movement that had long since become dispersed and defunct, although it has had continuing influence on the poetry of the entire twentieth century. The term, however, is certainly inadequate to characterize the substantial body of work she produced beginning with her first appearance in the January 1913 issue of *Poetry* magazine and ending with the long classical verse epic, *Helen in Egypt*, published in the year of her death.

This last work, as one critic has noted, made her "the first American woman to publish a major epic poem and the first American to create a female epic protagonist."[10] The sources and inspiration for this large body of work are threefold. First there are her imagist beginnings, greatly influenced by her early connection to Ezra Pound (they were engaged to be married, and he was a tireless champion of her poetry, promoting it especially through Monroe in his capacity as foreign correspondent for *Poetry* magazine). Second, there is her deep and intense absorption in Hellenic culture. Her poems are saturated with allusions to Greek gods and goddesses, but she modernizes the mythic dimensions of that world by blending mythology with an imagistic conception of the natural world and by connecting it to the events of her personal life. And third, there is the personal life, a truly remarkable one, characterized by intimate relationships with some of the great innovators of the twentieth century—Pound, D. H. Lawrence, and a year-long analysis with Sigmund Freud that infused her later work with a self-revelation that points toward the extremely personal, "confessional" poetry of the 1950s and 1960s.

H.D.'s early imagist poems, some of them classics of the genre, embody the basic principles of the movement. The most famous of these, "Oread," the title referring to a mountain nymph of Greco-Roman mythology, conveys a sense of the correspondences inherent in nature—the sea described in terms of the land, the land described in terms of the sea, and both evoked in terms of their imagistic impact:

> Whirl up, sea—
> whirl your pointed pines,
> splash your great pines
> on our rocks,
> hurl your green over us,
> cover us with your pools of fir.[11]

Kenneth Fields correctly observes that "it is pointless to ask whether this poem is about a pine forest seen in terms of the sea, or the other way around, for the standard ways of metaphor no longer apply. The poem is about both at once, both interacting: it is an instantaneous complex."[12] The last phrase recalls Pound's definition of the image as an "emotional and intellectual complex in an instant of time." The sea is solidified in terms of its shape, movement, and color, while the pine forest is liquefied by the active verbs that begin all but one line: *whirl, whirl, splash, hurl,* and *cover.* Motion, shape, color, and form interact in a dynamic, single vision.

This description of one entity of nature in terms usually applied to another underscores the density of H.D.'s imagistic method. Her imagism is not merely visual but textural as well, fully involving the reader's senses so that he or she seems transported into a palpable world of physical sensations. The second section of her early poem "The Garden" may be the most evocative description of a hot late summer day we have in all of American literature:

> O wind, rend open the heat,
> cut apart the heat,
> rend it to tatters.
>
> Fruit cannot drop
> through this thick air—
> fruit cannot fall into heat
> that presses up and blunts
> the points of pears
> and rounds the grapes.
>
> Cut the heat—
> plough through it,
> turning it on either side
> of your path.
>
> (H.D., 25)

The human longing for a cool breeze to "cut apart" and "plough through" the heat frames the middle stanza in which the heat itself frames and shapes the fruits of nature, outlining their contours and preventing them from falling. The breathy, plosive sounds of the stanza—the alliterative f's, th's, and p's—combine with the visual imagery to create a sense of suffocation and breathlessness.

From this evocation of the physicality of nature, it is but a short step to the second major characteristic of H.D.'s verse: its insistent renewal of the myths of the ancient world that embody the opposing forces of nature in a symbolic drama composed by the human imagination. In Greek religion, nature is charged with divinity; gods and goddesses represent natural elements in conflict. It is a pantheistic world, and the ritualistic events represented in Greek epics and dramas are enactments of universal mysteries made coherent by their presentation in human terms. The industrialized world of the early twentieth century had long lost touch with the cyclical sense of nature as reflected in Greek mythology, and many of the poets of the period—H.D., Pound, and Eliot particularly—lamented that loss and sought to revive the classical spirit by infusing their work with allusions to and reinterpretations of the Greek myths.

This immersion in Hellenic culture is evident throughout H.D.'s work and culminates in her last major poem, *Helen in Egypt*. But the sense in which she tries to relate it to the exigencies of the modern world is perhaps best illustrated by a poem written much earlier. "The Tribute" was initially published in *The Egoist*, a magazine she edited in London in 1916 before T. S. Eliot took over that position the following year. It is a long poem written in eleven sections contrasting the squalor of the marketplace, representing the commercial, power-driven, and military obsessions of the modern world, with the transcendent power of nature as embodied in the poetry, myths, and songs of the ancient world. The word *squalor* recurs nine times in the poem's first two sections, personified as an ox cart, a serpent, a jackass, trampling and overwhelming the natural physical beauty of the landscape that inspires poetry and myth. The poem begins:

> Squalor spreads its hideous length
> through the carts and the asses' feet,
> squalor coils and reopens
> and creeps under barrow
> and heap of refuse
> and the broken shards
> of the marketplace—
> it lengthens and coils
> and uncoils and draws back
> and recoils
> through the crooked streets.
>
> Squalor blights and makes hideous
> our lives—it has smothered
> the beat of our songs . . .
>
> (H.D., 59)

The poet's function in this squalid modern world is to restore a sense of sanctity and sanity to the blighted urban landscape, doubly blighted by the horrendous destruction of World War I, an event H.D. obliquely refers to at the end of section 2 by reminding her readers that "the boys have gone out of the city, / the songs withered black on their lips" (H.D., 60). And how is the poet to accomplish this transformation? In section 3 she enters the "temple space" of the city "to cry to the gods and forget /

the clamour, the filth" (H.D., 61) She recalls the origins of the modern city in ancient Athens, an urban civilization capable of retaining its connection to nature through the intervention of its deities:

> We turn to the old gods of the city,
> of the city once blessed
> with daemon and spirit of blitheness
> and spirit of mirth,
> we cry;
> what god with shy laughter,
> or with slender winged ankles is left?
>
> (H.D., 62)

And though she searches everywhere for the gods of antiquity in the modern city, she finds that but one god has survived, "one tall god with a spear-shaft, / one bright god with a lance" (H.D., 61). This warrior god epitomizes the spirit of an age of worldwide devastation, a god of death rather than a deity of light, beauty, and life:

> and we know his glamour is dross,
> we know him a blackened light,
> and his beauty withered and spent
> beside one young life that is lost.
>
> (H.D., 62)

But some in the city cannot accept this vast diminution of the human spirit; some cannot sing to or celebrate the god of the lance. She notices a "few old men," a "few sad women," "a few lads" "their white brows / set with hope / as light circles an olive-branch" (H.D., 63). With and for this meager handful she implores again the spirits of antiquity to revivify the modern world, to "heal us—bring balm for our sickness" (H.D., 63).

The final stanzas are a paean to whatever beauty may yet be recovered from a world that has substituted a devotion to money and power for a devotion to the miracle of life, the mystery of nature. "Beauty," Ezra Pound was to write much later in *The Pisan Cantos*, "is difficult." Here H.D. finds it difficult as well, but in the last lines of the poem she offers hope for its continual renewal in the youth of the world, who may yet transcend its modern depravity:

> could beauty be sacrificed
> for a thrust of a sword,
> for a piece of thin money
> tossed up to fall half alloy—
> then beauty were dead
> long, long before we saw her face.
> Could beauty be beaten out,—
> O youth the cities have sent
> to strike at each other's strength,
> it is you who have kept her alight.
>
> (H.D., 68)

"The Tribute" begins in squalor but ends with an assertion of beauty, a continuum in the human experience that endures despite massive human efforts to trample it underfoot.

Although imagism and Greek mythology are continuing sources of H.D.'s poetic energy, it is also true, as Louis Martz has observed, "that by 1916–17 H.D. was beginning to create a strongly personal voice, breaking out of the Imagist confines, breaking through the Greek mask" (H.D., xviii–xix). The beginning of this voice can be experienced in poems like "The Islands," written during her travels in Greece in 1920, and in many of the poems in her collection *Red Roses for Bronze*, published in 1931, shortly before her year-long psychoanalysis with Sigmund Freud, an experience that was to have an immeasurable impact on her later life and work. One feels in these late poems the palpable presence of the poet in the words on the page:

> No poetic phantasy
> but a biological reality,
>
> a fact: I am an entity
> like bird, insect, plant
>
> or sea-plant cell;
> I live; I am alive;
>
> take care, do not know me,
> deny me, do not recognise me,

shun me; for this reality
is infectious—ecstasy.

(H.D., 584)

The word ecstasy derives from the Greek *ekstasis*, a being put out of its place, and suggests a consciousness that has transcended its bodily habitat to cohabit instead with the natural world. As her biographer puts it, in much of H.D.'s work, "the human drama and the stage of nature upon which or in which it is enacted fuse into one perceptual whole."[13] This perceptual wholeness links the early work and the late and gives H.D.'s poetry an integrative fullness that sets it apart from the work of almost all the other modernists. As a poet of myth, the self, nature, and the modern urban world, she connected the elements that her peers saw as fragmented, dissonant realities.

Gertrude Stein

The place of Gertrude Stein (1874–1946) in the history of twentieth-century poetry is difficult to determine. Her major books, *Three Lives* (1909), *Tender Buttons* (1914), *The Making of Americans* (1925), and *The Autobiography of Alice B. Toklas* (1932), are essentially prose works, although whether Stein wrote prose, poetry, or "wrote writing" as she would have it is still open to question. Our preoccupation with genres and with classifying writers according to the genres they produce has caused her work to be ignored in many histories of modern and American poetry until recently. Her literary reputation seems to have equally vocal proponents and detractors. The negative critical view of her work is best summarized by Kingsley Widmer, who views her as a "shrewd self-publicist" and an *"avant*-kitsch writer."[14] On the other hand, it is equally possible to argue, as David Antin has, that she was the most radical of the modernists because more than any of the others, she realized that a truly revolutionary modern art needed "to begin from a radical act of definition or redefinition of the domain of the elements and the operations of the art or of art itself."[15] Put another way, Stein raised basic questions in her work about the nature and properties of language, or "more specifically, American English and how *else* its words might be used."[16]

The imagist movement, despite its emphasis on redefining poetry in the modern age, used words in essentially the same ways they have always been used—as signifiers of the people, things, and events they actually represent. Although most literary modernists retained this crucial mimetic function of the word, Stein did not. The primary concern of her work is not so much what words represent but rather with language itself and how words interact with one another to create their own aesthetic pleasure. As Kenneth Rexroth noted, "Gertrude Stein showed, among other things, that if you focus your attention on 'please pass the butter,' and put it through enough permutations and combinations, it begins to take on a kind of glow, the splendor of what is called an 'aesthetic object' " (Kostlanetz, xiv). The creation of aesthetic objects made out of words is in one sense a central definition of poetry, yet in another sense it seems a minor endeavor, sacrificing deeper emotional and intellectual possibilities for elaborate and sometimes highly technical wordplay that severs language from its personal and social moorings. As e.e. cummings put it, Stein "subordinates the meaning of words to the beauty of the words themselves," and as Sherwood Anderson observed, she lays "word against word, relating sound to sound, feeling for the taste, the smell, the rhythm of the individual word" (Kostlanetz, xx).

Stein's experiments with the disassembling and reconstruction of language unhinged from its conventional referential or narrative associations, has its most explicit source in her lifelong association with the major visual artists of her time, particularly the cubist painters. According to Richard Bridgman, "In spite of her voracity as a reader, Gertrude Stein remained remarkably free of literary influence in her writing, barren even."[17] She was, however, a passionate collector and patron of modern art, and her apartment in Paris, where she settled with her brother Leo in 1903, became a densely crowded gallery of modern paintings, as well as a salon for a generation of American writers and intellectuals living abroad in the first three decades of the twentieth century. It was Gertrude Stein who named this generation a "lost generation" for the disillusionment they faced following the devastation of World War I. In fact, Stein is probably better known for her memorable phrases than for her poetry or prose. Her description of the city of Oakland, California ("There's no there there"), has remained a staple evocation of American urban anonymity, and her famous "A rose is a rose is a rose is a rose" may be one of the most often-quoted lines ever written by an American.

Yet it is her contribution to twentieth-century poetry that interests us here, and that contribution was a substantial one, not so much to the poets of her own generation but to the vigorous linguistic experimentation that emerged later in the century in the innovative work of writers like John Ashbery, Robert Creeley, Jackson McLow, and David Antin. Stein gave these writers a sense of the fluidity and flux of the language, how loosely it held together compared to the static and traditional structures characteristic of its British counterpart. "Think about American writing," she told her students at the University of Chicago during a lecture tour of the United States in 1934–35,

from Emerson, Hawthorne, Walt Whitman, Mark Twain, Henry James, myself, Sherwood Anderson, Thornton Wilder and Dashiell Hammett and you will see what I mean, as well as in advertising and in road signs, you will see what I mean, words left alone more and more feel that they are moving and all of it is detached and is detaching anything from anything and in this detaching and in this moving it is being in its way creating its existing. This is then the real difference between English and American writing and this then can then lead to anything."[18]

Words detached from anything can lead to anything, and in Stein's poetry they almost always do. They are, in John Ashbery's phrase, a "hymn to possibility."[19] Here are the opening lines of "New":

> We knew.
> Anne to come.
> Anne to come.
> Be new.
> Be new too.
> Anne to come.
> Anne to come.
> Be new
> Be new too.
> And anew.
> Anne to come.
> Anne anew.
> Anne do come.

Anne do come too, to come and to come
not to come and as to
and new, and new too.

(Kostlanetz, 153)

While many readers dismiss this sort of self-generated wordplay
as gibberish, the very playfulness of the language interacting with
itself creates a sense of newness that gives the poem its title.
Knew, new, and *anew* interact throughout, and all rhyme with *to,
too,* and *do. Anne* and *and* have a close vocal affinity, as do *we*
and *be.* Most of these words recur in the final lines, which par-
odistically allude to "to be or not to be," transforming the question
of being into a question of turning repetitive events into novel
ones and adding as well a comic sexual pun. Rendering life meant
repeating words again and again in different contexts since "language itself is a complete analogue of experience because it, too,
is made of a large but finite number of relatively fixed terms
which are allowed to occur in a limited number of clearly specified
relations, so that it is not the appearance of a word that matters
but *the manner of its reappearance"* (Perloff, 86).

Stein herself differentiated between mere repetition and what
she called "insistence." "Is there repetition," she asks, "or is there
insistence? I'm inclined to believe there is no such thing as repetition. And really how can there be."[20] Stein argues that no event
in life recurs exactly the same way; there is always some difference
in emphasis. In "New," Anne appears and reappears anew, and
even exact recurrences carry different connotations because of the
context. For example, the repetition of "Anne to come" in lines
2 and 3 carries alternate possibilities of predictability, on the one
hand (because the first occurrence is preceded by "We knew"),
and hopeful anticipation, on the other hand (because the second
occurrence is followed by "Be new"). *Anne* goes through various
permutations and transformations in the poem until she seems
almost to emerge from the insistent pattern of recurrence as a
momentary physical presence:

Here.
Anne Anne.
And to hand.
For a while.

And to come.
In half or dark.
In half and dark.
In half a dark.
As to it.
In a line.
As fine a line.
Bestow.
Anne Anne
And to hand
As a while
For a while
Anne.
(Kostlanetz, 157)

We seem to be spending some actual time with Anne and of course we actually are, because Anne exists only "In a line," which Gertrude Stein has bestowed upon us, "As fine a line" as she could write.

Though Stein's writing is idiosyncratic and tedious to read in substantial doses, no other American writer in the twentieth century has called more attention to the process of composition itself and therefore drastically revised the way in which a great many contemporary American poets think of their art. Writing for Stein meant transforming the flow of language in the mind into the exactitude of language on the page. Composition itself is the subject of much of her writing in at least two senses. First, the attention of the reader is directed not to the meaning of the words themselves but to their interactions; hence questions raised about Stein's poetry are almost always compositional. Why is this word here? What is its relationship to the line before it? How are puns, echoes, rhymes, rhythms, and so on interrelated within the work? She is in this sense a poet's poet rather than a reader's writer. Second, the emphasis on composition roots her work in what William James called the "continuous present"—the idea that "all knowledge (whether of the present or the past) is held within the experience of the present. This is what is real. Reality is *now*, and this present is in continual flux."[21] This second sense of composition means that the only "real" or "live" subject for a writer is the internal state of his or her mind at the moment the writing is taking place.

Only if the traces of the moment can somehow find their way on to the page will the writing be "real."

This sense of flux, of word-to-word and line-to-line determinations, creates in her work what John Ashbery describes as "an all-purpose model which each reader can adapt to fit his own set of particulars" (Perloff, 105). From this perspective, it is usually fruitless to try to paraphrase or extract particular meanings or themes from Stein's work. Despite the voluminous critical literature that has recently surrounded that work, taming it and domesticating it like a white picket fence, the work remains stubbornly itself, impervious to explication that reduces it to the banalities that it raises to the status of high art:

Anyone being one is one. Anything put down is something. Anything being down is something and being that thing it is something and being something it is a thing and being a thing it is not anything and not being anything it is everything and being that thing it is a thing and being that thing it is that thing it is that thing. Being that thing it is that thing and being that thing it is coming to be a thing having been that thing and coming to be a thing having been that thing it is a thing being a thing it is a thing being that thing. (Hass, 143)

It seems fitting that Gertrude Stein's last words, spoken on her deathbed to her lifelong companion, Alice B. Toklas, capsulize the exactitude and directness of so much of her work. As her biographer describes the scene, "She turned to Alice and murmured, 'What is the answer?' Alice, unable to answer, remained silent. Gertrude said, "In that case, what is the question?' " (Mellow, 468).

Marianne Moore

Although she is sometimes associated with the imagists because she attended Bryn Mawr with H.D. and her poetry is certainly strewn with imagery, Marianne Moore (1887–1972) had little use for literary movements, and she thought *imagism* was a questionable term since images are central to almost all poetry (Gould, 183). Of the innovative poets of the first part of the century, she certainly had the greatest humility. Her first book, *Poems*, was published by H.D. and her friend Bryher Winifred Ellerman in 1921 without Moore's knowledge or permission. She later told an interviewer about her reaction to her friends' zeal: "To issue my slight product—conspicuously tentative—seemed to me premature. I disliked the term 'poetry' for any but Chaucer's or Shakespeare's or Dante's."[22] The originality of her work commanded immediate attention. A year after the publication of *Poems*, Harriet Monroe published a "Symposium on Marianne Moore" in *Poetry* that recognized that a clearly new and distinctive voice had appeared on the American scene.

The components of that voice are not easy to identify, though they include a meticulous attention to precise detail, a new kind of metric based on syllables rather than stresses or accents in a line, unorthodox line breaks, with lines often ending on unemphasized words like *a* and *in* and *the*, and a penchant for unfashionable subject matter—exotic animals, real and imagined, strange flowers and herbs, and even baseball. She endlessly revised her poems, even after book publication, and her critics and biographers have their hands full trying to determine which version of a Moore poem is the definitive version. The most conspicuous case of this is her famous and often reprinted poem "Poetry," which appeared as a poem of twenty-nine lines in *Poems*, a drastically revised and trimmed version of thirteen lines in her second collection, *Observations* (1925), a return to a slightly modified version of the original in the *Selected Poems* of 1935, and an unmercifully truncated version of only three lines in the *Complete Poems* of 1967. That last volume appears with a characteristically terse and understated "Author's Note": "Omissions are not accidents."

In the case of "Poetry," while the omissions are clearly not accidental, they are certainly detrimental and demonstrate that Moore's humility and uncertainty about her work did not always serve her well. The first version of the poem is quintessential Moore. Here are the first stanza and part of the second:

I, too, dislike it: there are things that are important
    beyond all this fiddle.
  Reading it, however, with a perfect contempt for it, one
    discovers in it after all, a place for the genuine.
      Hands that can grasp, eyes
      that can dilate, hair that can rise
        if it must, these things are important not because a

high-sounding interpretation can be put on them but because they
are
useful.[23]

The direct and surprising statement of the first phrase identifies
the poet with every reader who has had difficulty enjoying poetry,
and it is one of the reasons that the poem is so popular with
students at all levels who tend to groan when they hear the word
poem. The slangy informality and self-deprecating modesty of the
second phrase heightens that identification and leads to another
surprise in the second line, which contrasts "a perfect contempt"
for poetry with discovery and "the genuine." The reluctant reader
of poetry is in a sense seduced by the poem. This seduction,
which continues for the remainder of "Poetry," is true of much
of Moore's other work. It is a poetry of genuine discovery and is
important "not because a / high-sounding interpretation can be
put on [it] but because it is useful."

The "use" of Marianne Moore's poetry is to make the reader
more attentive to the surprising peculiarities of the world of things,
objects, people, animals, and plants that surrounds us. It is a
poetry, as a recent critic has observed, of "sincerity and gusto,"
the object of which is "to keep the mind alert and free, the world
large and abundant."[24] "The Mind Is an Enchanting Thing" is the
title of one of her most memorable poems. The first line of it
modifies the title to indicate that the mind is capable not only of
casting a spell but of being itself enchanted:

> is an enchanted thing
>   like the glaze on a
> katydid-wing
>   subdivided by sun
>   till the nettings are legion.[25]

In response to a question about how she begins poems, Moore
told an interviewer, "A felicitous phrase springs to mind—a word
or two, say—simultaneous usually with some thought or object
of equal attraction: . . . 'Kattydid-wing [*sic*] subdivided by *sun* till
the nettings are *legion.*' I like light rhymes, inconspicuous rhymes
and unpompous conspicuous rhymes" (Tomlinson, 28). That a

poet so admired by the literary avant-garde of her time should be so concerned with rhyme is surprising, but as the remark indicates, Moore's rhymes are distinctly her own. *Thing* and *wing* in this passage is an "unpompous conspicuous" rhyme, while *sun* and *legion* is clearly "inconspicuous." And the *a* that ends line 2 is lightly rhymed with a *the* in the next stanza:

> like the apteryx-awl
>   as a beak, or the
> kiwi's rain-shawl
>   of haired feathers, the mind
>   feeling its way as though blind,
> walks along with its eyes on the ground.
>   (Moore, 134)

The reader may not know what an apteryx is upon first reading this stanza, (or what a katydid is, for that matter), but these exotic creatures certainly enchant the mind and make us want to find out. An apteryx, it turns out, is just another name for a kiwi, so the apteryx-awl is the kiwi beak, characteristically poking along the ground as it walks; the bird's haired feathers are its rain shawl, a protective and comforting garment. The entire stanza, a single image of a kiwi walking along, beak and eyes facing the ground, is likened to the mind enchanted by the objects before it.

The spritely and playful sense of language in Moore's poems makes them often appear perilously close to light verse, a genre that most "serious" poets eschew. But her poetry is also infused with a moral and aesthetic sense that rises above the play of words like a steeplejack viewing the broad expanse of the physical landscape below and discovering a certain calm and order in the contours of the human and natural world. This order and tranquility provide for Marianne Moore an essential "reason for living." I am describing here the opening lines of the first poem in Moore's *Complete Poems*, "The Steeplejack":

> Dürer would have seen a reason for living
>   in a town like this, with eight stranded whales
> to look at; with the sweet sea air coming into your house
> on a fine day, from water etched
>   with waves as formal as the scales
> on a fish.
>   (Moore, 5)

To observe the world as a visual artist must—fascinated by its particulars, intrigued by its correspondences and relationships, noticing patterns and connections that most of us are oblivious to—is for Moore the role of the poet as well.

> One by one in two's and three's the seagulls keep
>   flying back and forth over the town clock,
> or sailing around the lighthouse without moving their wings—
> rising steadily with a slight
>   quiver of the body—or flock
> mewing where
>
> a sea the purple of the peacock's neck is
>   paled to greenish azure as Dürer changed
> the pine green of the Tyrol to peacock blue and guinea
> gray. You can see a twenty-five-
>   pound lobster; and fish nets arranged
> to dry. The

(Moore, 5)

It is awkward to end a quotation with *the*, but Moore ends her stanzas with such nondescript articles, giving the images an interconnectedness that mirrors the connections between the things she observes in the world. Everything in the poem is connected to something else by actual rhymes or parallel images, and these correspondences evoke the sort of etched landscape that Dürer himself might have drawn. The "eight stranded whales" form a pattern; the motion of the "sweet sea air" ripples along the water, creating a repetitive sense of movement that is "as formal as the scales / on a fish." The quiet, floating movement of the seagulls over the town clock echoes the drowsy progression of time "in a town like this," where the smallest movement—"a slight quiver of the body"—is recorded. Gradations of the sea's color are observed, as well as its motion, and these in turn are likened to the way Dürer "changed / the pine green of the Tyrol to peacock blue and guinea / gray." Both the sea and the pine trees (as in H.D.'s "Oread") are seen in terms of one another, both have the spectacular variety of peacock feathers, and both are manna for the artist's imagination, which transforms nature merely by observing the correspondences among its particularities. For the poet, the very act of naming the things of nature differentiates and particularizes the surface confusion of the natural world by setting

things in their proper place. The next four stanzas of "The Steeplejack" are a naturalist's catalog of the abundance of the physical
world:

> whirlwind fife-and-drum of the storm bends the salt
>   marsh grass, disturbs stars in the sky and the
> star on the steeple; it is a privilege to see so
> much confusion. Disguised by what
>   might seem the opposite, the sea-
> side flowers and
>
> trees are favored by the fog so that you have
>   the tropics at first hand: the trumpet vine,
> foxglove, giant snapdragon, a salpiglossis that has
> spots and stripes; morning-glories, gourds,
>   or moon-vines trained on fishing twine
> at the back door:
>
> cattails, flags, blueberries and spiderwort,
>   striped grass, lichens, sunflowers, asters, daisies—
> yellow and crab-claw ragged sailors with green bracts—toad-plant,
> petunias, ferns; pink lilies, blue
>   ones, tigers; poppies; black sweet–peas.
> The climate
>
> is not right for the banyan, frangipani, or
>   jack-fruit trees; or for exotic serpent
> life. Ring lizard and snakeskin for the foot, if you see fit;
> but here they've cats, not cobras, to
>   keep down the rats.
>
> (Moore, 5–6)

These stanzas reveal Moore's fascination with exotic flora and
fauna. They evoke not only what can be seen in a town like this
but also things that "The climate / is not right for." And words
like *salpiglossis, spiderwort, lichens,* and especially *frangipani* (a
tropical American shrub with large fragrant flowers) are a pleasure
to roll across one's tongue. Moore makes her readers feel that it
is "a privilege to see so / much confusion" because her artful
enumeration of specifics is a momentary stay against that confusion.
She reminds us that language is the human instrument by which
we give shape, order, and meaning to both the physical world
that surrounds us and the imaginative world that lives within us.

Her poetry connects these two worlds. There is no better terse description of its genuine originality than her own famous phrase from the original version of "Poetry." Hers is a body of work that presents for our inspection "imaginary gardens with real toads in them."

· FIVE ·

A Grrrreat Littttttttterary Period: T. S. Eliot and Ezra Pound

> It was an intense literary atmosphere, which though it was thrilling, every minute of it, was fatiguing in the extreme. I don't know how Ezra Pound stood it, it would have killed me in a month.
>
> —William Carlos Williams, *Autobiography*

No other poets have had a greater impact on the sensibility of their age than T. S. Eliot (1888–1965) and Ezra Pound (1885–1972), and it is equally appropriate to label the first half of the twentieth century "The Pound Era," as Hugh Kenner has done, or "The Age of Eliot" as Russell Kirk has called it. Both radically changed the direction of American literature. It is ironic that these American midlanders—Pound from Hailey, Idaho, Eliot from St. Louis, Missouri—were most responsible for turning the attention of American writers away from their indigenous experience and toward European and Oriental traditions. Both sought to revive a sense of history and tradition in American culture, and both found Europe a more congenial and cosmopolitan home than the uncultured American heartland they left behind. "London may not be the Paradiso Terrestre," Pound wrote to Eliot in 1914, "but it is some centuries nearer it than is St. Louis."[1] Together with H.D. and Gertrude Stein, they attempted to reverse the nativizing trends in American literature begun with Walt Whitman and continuing through writers like Edgar Lee Masters and Carl Sandburg. Though Pound was able to make "a pact" with Whitman in a brief lyric he published early in his career, the tone of the poem is grudging and hesitant:

> I make a pact with you, Walt Whitman—
> I have detested you long enough.

> I come to you as a grown child
> Who has had a pig-headed father;
> I am old enough now to make friends.
> It was you that broke the new wood,
> Now is a time for carving.
> We have one sap and one root—
> Let there be commerce between us.[2]

The new wood that Whitman broke was free verse, and the carving that Pound refers to indicates his intention to find newer, more sophisticated uses for that form. Pound and Eliot did find new uses for free verse. *The Waste Land* and *The Cantos*, the two major works they produced, virtually redefined the term for twentieth-century readers. Here were writers attempting to summarize and synthesize a vast array of poetic traditions, from the troubadour lyrics of twelfth-century Provence to the Greek and Roman epic traditions, to the vast, unexplored body of Oriental literature. For both writers, all the world's literature was a single aesthetic legacy. The modern poet's task was to absorb it and, as Pound said again and again, "make it new."

T. S. Eliot and Tradition

In his enormously influential essay, "Tradition and the Individual Talent," originally published in 1919, Eliot redefined the word *tradition* for modern writers. He argued that poets should discover their relationship to literary works of previous generations before undertaking their own work. In order to find out what needs to be done in any given literary genre, writers must understand what has been accomplished. Instead of admiring writers for their originality, Eliot urged his peers to look for the ways writers assimilated and built upon the work of their predecessors. He believed that if we approach a poet's work without the "prejudice" of seeking originality, "we shall often find that not only the best, but the most individual parts of his work may be those in which the dead poets, his ancestors, assert their immortality most vigorously."[3] "Tradition," for Eliot, meant developing a historical sense, which he felt was indispensable to serious poets. A writer needed to write "not merely with his own generation in his bones, but with a feeling that the whole of the literature of Europe from Homer and within it the whole of the literature of his own country has a simultaneous existence and composes a simultaneous order" (Shapiro, 66). This notion of discovering the prevailing order of the world's literature and understanding the individual writer's relation to that order permeates nearly everything Eliot wrote. He believed that "no poet, no artist of any art, has his complete meaning alone. His significance, his appreciation is the appreciation of his relation to the dead poets and artists" (Shapiro, 67). The idea of finding an abiding order and pattern in human experience is, for Eliot, a central and commanding need.

"Tradition and the Individual Talent" is an eminently quotable essay; it contains the precepts that guided a generation of poets who felt that Eliot had hit upon a formula for bringing American writing into the world arena. Instead of concentrating on what differentiates American literature from that of Europe, Eliot sought to reconnect it to the very conventions it had been jettisoning. Where Whitman, Emerson, and, later, William Carlos Williams had urged American artists to rivet their attention on the present and write about the experience they knew, Eliot insisted that the poet must surrender personal experience to something larger— what he called the "impersonal" emotion of art. His famous reversal of the romantic idea of poetry as the spontaneous overflow of powerful feelings that derive from emotion recollected in tranquility underscored T. E. Hulme's contention that the modern period was to be essentially a classical age. "Poetry," Eliot wrote, "is not a turning loose of emotion, but an escape from emotion; it is not the expression of personality, but an escape from personality" (Shapiro, 71). He felt that subjectivity is debilitating because it separates the individual from both the social and natural world. As Peter Ackroyd puts it, Eliot believed "the only way out of [the] subjective trap is in the idea of system and order: there is, on the one hand, the invasive power of subjective feeling which cannot be communicated and, on the other, the need for order and ritual which may counteract that subjective consciousness. Indeed, the notion of ritual permeates both Eliot's work and the meticulous routines of his adult life."[4]

The idea that poetry should be impersonal and express neither private feelings nor personality led to a highly cerebral and "literary" poetry that quickly gained adherents in university circles because it was the sort of work that lent itself to academic study.

Eliot's poetry (and Pound's) required a vast background in literary history in order for readers to comprehend its most fundamental allusions. William Carlos Williams, who was trying to define a totally different direction for American verse, said that Eliot "wiped out our world as if an atomic bomb had dropped on it" because the intellectual attraction of Eliot's work proved irresistible to emerging young American poets. Eliot's taut, ironic tone, his richly allusive style, and his collage-like juxtaposition of striking images became the dominant mode in American poetry until mid-century.

The Love Song of J. Alfred Prufrock

Among the early influences on Eliot's work was the radical poetic style of the French symbolist poets: Baudelaire, Rimbaud, Verlaine, Corbière, and especially Jules Laforgue. Eliot says that he learned from these writers "that the business of the poet was to make poetry out of the unexplored resources of the unpoetical."[5] And the first thing that may strike most readers about Eliot's early work is its "unpoetical" quality. This is an urban poetry rooted in the tawdriness of the twentieth-century urban landscape. One of his earliest poems, "Rhapsody on a Windy Night" (1911), introduces images that Eliot was to utilize with variations in much of his other early work. The lovely, musical title leads the reader to expect a romantic evocation of an evening, but the poem almost immediately undercuts these expectations with striking, anxiety-ridden images, as the following lines show:

> Midnight shakes the memory
> As a madman shakes a dead geranium.[6]

Ironically, this nervous, tense, antiromantic poem, filled with images of torn, stained dresses, rusty, broken mattress springs, a cat licking rancid butter, an old crab "with barnacles on his back," and others equally tawdry, became the source for the haunting and lovely song "Memory" in the musical *Cats*, based on Eliot's *Old Possum's Book of Practical Cats*.

In "Rhapsody" the technique emerges that was to become Eliot's trademark and revolutionize twentieth-century American verse: the juxtaposition of surprisingly different, often contradictory or contrasting images and ideas. His first collection of poems, *Prufrock and Other Observations* (1917), is characterized by "great shifts of tone . . . and . . . by the rapid succession of images. There are constant modifications of thought and emotion, moving from half-comic expressions of regret and nostalgia to cruel or simply impersonal observations" (Ackroyd, 92). Nowhere are these shifts and constant modifications more evident than in "The Love Song of J. Alfred Prufrock," a poem that has become perhaps the most famous ever written by an American. Pound immediately recognized it as a major work, and in his capacity as foreign correspondent for *Poetry* magazine, wrote to the editor, Harriet Monroe, informing her that Eliot produced "the best poem I have had or seen from an American. . . . He has actually trained himself *and* modernized himself *on his own*" (Ackroyd, 56). Pound's incredulity underscores the revolutionary nature of "Prufrock," a poem that wedded imagist doctrine to a modern urban sensibility as well as to a sensibility steeped in long-developed European literary traditions.

The clash of language in the poem begins with the title: a love song but not a lover's song; it is the love song of a man with the formal, antiromantic name of J. Alfred Prufrock. The quotation following the title, from Dante's *Inferno*, heightens this sense of disjunction: here is a love song that begins with an allusion to Hell. And the poem's first image—likening a beautiful evening sky to "a patient etherised upon a table"—assures the reader that something is very wrong.

Formally, the poem is a dramatic monologue, a genre perfected by nineteenth-century British poet Robert Browning, whose "My Last Duchess" and "Fra Lippo Lippi," are classics of the form. The speaker in Eliot's poem is J. Alfred Prufrock, a highly self-conscious, twentieth-century man, wracked by indecision about almost everything. To whom he is speaking in the poem is purposefully ambiguous. It is possibly someone else in the room, most likely a woman he is trying to seduce; it could be to the reader, so that the "you" in the first line—"Let us go then, you and I"—becomes everyone who reads the poem; and it could be to another part of Prufrock himself, so that the poem becomes an internal monologue between two parts of a self—a nervous chat between the Ego and the Id. Each of these interpretations has advocates. It is a measure of the poem's strength that it can be read consistently with any of these three premises in mind.

"The Love Song of J. Alfred Prufrock" remains a powerful poem for contemporary readers because it captures the anxiety, indecision, and social falsity that Eliot felt characterizes twentieth-century life. It is a psychic journey through a collective male consciousness that sees the modern world bereft of meaning, desperate for human connections. The imagery shows us a world saturated by ugliness: yellow fog and smoke (the poem is set in early twentieth-century London), cheap hotels, half-deserted streets, soot falling from chimneys. The narrator is preoccupied with the passage of time, his appearance, and with what others think of him. Echoing the famous passage from Ecclesiastes ("To every thing there is a season") Prufrock seems obsessed by time. Allusions reverberate throughout the poem, illustrating how much of Prufrock's consciousness of life is shaped and conditioned by literature. Our impression reading it today is of a highly self-conscious literary intellectual, inwardly tortured by his anxiety, paranoia, and the inability to make decisions.

As the monologue begins, he is preparing to leave some social situation—possibly a cocktail party, where "In the room the women come and go / Talking of Michelangelo." The singsong, jingly rhythm and rhyme of the couplet suggests small talk rather than a serious discussion of art. Prufrock invests every inconsequential decision he considers making with heavy emotional weight. "Do I dare / Disturb the universe?" he asks when he is merely considering descending a staircase. He worries incessantly about his appearance ("They will say, 'But how his arms and legs are thin!' ") and is paranoid about being stereotyped.

It soon becomes clear that the poem is less about an individual than it is about a representative modern man, paralyzed by the confusion and enormity of twentieth-century life and culture. He is unable to act as a force for change because he feels ineffectual and threatened on every side. His inability to act is not tragic in the classical sense, though, for Prufrock is an individual who lives in a mass society, and his individuality has been devoured by it. "I am not Prince Hamlet, nor was meant to be," he concludes, but rather "an attendant lord, one that will do / To swell a progress, start a scene or two, / Advise the prince." In other words, Prufrock is not a heroic tragic hero but rather a bit player on the historical stage. He is a representative citizen of a Western civilization that has passed its prime ("I have seen the moment of my greatness flicker") and can look forward only to aging and death. The poem's final lines beautifully evoke those past imaginative and creative periods of human history (Eliot has a consistent tendency to romanticize the past) that have culminated in the harsh, human realities of the present. Prufrock continues to be indecisive about the trivial concerns of his present and future, but he momentarily recalls a time when life was enriched by the myths that nourished it:

> Shall I part my hair behind? Do I dare to eat a peach?
> I shall wear white flannel trousers, and walk upon the beach.
> I have heard the mermaids singing each to each.
>
> I do not think that they will sing to me.
>
> I have seen them riding seaward on the waves
> Combing the white hair of the waves blown back
> When the wind blows the water white and black.
>
> We have lingered in the chambers of the sea
> By sea-girls wreathed with seaweed red and brown
> Till human voices wake us and we drown.
>
> (Eliot, 7)

These lovely images, contrasted with the tawdriness of most of the earlier imagery, posit a civilization that had once been able to create and experience beauty but is now drowning in the cacophonous human reality of the present.

The Waste Land

J. Alfred Prufrock's conception of Western civilization in its decaying phase is developed in Eliot's difficult but unquestionably seminal poem, *The Waste Land*. Because of Eliot's insistence on the "impersonality" of modern poetry, for many years the poem was seen primarily as a work about the decline of spirituality and the loss of a mythic dimension in twentieth-century life, but the more that scholars learn of Eliot's personal life, the more *The Waste Land* appears to be tied to specific events in that life, particularly his "nervous breakdown" and his troubled marriage to his first wife, Vivien. Eliot himself supported this view of it. In a lecture at Harvard, he remarked that "various critics have done me the honour to interpret the poem, considered it, indeed, as an important bit of social criticism. To me it was only the relief of a personal and wholly insignificant grouse against life; it is just a piece of rhythmical grumbling."[7]

Although details of the poem's conception are sketchy, Eliot apparently began it shortly after his father's death in January 1919.[8] He worked on it sporadically for the next year, while his mental and physical health, as well as his marriage, deteriorated. His mother, sister, and brother visited him in London in 1920, making the long journey from the United States and hoping to provide mutual familial support during a time of tragedy. But his mother and Vivien quarreled, and the visit created more tension than it relieved. According to Ronald Bush, "By September he was weak and ill, and wrote that he felt extremely 'shaky, and seem to have gone down rapidly since my family left' " (Bush, 55). He decided to spend some time in Margate, a resort town on the Kent coast of England, where he and Vivien went for a long rest in October. While there, Eliot gathered some previous fragments and wrote some of the most memorable lines in *The Waste Land*, including the famous statement that epitomizes the disconnection and fragmentation that characterizes it: "On Margate Sands, / I can connect / Nothing with nothing." After returning to London briefly in November, Eliot decided to undergo further treatment for his depression at a sanatorium in Lausanne, Switzerland, where he composed most of the poem's concluding sections.

It is important to understand that *The Waste Land* was conceived and written during a time of acute personal stress. The discontinuities within the poem reflect a distracted state of mind as well as an avant-garde aesthetic choice. One of the lines from Eliot's later *Four Quartets* seems relevant here: he was a man "distracted from distraction by distraction."

Until 1971, when the facsimile of the original drafts and manuscripts of the poem was published, little was known about the circumstances of its composition, particularly of the roles played by John Quinn, a lawyer and art patron who supported the development of Eliot's career, as well as Ezra Pound, who made significant changes in the manuscript. Upon completing a long, diffuse poem of over a thousand lines, Eliot returned to London via Paris where he showed the manuscript to Pound, who made substantial editorial cuts, trimming the poem to its final version of 433 lines. Pound and Eliot corresponded further about the manuscript, and Pound wrote a witty letter complimenting Eliot on the final version, saying he was "wracked by the seven jealousies" and speaking of their collaboration as part of "a grrrreat litttttttterary period."[9]

Eliot intended to call the poem "He Do the Police in Different Voices," after a line from Charles Dickens's *Our Mutual Friend* referring to a character who reads aloud police blotter stories from the newspaper. The original title emphasized the cacophony of voices within the poem, certainly one of its most striking qualities. As Lionel Trilling observed, "If we are introduced to *The Waste Land* by listening to it, inevitably we are struck by the large variety of its vocal modes, its many different kinds of utterance—we hear speech that is sometimes grave and simple, sometimes lyric and tender, sometimes hysterical, sometimes toneless, sometimes querulous, sometimes awed"[10] (Trilling, 939). This wide range of voices is drawn from many sources, both literary and personal. Eliot was unapologetic about his use of other writers' lines and sentiments. In *The Sacred Wood*, he wrote, "Immature poets imitate; mature poets steal; bad poets deface what they take, and good poets make it into something better or at least something different."[11]

To give his readers some help locating the literary sources and understanding their importance in the poem, he appended a set of "Notes" to the poem, an unprecedented literary gesture, underscoring the difficulty of the work. The notes have sent generations of critics to the library stacks tracing each of the allusions to its source, and although this academic study has unquestionably contributed to our understanding of the poem, it may also have diminished its emotional impact. *The Waste Land* is a powerfully moving poem, dense with unforgettable lines and images. From its startling opening lines reversing the traditional associations of spring ("April is the cruellest month") to its concluding Sanskrit chant ("Shantih, shantih, shantih"), the poem is a repository of the mythic remnants of Western civilization that seemed so tattered following the devastation of World War I. It is also an intensely personal poem, chronicling the torturous inner life of a deeply troubled man. As Ronald Bush observes, "From the summer of 1915, when Eliot married Vivien Haigh-Wood and decided for England and a life of poetry, his 'inner world of nightmare' had all too many correspondences with the world of outer events" (Bush, 53).

To readers of the poem today, its allusions seem even more esoteric than they appeared to Eliot's contemporaries, but its emotional impact remains strong. The first section, "The Burial of the Dead," the title taken from the burial service of the Church of England, serves as a prelude to the description of a "dead" civilization—the Western world following World War I. It also reflects the state of the narrator's psyche: depressed and lifeless, out of touch with even the possibility of vitality and pleasure. April, the time of year traditionally associated with rebirth and renewal, is here described as the "cruellest month" because it is a reminder of the vigorous life forces that have been diminished by the complexities, neuroses, and anxieties of twentieth-century civilization. The awakening earth mixes "memory and desire." It is a reminder of past times when humankind was more in touch with the natural processes of the seasons, and it awakens the desire for life within us.

The narrator of the poem's early lines takes the reader through the seasons, ironically observing, "Winter kept us warm, covering / Earth in forgetful snow." From the generalized opening, the poem moves to a specific locale, the city of Munich (which Eliot visited in 1911), evoked by mention of the Starnbergersee, a lake near Munich, and the Hofgarten, a public park there. In this park the speaker, here identified as Marie, a woman from the upper social classes, speaks of her childhood when she sledded in the mountains with her cousin, the "archduke." She is the first of many "characters" in the poem whose voices blend and become almost interchangeable. But there is one consistent, ominous voice throughout: that of a narrator who raises questions about the nature of the Waste Land and comments on the spiritual emptiness he sees all around him. The Waste Land is a symbol of that emptiness: a barren landscape devoid of even the possibility of life.

The first powerful and memorable description of the Waste Land follows the conversation in the Hofgarten:

> What are the roots that clutch, what branches grow
> Out of this stony rubbish? Son of man,
> You cannot say, or guess, for you know only

A heap of broken images, where the sun beats,
And the dead tree gives no shelter, the cricket no relief
And the dry stone no sound of water.

(Eliot, 38)

The stony rubbish, the broken images, the relentless heat, the dead tree, and the dry stone are all evocations of barrenness—a stony, dessicated landscape where nothing worthwhile lives or grows. In this landscape, modern humanity exists without the comfort or solace of religious faith. And without an abiding faith in an afterlife, the brevity and transitoriness of human life make daily living charged with anxiety. Echoing John Donne's haunting *memento mori* from *Devotions on Emergent Occasions*, a series of meditations Donne wrote when he believed he was dying, the narrator confronts mortality directly: "I will show you fear in a handful of dust." This chilling line is followed by another tone entirely: lines from the libretto of Richard Wagner's *Tristan und Isolde* in which a sailor laments the love he left behind. The lament fades into some dialogue about "the hyacinth girl," a lyrical interlude in "The Burial of the Dead" associated with rebirth and resurrection rather than with the finality of "a handful of dust." But the lyrical respite is brief; the poem gathers again the energy of desolation in another refrain from *Tristan and Isolde*, this time the lines spoken to Tristan while he is dying and waiting for a ship to bring Isolde to him. A lookout reports there is nothing on the horizon; the sea is desolate and empty (*"Oed' und leer das Meer"*). The hopeful anticipation of the lover becomes an expression of emptiness. So the first part of *The Waste Land* pieces together, in collage fashion, segments of language associated with death, the possibility of resurrection and renewal through love and faith, and the actuality of modern existence, which for Eliot seemed bereft of both love and faith.

The second part of "The Burial of the Dead" introduces another "character," Madame Sosostris, a "famous clairvoyante" who uses the Tarot deck of cards, originally associated with ancient fertility rites, to tell fortunes. Eliot refers to the several cards mentioned in this sequence in his notes: he associates the "hanged man" with the hanged god mentioned in Frazer's *Golden Bough*, a repository of ancient myth and ritual that was a major source of the poem, along with Jesse Weston's *From Ritual to Romance*. Both of these important scholarly works argued that myths are recurrent attempts to explain life's mysteries.

The recurrence of a sacrificial god figure in the history of myth leads Eliot to associate the hanged man as well with Christ, mentioned directly in section V of the poem. The line here, "I do not find / The Hanged Man," refers to the absence of a sacrificial presence in the vulgar world represented by Madame Sosostris. Eliot's note on this section is important because it underscores the method of *The Waste Land:* how the characters in the poem fade into one another, creating a panorama of human history. From the ancient gods mentioned in Fraser and Weston, through the Christian adaptation of pagan rituals associated with death and resurrection, "The Burial of the Dead" moves to the modern spurious spirituality represented by a carnival fortune-teller and the secularized world, represented in the final part of this section by the crowds flowing over London Bridge to the city's business and financial district.

The second section of *The Waste Land,* "A Game of Chess," though it alludes to Shakespeare's *Antony and Cleopatra* and *Hamlet,* as well as to other Elizabethan dramatists (the title is from a play by Thomas Middleton), seems closely connected to Eliot's personal life, particularly his anguished relationship with Vivien. It begins with a long descriptive passage of an elegant boudoir where a woman, surrounded by opulent grandeur, brushes her hair. This elegance is undercut by the tension and anxiety that characterizes the dialogue:

> 'My nerves are bad tonight. Yes, bad. Stay with me.
> 'Speak to me. Why do you never speak. Speak.
> 'What are you thinking of? What thinking? What?
> 'I never know what you are thinking. Think.'
>
> (Eliot, 40)

This is the language of desperation that Eliot associated with Vivien's more frantic moments. (In the 1930s, after separating from her, he was instrumental in having her committed to Northumberland House, a private mental hospital in London [Ackroyd, 233].) The woman's desperate anxiety, urging her husband or lover to "Speak" and "Think," provokes the man's response, two of the most chilling lines in the poem: "I think we are in rat's alley /

Where the dead men lost their bones" (Eliot, 40). That terrifying image, however, is merely a prelude to the existential confrontation with nothingness that follows as the dialogue between the man and woman continues:

> 'What is that noise?'
> > The wind under the door.
> 'What is that noise now? What is the wind doing?'
> > Nothing again nothing.
> > > 'Do
> 'You know nothing? Do you see nothing? Do you remember
> 'Nothing?'

> (Eliot, 40–41)

The repetition of *nothing* propels the anxiety level to a cosmic scale. This is not merely a confrontation between a man and woman in a tense, loveless marriage (though it certainly is that) but also humanity's confrontation with the nothingness that surrounds a purely physical—and therefore nonspiritual—existence.

As a parallel to the scene between the upper-class husband and wife in "A Game of Chess," Eliot concludes the section with an overheard conversation concerning "Lil" and "Albert" in a British working-class pub, punctuated by the bartender's closing time cry, "Hurry up please it's time," a refrain that becomes increasingly urgent as the time passes. As James Miller has observed, "The passage is harsh, pitiless, ugly—and perhaps more revealing of the speaker-poet than of Lil, Albert, and their friend the monologuist. His [Eliot's] empty relationship with his wife has colored his view of all marriage, all man-woman relationships. His imagination seizes on an overheard conversation as providing a universal insight, marriage stripped of meaning, sex stripped of joy."[12] This is a highly personal reading of the passage to be sure, but "A Game of Chess" may be the most personally revealing section of the poem. It is Eliot's view of marriage in the Waste Land, one shaped by the difficulties of his own marriage.

The long third section of the poem, "The Fire Sermon," takes its title from a sermon preached by Buddha against the fires of lust, envy, and other passions. It combines lyricism and tawdriness throughout, moving easily back and forth in time from present (early 1920s) London to Elizabethan times. The Thames, London's river, is a witness to the panorama of human folly, particularly sexual folly, that Eliot seems obsessed by. Echoing Spenser and Andrew Marvell's great *carpe diem* "seduction" poem, "To His Coy Mistress," the narrator searches for satisfying man-woman relationships in the Waste Land but finds only anxiety, vulgarity, and mechanical and empty sex. The section is especially important because it identifies the narrator as Tiresias, the Greek prophet in *Oedipus* who has experienced life as both a man and a woman. Eliot writes, "Tiresias, although a mere spectator and not indeed a 'character,' is yet the most important personage in the poem, uniting all the rest. Just as the one-eyed merchant, seller of currants, melts into the Phoenician Sailor, and the latter is not wholly distinct from Ferdinand Prince of Naples, so all the women are one woman, and the two sexes meet in Tiresias. What Tiresias *sees*, in fact, is the substance of the poem" (Eliot, 52). What Tiresias does see in the poem is an episode of "loveless lovemaking" between a "young man carbuncular" and a typist "home at teatime." The passage describing this lovemaking may be the least passionate description of sexuality in modern literature:

> The time is now propitious, as he guesses
> The meal is ended, she is bored and tired,
> Endeavours to engage her in caresses
> Which still are unreproved, if undesired.
> Flushed and decided, he assaults at once;
> Exploring hands encounter no defence;
> His vanity requires no response,
> And makes a welcome of indifference.
>
> (Eliot, 44)

If this is indeed the substance of *The Waste Land*, then it is a poem about sexuality devoid of love, about physical union without spiritual assent.

The puzzling, brief, fourth section of the poem, "Death by Water," seems drawn from Jesse Weston's *From Ritual to Romance*, which describes an Alexandrian ritual involving an effigy of the fertility god thrown into the sea as a symbol of the death of the powers of nature. Eliot had originally written (in 1916–17) a version of this lyric in French called *Dans le Restaurant*.[13] The water imagery contrasts sharply with the fire imagery in "The Fire Sermon," and the death by water as explained by Weston suggested a redemptive death. The poem here seems to be moving away from the dessicated imagery that characterizes the first three sections, but it is in fact a *death* by water that is emphasized. It is not far from "rat's alley where the dead men lose their bones" to the story of Phlebas where "A current under sea / Picked his bones in whispers" (Eliot, 46). Again Eliot seems to be confronting death without illusion, as the narrator addresses the reader directly (for the second time in the poem):

> Gentile or Jew
> O you who turn the wheel and look to windward,
> Consider Phlebas, who was once handsome and tall as you.
>
> (Eliot, 46–47)

The remarkable conclusion of *The Waste Land*, "What the Thunder Said," alternates, as Eliot's note points out, between a description of the journey to Emmaus taken from the Gospel according to Luke, the approach to the "Chapel Perilous" taken from Jesse Weston's description of the Legend of the Holy Grail, and "the present decay of Eastern Europe," presumably what Eliot regarded as the unfortunate consequences of the Russian Revolution. Additionally, it draws from Indian legend of the Thunder from a Hindu sacred book. Images of lifelessness and sterility dominate a landscape where there "is no water but only rock," where there is a longing for the April rains to stir the dry land into life:

> If there were the sound of water only
> Not the cicada
> And dry grass singing
> But the sound of water over a rock
> where the hermit-thrush sings in the pine trees
> Drip drop drip drop drop drop drop
> But there is no water.
>
> (Eliot, 48)

The lack of water, a symbol of life and rebirth throughout the poem, emphasizes the continuing sterility of the Waste Land, which Eliot here universalizes. One city is every city; one human being is all human beings; one person on the brink of madness is a mad civilization:

A Grrrreat Littttttttterary Period

Falling towers
Jerusalem Athens Alexandria
Vienna London
Unreal

A woman drew her long black hair out tight
And fiddled whisper music on those strings
And bats with baby faces in the violet light
Whistled, and beat their wings
And crawled head downward down a blackened wall
And upside down in air were towers
Tolling reminiscent bells, that kept the hours
And voices singing out of empty cisterns and exhausted wells.
                                                  (Eliot, 48).

This passage recapitulates much of the imagery presented earlier in the poem: the "unreal" city of "The Burial of the Dead" and "The Fire Sermon" (London) becomes all the "unreal" cities that have been centers of Western civilization. The "broken images" and "white towers" mentioned earlier become the "falling towers," emblematic of both the decline of civilization and the impotency of the individual; the woman combing her hair repeats the image from "A Game of Chess," but the desperation there becomes absolute madness here—a world turned upside down, empty and exhausted.

There is no water, but there is moonlight, wind blowing through the grass, a cock crowing, a flash of lightening, and finally "a damp gust bringing rain." These are all harbingers of a new way of being—a way out of the Waste Land. Drawing on the wisdom of the East rather than the decadence and decay of the West, the narrator interprets the thunder by alluding to the Sanskrit legend in which the divine voice (thunder) is indicated by the work *Da* but interpreted variously as *damyata* ("restrain yourself"), *datta* ("give"), and *dayadhvam* ("be compassionate"). Eliot uses this wisdom as the key to unlock the personal prison that confines the inhabitants of the Waste Land. By giving of oneself, by sympathizing with others, by controlling one's life and destiny (to the degree that that is possible), the sterile and depressive vision of life epitomized by the arid landscape of the Waste Land may be overcome. In the final stanza, the narrator sits on the shore fishing "with the arid plain behind" him. Although his cultural memory remains fragmented and inconclusive (snippets of nursery rhymes, Dante, Elizabethan plays, and other echoes of past culture make up his reverie), he comments on the poem itself as "fragments shored against my ruins" and concludes by repeating *Shantih*, which Eliot translates in his notes as "The Peace which passeth understanding" (Eliot, 55).

Thus *The Waste Land* ends on an accepting note. It is a psychic portrait of Eliot as a very troubled man but one on the road to recovery; as well, it is a cultural record of a society shattered by the trauma of World War I (and one that will never be the same again) but nonetheless must find a way to renew itself. "Its parts," Conrad Aiken wrote in an early review of the poem, "are not important parts of an important or careful intellectual pattern, but they are important parts of an important emotional ensemble."[14] Although contemporary students will find much of the poem intellectually obscure, its emotional impact seems to have actually been heightened by familiarity. No longer does it seem so important to trace every allusion to its source but rather to respond to the shifting tones and moods that embody the anxiety, melancholy, and diminished hope of much of twentieth-century life.

The Four Quartets

The poetry of *The Waste Land* is the poetry of a troubled, depressed, emotionally fragmented man searching for a sense of cohesiveness and purpose in his life. The poem records the various stages of that search, and its conclusion points to at least the possibility of resolution through some sort of spiritual renewal. After completing and publishing the poem, Eliot turned increasingly toward the Anglican church, seeking a sense of order and stability he had felt so lacking in his personal life and the modern world generally.

Although his marriage continued to disintegrate as Vivien's emotional and physical health deteriorated, he made a series of major life changes clearly intended to strengthen and solidify his blurred psychic identity. In 1927 he was baptized and became a member of the Church of England and a naturalized British citizen. In the preface to a collection of essays published the following year, he described his intellectual orientation as "classicism in literature, royalist in politics, and anglo-catholic in religion."[15] He edited the *Criterion*, an influential literary periodical during these years, and left his long-term job at Lloyd's Bank in London for a position at Faber & Gwyer (later Faber & Faber) publishers, where, as poetry editor, he increasingly shaped the poetic values of the next generation of English-language poets. In 1933, after a trip to America, he separated from his wife and returned to England to begin a "new" life.

He turned increasingly to writing drama and literary criticism during this period, although he did produce some memorable poetry, notably "The Hollow Men," "The Journey of the Magi," and "Ash Wednesday," all asserting the need for spiritual renewal in a materialistic and misdirected world. But it was not until the mid-1930s—when he turned his attention to writing what was to become a long, discursive philosophical poem, *The Four Quartets,*—that a sustained effort comparable to *The Waste Land* began to emerge.

The Four Quartets, like much of Eliot's other poetry, was not originally conceived as a single work. He began writing it in 1935 and published various parts of it as separate poems. It was not published as a unified poem until 1943 when the first edition appeared in America.[16] The overall title is a bit misleading, since each of the four poems in the sequence has five, not four, sections; "Four Quintets" would more accurately describe the whole. Each of the poems is associated with a particular locale. "Burnt Norton" is a country house in Gloucestershire that Eliot visited in 1934; "East Coker" is a village in Somerset where one of Eliot's ancestors left from for America in 1669; "The Dry Salvages" is "the name of a group of three rocks off the eastern corner of Cape Ann, Massachusetts" (Gardner, *CFQ*, 120); and "Little Gidding" is a chapel in Huntingdonshire, once the center of a religious utopia founded in the early seventeenth century by Nicholas Ferrar. Each of these places has important personal associations for Eliot, and like *The Waste Land, The Four Quartets* is highly personal despite its sometimes distant and neutral philosophical language and tone.

"BURNT NORTON". Like many other modernist writers, Eliot became preoccupied with the struggle of the artist to arrest the passage of time. He also was haunted by his own inability to put his past behind him and begin life anew. The first lines of "Burnt Norton" announce the poem's theme:

> Time present and time past
> Are both perhaps present in time future
> And time future contained in time past.
> If all time is eternally present
> All time is unredeemable.
>
> (Eliot, 117)

Both the tone and diction of these lines are entirely new in Eliot's poetry and in the poetry of the modern period generally. Here is a new imageless, discursive, nonfragmented sequence of lines that conceptualizes the difficulty of trying to understand the continuity of time in human experience. Much of the language of "Burnt Norton" is abstract and even academic, but when Eliot "translates" his abstruse speculations into poetic imagery, he achieves an unprecedented union of physical sensation and disembodied language. It is as if the poem reaches out from some eternal world into the transitory world we all occupy to embody its ideas:

> Footfalls echo in the memory
> Down the passage which we did not take
> Towards the door we never opened
> Into the rose garden. My words echo
> Thus in your mind.
>
> (Eliot, 117)

These haunting, self-reflexive lines force the reader to realize that these words were composed in a past that was someone else's present, and that has become, through the act of reading, the reader's present. They are an echo in time, as all poetry is. In this sense, poetry disturbs the flow of time by creating a continuing present each time we read a poem anew. This seems reason enough to write it, but the narrator of *The Four Quartets* questions the point of it:

> But to what purpose
> Disturbing the dust on a bowl of rose-leaves
> I do not know.
>
> (Eliot, 117)

"Burnt Norton" disturbs the dust further by venturing back in time to the narrator's "first world," the spring of human life, filled with promise, excitement, discovery. Although Eliot's descriptive details are taken literally from the gardens at Burnt Norton that he visited in the mid-1930s (Gardner, *CFQ*, 37–38), they are also metaphoric in that they reflect the seasons of a life—a man in autumn called back to the physical sensations associated with childhood. A bird, as in Walt Whitman's "Out of the Cradle Endlessly Rocking," leads the way:

> Other echoes
> Inhabit the garden. Shall we follow?
> Quick, said the bird, find them, find them,
> Round the corner. Through the first gate,
> Into our first world, shall we follow
> The deception of the thrush?
>
> (Eliot, 117–18)

The word *deception* sounds an ominous note, a reminder that the transcendence of time is one of the primary illusions art makes possible. All art, Eliot wrote elsewhere, "aspires to the condition of the timeless" (Bush, 198). The echoes mentioned twice already in the poem are, in the first instance, echoes from Eliot's present (our past) reaching into his future (our present), and in the second instance, echoes from his past that create the poetry of his present and become his legacy to posterity.

But in Eliot's evocation of childhood is also his awareness of its demise. This sense of transitoriness is conveyed through what he called "objective correlatives," images that evoke universal feelings. A dry pool is filled with water, its surface glittering in the sunlight; a cloud passes overhead, and the pool is empty again. In a remarkable sequence of images, the life cycle is traversed, from nothingness to birth, flourishing, death, and nothingness again:

> Dry the pool, dry concrete, brown edged,
> And the pool was filled with water out of sunlight,
> And the lotos rose, quietly, quietly,
> The surface glittered out of heart of light,

And they were behind us, reflected in the pool.
Then a cloud passed, and the pool was empty.

(Eliot, 118)

This is highly concentrated poetry, with a stark, unflinching vision of human reality. But in "Burnt Norton's most startling and memorable lines, Eliot has his "bird" observe that "human kind / Cannot bear very much reality" (Eliot, 118).

It is surely correct to speak of "Burnt Norton," and of *The Four Quartets* generally, as "an event in Eliot's inner life, and as part of that expanded life he lived in his poetry" (Bush, 192). But poems are literary artifacts that involve us, as Ronald Bush notes, through "effects that construct a new reality out of language" (Bush, 193). Although humankind cannot bear much reality, through the mediation of language, that reality becomes more palatable, orderly, and even aesthetically pleasing. "Burnt Norton" moves toward what Eliot called "the still point," that axis between past and future that is an eternal present but a present becalmed and ordered by art, rather than in constant flux as is the actual present. Only through art can human experience be made timeless and achieve the stillness impossible to arrive at in the transient world.

So Eliot proposes to escape from time at the same time as he asserts the impossibility of living in a timeless world. Only through a kind of disembodied, eternal language—a phrase that almost defines what Eliot thought poetry was—can human beings approach the still point, but approaching it does not mean they will ever get there:

> Words move, music moves
> Only in time; but that which is only living
> Can only die. Words, after speech, reach
> Into the silence. Only by the form, the pattern,
> Can words or music reach
> The stillness.

(Eliot, 121)

But paradoxically, "Words strain, / Crack and sometimes break under the burden" (Eliot, 121). Anticipating later postmodern poets (see especially John Ashbery's "Self Portrait in a Convex Mirror"), Eliot here seeks words that both exist in time and transcend it.

It is this "systematic doubleness" (Bush, 206) of *The Four Quartets* that gives the poem its power.

"EAST COKER".   In "East Coker," Eliot describes his visit to the small village in Somerset where his ancestors lived before they set off to America. The first line of the poem, "In my beginning is my end," signals the narrator's intent to trace his origins. Eliot evokes the spirit and language of a Tudor village, quoting from Sir Thomas Elyot's *Book of the Governor*. The lines Eliot cites are about marriage. Given his own disastrous first marriage, they reverberate with irony:

> The association of man and woman
> In daunsinge, signifying matrimonie—
> A dignified and commodious sacrament.
> Two and two, necessary coniunction,
> Holding eche other by the hand or the arm
> Which betokeneth concorde.
>
> (Eliot, 124)

The formal, stately cadence of this language, as well as the archaic diction, gives way to a more troubled view of marriage that almost certainly reflects Eliot's own resistance to sexuality and fear of a meaningless, monotonous life leading only to death—a life, as Prufrock would have it, "measured out in coffee spoons":

> The time of the coupling of man and woman
> And that of beasts. Feet rising and falling.
> Eating and drinking. Dung and death.
>
> (Eliot, 124)

Later in the poem Eliot questions not only his ancestors' views of marriage but also the whole "polite" literary tradition he inherited from them, with its emphasis on formal exactitude, on the surface rather than the psychological realities of life:

> Had they deceived us
> Or deceived themselves, the quiet-voiced elders,
> Bequeathing us merely a receipt for deceit?
>
> (Eliot, 125)

The word *receipt* here is used in its archaic Elizabethan sense meaning "recipe," and the lines seem to reverse Eliot's almost sacred reverence for tradition and a continuous literary heritage. Here he seems to have considerable doubts about the very point of literature and literary conventions. The conventionally structured seventeen-line lyric that opens the second section of "East Coker" reminds the narrator of how difficult, if not impossible, it is for traditional poetry to capture modern experience. Although we depend on the past for knowledge of who we are, the twentieth century seems an age in which the traditional patterns of order and form have been shattered. Knowledge of our heritage

> imposes a pattern, and falsifies
> For the pattern is new in every moment
> And every moment is a new and shocking
> Valuation of all we have been.
>
> (Eliot, 125)

Because "every moment is a new and shocking / Valuation of all we have been," life requires constant renewal and reexamination. So although the narrator of "East Coker" searches to find a sense of personal and poetic identity by seeking its historical origins, that identity is not fixed and is subject to continual flux. The attempt to capture or present reality is a "raid on the inarticulate," in Eliot's famous phrase. The last section of the poem makes these frustrations explicit:

> So here I am, in the middle way, having had twenty years—
> Twenty years largely wasted, the years of l'entre deux guerres—
> Trying to learn to use words, and every attempt
> Is a wholly new start, and a different kind of failure
> Because one has only learnt to get the better of words
> For the thing one no longer has to say, or the way in which
> One is no longer disposed to say it. And so each venture
> Is a new beginning, a raid on the inarticulate
> With shabby equipment always deteriorating
> In the general mess of imprecision of feeling,
> Undisciplined squads of emotion.
>
> (Eliot, 128)

Although this process is difficult and even torturous, each "new beginning" brings something new into poetry and creates a sense of contemporaneity. The final lines of "East Coker" reverse the formulation of the opening lines; instead of anticipating the end of things in their inception, the narrator sees ending as a new kind of emergence: "In my end is my beginning."

"THE DRY SALVAGES". The reader may realize, by the time he or she arrives at the third of the four quartets, that this is an elemental poem in the most literal sense. As one critic has noticed, "The Dry Salvages" "adds to the *air* which stirred the dust on the bowl of rose leaves in *Burnt Norton* and to the soil or *earth* of *East Coker*, another of the four elements of Heraclitus: the *water* of the river and the ocean" (Headings, 169). The title is taken from a group of rocks near Cape Ann that Eliot remembered from his youth, but the water of the poem is used symbolically throughout in much the same sense that it appears in *The Waste Land*— as a life-sustaining force within and around us and also as an ancient chronometer, measuring time independent of human conceptions of it. The sea is an image that links past and future in a perpetual, fluid present.

"We cannot think," Eliot writes, "of a time that is oceanless" (Eliot, 132). Time, like the ocean, is a perpetual flux, and "our own past is covered by the currents of action" (Eliot, 133). We seek permanence and stability—the rocks rather than the water that surrounds and engulfs them—but the immensity of the water (eternity) dwarfs the formed shapes of the Dry Salvages. Human beings are destined to seek meaning by understanding the past and planning for the future,

> But to apprehend
> The point of intersection of the timeless
> With time, is an occupation for the saint—
> (Eliot, 136)

There are in this world only "hints and guesses" of a timeless, permanent, coherent world, and the poet of *The Four Quartets* seeks comfort in them.

"LITTLE GIDDING". One of those comforts is a small chapel in Huntingdonshire, the center of a utopian religious community founded by Nicholas Ferrar in the seventeenth century. Eliot, who visited "Little Gidding," as this chapel and community was called, in spring 1936, was apparently deeply moved by the experience.

He set out to conclude his *Four Quartets* on a note of timelessness, and he saw in the commitment to devotion and worship represented by Little Gidding a "communication / Of the dead . . . tongued with fire beyond the language of the living" (Eliot, 139). In Little Gidding, he felt that he had found "the intersection of the timeless moment" (Eliot, 139). This last poem of the sequence thus draws together images that have appeared earlier; the earth, air, and water of the first three poems are here "tongued with fire."

The opening of "Little Gidding" describes Eliot's approach to this place in the "Midwinter spring" of May, a time that "is its own season" because though it is literally spring, Eliot came here to connect with the spirit and tradition of the dead who once lived here. He addresses the reader in a hypnotic incantatory phrase, repeated again and again in the first part of the poem:

> If you came this way,
> Taking the route you would be likely to take
> From the place you would be likely to come from
> If you came this way in May time, you would find the hedges
> White again, in May, with voluptuary sweetness.
> It would be the same at the end of the journey,
> If you came at night like a broken king,
> If you came by day not knowing what you came for,
> It would be the same, when you leave the rough road
> And turn behind the pig-sty to the dull facade
> And the tombstone.
>
> (Eliot, 139)

This place that is always the same provides comfort for Eliot and is contrasted with the second section of the poem, which begins with three rhymed octets describing the various "deaths" of earth, air, water, and fire. This description is followed by a long passage drawn from Eliot's experience as an air raid warden in World War II. The narrator encounters another walker in the predawn London streets and recognizes a kindred spirit, a "familiar compound ghost / Both intimate and unidentifiable" (Eliot, 140). Like Stetson in *The Waste Land*, the figure represents the human spirit from the past struggling to make sense of existence in the darkest hours of humanity. The narrator seeks to learn something from the stranger's experience; the apparition offers him the most important advice any poet can get:

> For last year's words belong to last year's language
> And next year's words await another voice.
>
> (Eliot, 141)

Eliot, the modern poet, becomes the vehicle for this "familiar compound ghost" whose words echo the words of earlier poets. The figure fades with the coming of dawn and the end of the air raid patrol.

Part III of "Little Gidding" is a falling off from this dramatic encounter and offers a meditation on history that has in common the death of all things, but the poem's power is restored by the short double octet of Part IV, paradoxically identifying love as the source of human torment since it ties us to one another and to the transitory things of this world. The poem concludes with another play on beginnings and endings, life and death, words and their meaning. The poet has "come home" to "Little Gidding" where he has found the pattern of timeless moments in history. He identifies with all of humanity, living and dead, and in this revelation finds solace in the idea of life as a continuing, timeless cycle:

> We die with the dying;
> See, they depart, and we go with them.
> We are born with the dead:
> See, they return, and bring us with them.
>
> (Eliot, 144)

In these lines is the essential Eliot: the voices of the living and the dead entwined in a new and unique voice that became the voice of modernity.

Pound's Ideas about Literature

To link the Eliot of *The Four Quartets* to Ezra Pound is to create a very odd couple because Pound never was attracted to the formal organized religion that so comforted Eliot or to the anglocentric literary tradition that meant so much to "Ol' Possum" (Pound's nickname for Eliot). Yet their early ideas evolved along similar paths, and Pound's insistent sense of a need in human affairs for the assertion of order and tradition, though different from Eliot's, was equally strong.

Perhaps the best place to begin understanding this need and how it is significant in Pound's work is a little book called *The ABC of Reading*, originally published in 1934. Pound was a great aphorist, and some of his ideas about literature are among the most cogent definitions of literary matters anyone has ever produced. Though he despised universities (he called them "institutions for the obstruction of learning"), he established what his publisher, James Laughlin, called the "Ezuversity." Pound gave lessons in literature to anyone who would listen. He was relentless in his tendency to impose his ideas about almost everything on others. Gertrude Stein called him "a village explainer, excellent if you were a village, but if you were not, not."[17] The very title of *The ABC of Reading* or of his important essay, "How to Read," reflects his pedagogical tendencies. "The proper METHOD for studying poetry and good letters," he wrote, "is the method of contemporary biologists, that is careful first-hand examination of the matter, and continual COMPARISON of one 'slide' or specimen with another."[18] Pound intended to reassert for literature some of the intellectual authority it had lost to science. Therefore it needed to be studied like a science, not merely read and enjoyed. Further, it needed to be studied comparatively; the study of individual national literatures was provincial and separated writers from the international community and traditions to which they belonged and that belonged to them. The only literature worth studying was that which made a definite contribution to the art of verbal expression.

These were not novel ideas for a literary scholar, but they were novel for a poet to be expressing. Pound urged writers to "go in fear of abstractions" and argued that "abstract arguments didn't get mankind rapidly forward, or rapidly extend the borders of knowledge" (*ABC* 26). He offered two concise and exact definitions of literature: "Great Literature is simply language charged with meaning to the utmost possible degree," and "Literature is news that STAYS news" (*ABC* 28–29). He spoke of the social and political function of literature and saw it as an index of the state of any civilization: "Good writers are those who keep the language efficient. That is to say keep it accurate, keep it clear. . . . If a nation's literature declines, the nation atrophies and decays" (ABC 32).

One of Pound's most valuable conceptions of poetic language is his idea of three aspects of poetry—what he called (using the original Greek terms) *melapoeia, phanopoeia,* and *logopoeia.* The first, *melapoeia,* refers to the musical properties of language, the melodic or lyric components of poetry that are its very source. Pound's own melodic sense of language is evident in his work, and it can be reasonably asserted that he had the best ear for poetry of any other twentieth-century writer. *Phanopoeia* refers to the image-evoking properties of language—the ability of words to cast images on our visual imagination. Pound was one of the founders of the imagist movement, and the best of his work is both melodic and visual; that is, it utilizes both *melapoeia* and *phanopoeia.* The third aspect of poetry, *logopoeia,* what Pound called "the dance of the intellect among words," is a major factor in his epic poem, *The Cantos.* Poetry for Pound involved the sounds of words, the images they convey, and the meanings they contain. Lyric poetry is strongest in *melapoeia; phanopoeia* is an essential component of modern verse; and *logopoeia* enables poetry to convey ideas and embody history. The twentieth-century poet, to be truly modern, needed to utilize fully all these elements.

The difficulty of modern poetry is explained by Pound in an important essay, "I Gather the Limbs of Osiris": "If a book reveal to us something of which we were unconscious, it feeds us with its energy; if it reveal to us nothing but the fact that its author knew something which we knew, it draws energy from us."[19] For poetry to be energizing, it must break new ground, create new awareness in its readers. If we read only to reinforce our received knowledge, our intellectual and emotional capacities are not expanded but diminished. In the middle of one of his particularly difficult *Cantos,* written much later in his life, Pound continues to assert this principle: "*If we never write anything save what is already understood, the field of understanding will never be extended. One demands the right, now and again, to write for a few people with special interests and whose curiosity reaches into greater detail.*"[20] To some this argument may seem disingenuous and elitist, but it is clearly at the center of Pound's literary worldview.

Pound's Early Life and Work

Pound's elitism and ambition surfaced early in his life. He decided to become a poet at about age fifteen and determined that by the time he turned thirty, "he would know more about poetry than any man living: would know the 'dynamic content' from the 'shell', what was accounted poetry everywhere, what part of it was indestructible and could not be lost in translation, and what effects were obtainable in one language only and were incapable of being translated at all."[21] He attended the University of Pennsylvania in 1901, where he met William Carlos Williams, but transferred to Hamilton College in upstate New York in 1903 where he completed his B.A. degree. He returned to the University of Pennsylvania to do graduate work in comparative literature in 1905. After completing an M.A., he was awarded a traveling fellowship to spend the summer of 1906 in Europe. Upon returning to the United States, he took a teaching position at Wabash College in Crawfordsville, Illinois, but this provincial midwestern town was hardly congenial to his cosmopolitan spirit. In an early poem composed during this period he wrote:

> And I am homesick
> After mine own kind that know, and feel
> And have some breath for beauty and the arts.
> (Stock, 37)

Because of a local scandal (a woman spent the night in his apartment) his tenure at Wabash was brief, and he left in early 1908, stopping briefly in New York before sailing for Europe where he spent three months in Venice, which he loved more than any other European city. He published his first book of poems, *A Lume Spento* ("With Tapers Quenched"), there and then traveled to London during the same year and published a second small collection, *A Quinzaine for This Yule*. In 1909, two more significant collections, *Personae* and *Exultations*, were published in London.

It is hard to imagine that the radically innovative poet of *The Cantos* emerged from such traditional, even archaic beginnings. These poems are imbued with what Pound called "The Spirit of Romance," the title of his first book-length prose work. He believed that poetry needed to be reconnected to its musical roots and looked to the Provençal troubadours for lyrical inspiration. The language of these poems is lush, even overripe, and a far cry from the clear, direct expression he was to champion in his "imagist" phase. But it is unquestionably a *melapoeic* verse that calls attention to its repetitive sound patterns, its outmoded diction, its restrictive formal organization. He sought to revive traditional forms like the sestina, the ballad, the villanaud, and others to recreate the musical urgency of the medieval poetry in the modern world. Particularly impressed with the work of the Provençal poet Bertan de Born, he adopted the troubadour as a persona to express and display his own poetic skills. In an essay called "How I Began," he describes the way in which he composed one of the best of these early poems, "Sestina: Altaforte," in the Reading Room of the British Museum: "I had had De Born on my mind. I had found him untranslatable. Then it occurred to me that I might present him in this manner. I wanted the curious involution and recurrence of the Sestina. I knew more or less of the arrangement. I wrote the first strophe and then went to the Museum to make sure of the right order of permutations. . . . I did the rest of the poem at a sitting. Technically it is one of my best, though a poem on such a theme [the stirring up of war] could never be very important" (Stock, 68). It is important to note that Pound is more interested in the technical elements of the poem than its subject. His poetry of this period is a learned poetry rather than one that grows from personal experience. Yet Pound animated these virtually extinct poetic forms with a bravura and an intensity that was unique. An early anonymous reviewer commented that "his style . . . is often involved, obscure, and pedantic, and there is a certain disagreeable insistence upon the value of the poetic rind itself. But on the other hand the lines are almost oppressive with their unexpanded power, with their intensity and passion, and they are full to the fingertips with an extremely interesting personality" (Raffel, 72).

Pound was a flamboyant performer of his work as well. He read "Sestina: Altaforte" "so forcefully at a poets' dinner arranged by [T. E.] Hulme at the Tour Eiffel restaurant in Percy Street in 1909 that the management placed a screen around the table" (Stock, 72). After the experience of World War I in Europe, Pound, like most of his peers, could no longer write about war so impersonally. In his long, difficult poem, "Hugh Selwyn Mauberley," he lamented the impossibility of trying to sustain poetry in a war-torn world. "The age demanded an image," he wrote,

> Of its accelerated grimace,
> Something for the modern stage,
> Not, at any rate, an Attaic grace.
>
> (*SP* 62)

In the same poem he offers a tribute to all the men who died during the war "believing in old men's lies":

> There died a myriad,
> And of the best, among them,
> For an old bitch gone in the teeth,
> For a botched civilization.
>
> (*SP* 64)

Like Eliot, Pound viewed Western civilization as a cultural waste-land, and he took it as a personal mission to try to "resuscitate the dead art / Of poetry" (*SP* 61).

Pound and Vorticism

Pound began this attempt at resuscitation in the prewar years and continued it throughout the war as a kind of creative counter to the physical destruction taking place on the Continent. In a 1916 letter to lawyer and art patron John Quinn describing the art of Wyndham Lewis, Pound speaks of Lewis's remarkable artistic talent as emblematic of a new kind of modern art. Lewis's genius, he writes, is "not merely knowledge of technique, or skill, it is intelligence and knowledge of life, of the whole of it, beauty, heaven, hell, sarcasm, every kind of whirlwind of force and emotion. Vortex. That is the right word, if I did find it myself" (Paige, 74). His very large ego bruised by Amy Lowell's takeover of the imagist movement, Pound reformed Imagism as a larger, more encompassing movement that would epitomize the dynamic energy he saw as the primary characteristic of the newly emerging art forms of the twentieth century in all of their various aesthetic manifestations. The early poetry that looked backward toward reviving the "spirit of Romance" of the Middle Ages was to be supplanted by a vigorous modern poetry, hardened and enspirited by the rapidly changing tempo of the new era. This movement crystallized in a magazine edited by Lewis and appropriately called *Blast.*

Pound, Lewis, and sculptor Gaudier-Breska were the central figures associated with vorticism, and it is significant that each artist worked in a different medium. In an essay defining vorticism, Pound contended that the avant-garde emerged simultaneously in the various arts: "Every concept, every emotion presents itself to the vivid consciousness in some primary form. It belongs to the art of this form. If sound, to music; if formed words, to literature; the image to poetry . . . colour in position, to painting; form or design in three planes, to sculpture."[22] The various art forms were to pollinate and interact with one another so that artists could indeed be "the antennae of the race," the harbingers of the new. The notion of simultaneity in vorticism extended as well to a revolutionary sense of time, dealt with at length in Wyndham Lewis's *Time and Western Man* (1927) but best illustrated by Pound's newly developed poetic technique in which historical epochs are layered collage style one next to the other without regard to their chronological order. This became the dominant method in *The Cantos* but is apparent in some of the earlier work as well, especially "Hugh Selwyn Mauberley" and "Homage to Sextus Propertius." The vortex in Pound became simply another name for the modern, the center of a whirlwind of creative energy from which the newest developments in all the arts would emerge.

The Cantos

Although Pound's early work is of some historical interest, and a few poems—"Na Audiart," "Portrait D'une Femme," "The Seafarer," "Ballad of the Goodly Fere," "Ancient Music," and "Hugh Selwyn Mauberley"—are memorable, had he not turned his attention to the larger design of *The Cantos* he would be remembered primarily as a discoverer of poetic talent (he championed the work of Robert Frost, T. S. Eliot, H.D., Marianne Moore, James Joyce, and many of the other major writers of the modern period). But in 1925 "after a false start and ten years' work" (Bush, 3), Pound published *A Draft of XVI Cantos for the Beginning of a Poem of*

Some Length, and *The Cantos* remained at the center of his life's work until his death in Venice in 1972. He issued sections of the poem sporadically and in fragmentary fashion. The final section, published a few years before his death, was issued as *Drafts and Fragments of Cantos CX–CXVII*. Shortly after Pound's death, James Laughlin, his publisher at New Directions, issued a complete edition of the poem, a volume of 803 pages, making it the longest notable poem written by an American and probably the most difficult.

The reader of *The Cantos* enters a world apart—there is no other poetry quite like it in English—and usually with misgivings. Its sheer bulk is intimidating, as well as its dense thicket of allusions, its collage-like structure, its uncertain continuity, and its private and cryptic references. This is not a poem one reads from beginning to end but rather one to browse through as one would through a museum, stopping in places to admire something special, moving more quickly through areas of little interest.

There is a lively debate among Pound scholars as to whether the poem has an overall unity. The best summary of the poem's unity comes from Carroll Terrell, whose *Companion to the Cantos* is an essential supplement for the contemporary reader. Terrell sees *The Cantos* as a "great religious poem. . . . an account of man's progress from the darkness of hell to the light of paradise. . . . Thus, the central conflicts and tensions of the poem are the same as those of all other great epics . . . of the past: the eternal struggle of the forces of good against the forces of evil."[23] The counterstatement to this position comes from Pound himself, who late in his life told his biographer, Noel Stock, that *The Cantos* were a "botch." He emphasized the poem's lack of continuity: "I picked out this and that thing that interested me, and then jumbled them into a bag. But that's not the way . . . to make . . . a work of art" (Stock, 457–58). An intermediary view, shared by many readers, is that the poem is intermittently brilliant and tedious, luminous and obscure. In the end, there are about as many interpretations of *The Cantos* as there are readers of it. Because of Pound's obsessive and disjointed poetics, his encyclopedic but erratic worldview, and his incessant literary posturing, it is impossible to find general agreement as to the value of the poem or its many meanings. Unquestionably it contains some of the most beautifully lyrical lines of twentieth-century poetry, but it also has long, barren stretches of impenetrable, arcane, even antipoetic cryptograms.

Because of its difficulty, there is a major critical industry devoted to explicating *The Cantos*. All of this exegesis has helped clarify some of the obscurity of the poem, but it has also underscored the contention that it is a poem for scholars and specialists rather than for those who read poetry for pleasure. For many, criticism of the poem has become a substitute for the poem itself. This state of affairs is hardly surprising because clearly part of Pound's intention in *The Cantos* is to introduce the reader to a wide range of the world's literature and cultural history. He intended to reassert for English-language poetry some of the authority it had surrendered to prose and other art forms. Before the eighteenth century and the rise of the novel as a major literary form, poetry had prevailed as the dominant literary form. What is most alive about the distant past, he believed, is its poetry. We can learn more about the ancient Greeks from Homer than we can from a shelf of historical works and more about the Middle Ages from Dante than from almost any other source. Epic poetry particularly, since it transmits what Pound called "the tale of the tribe," is the highest form of verbal achievement. But since the middle of the eighteenth century, "the serious art of writing" went over to prose. Pound's intent in *The Cantos* is to revive the epic tradition by keeping the present alive for the future through poetry, just as the past has remained vital through its poetry.

This extremely ambitious agenda informs *The Cantos* throughout, but it is only sporadically successful. There are few who would disagree that apart from *The Pisan Cantos*, written under the most trying personal circumstances, the most memorable parts of the poem appear very early. But as the poem progresses, the reader senses a dissipation of energy, a moving away from the poem's initial conception, and the emergence of themes and images that seem almost antithetical to the earlier parts. Pound became absorbed by economic theories, fascist politics, and an obsessive account of Oriental and American history that dragged the poetry into ideologies smothering its language with self-indulgent blather.

GRAPPLING WITH *THE CANTOS*. It is obviously beyond the scope of this chapter to provide a close reading of this enormously complex poem, but we can suggest a way into the poem—a method for reading it—and then simply point out a number of its primary themes that emerge further along.

Opening to the first canto, the reader finds an odd-*sounding* language, highly alliterative and reminiscent of an earlier form of English. Anyone who has read some of Pound's earlier work will recall his translation of the Old English masterpiece, "The Sea-farer." Both poems are about a sea voyage, and both make extensive use of the Old English alliterative line. *The Cantos* begins:

> And then went down to the ship
> Set keel to breakers, forth on the godly sea, and
> We set up mast and sail on that swart ship,
> Bore sheep aboard her, and our bodies also
> Heavy with weeping, and winds from sternward
> Bore us onward with bellying canvas,
> Circe's this craft, the trim-coifed goddess.
>
> (*Cantos*, 3)

This description of an embarkation seems to begin in the middle of an ongoing story. Pound makes use here of a central convention of epic poetry, plunging the reader into the middle of the action. An epic, in Pound's view, holds the collective memory of a civilization and as such exists outside time proper. Its treatment of time is not chronological but rather akin to the way we hold our personal temporal experience in memory, with some events that happened in the distant past being more vivid and accessible than those that happened yesterday. But what exactly are we beginning in the middle of? The reference to Circe makes it clear that the voyage is that of Odysseus, and it does not take long to discover that the passage is a "translation" of Book XI of that epic, the famous *Nekuia* section in which Odysseus, following Circe's command, seeks out Tiresias, the ancient prophet, by journeying to the underworld in order to discover the route to return to his native land. The journey to the underworld is another traditional epic convention: the epic hero confronts and learns from the dead souls of the past. It is a sacrificial human journey, the present paying homage to the past, acknowledging its formative role in the unfolding and continuous human drama.

The Cantos begins in the middle of another epic poem, and Pound adds the Old English style to remind the reader of still another epic tradition (Old English is the language of *Beowulf*) and to link the poem to modern English as well. Here is the beginning of a modern epic that acknowledges its roots both in language and literary traditions. Later in the first canto, still other levels of language enter the poem when the reader is informed that Pound is translating *The Odyssey* not from the original Greek but from a Latin edition of the poem published during the Renaissance. Here, however, the reader is plunged into the classical world of Odysseus via the Anglo-Saxon epic tradition.

The ship soon arrives at the mythic Kimmerian lands that lie at the entrance to the underworld and are always described in Greek mythology as being shrouded in darkness. Pound maintains that tradition by creating a nearly palpable sense of darkness and impenetrability. The lands here are

> Covered with close-webbed mist, unpierced ever
> With glitter of sun-rays.
>
> (*Cantos*, 3)

When they arrive at the entrance to Hades, Odysseus and his crew perform a ritual—the sacrifice of a sheep—to gain entrance to the underworld and obtain an audience with Tiresias. Odysseus sees the souls of the dead all around Erebus, the outer portal of Hades, and they demand more sacrifices. He satisfies their demands while waiting to hear from Tiresias and sees his friend Elpenor, who had died in a fall from the roof of Circe's dwelling. Elpenor wants a proper burial reflecting Greek belief that the soul cannot rest until the appropriate rituals are performed.

This is an early statement of one of the poem's recurrent themes. Throughout *The Cantos* Pound emphasizes the importance of ordering things, of linking present and past, and especially of putting one's own life in order. That order may not be easily discernible, but it needs to be discovered and asserted. The much-anthologized Confucian canto, Canto XIII, is the most explicit statement of this theme. Here, Elpenor, "Unburied, cast on the wide earth," is a "Pitiful spirit" because the burial rituals have not been performed. Odysseus is about to respond to his request, when Tiresias arrives and recognizes a new Odysseus, transformed by the energy of Pound's poetic imagination:

A Grrrreat Littttttttterary Period

'A second time? why? man of ill star,
'Facing the sunless dead and this joyles region?'

(Cantos, 4)

Tiresias accepts the blood sacrifice and then prophesizes that Odysseus shall return to Ithaca but that he shall lose all his friends.

This entire beginning can be seen as a metaphor for the modern poet in search of a lost tradition. Pound begins his masterwork with a tribute to the writer who invented epic poetry for Western civilization, but he does so at great personal cost: the submersion of his own identity in the various personae that embody the traditions extended by *The Cantos*.

Toward the end of Canto I, there is a definite shift; the reader is almost literally uprooted from the mythic land of the Greek underworld to another world altogether:

Lie quiet Divus. I mean, that is, Andreas Divus,
In officina Wecheli, 1538, out of Homer.

(Cantos, 5)

These initially puzzling lines are actually quite explicit. Andreas Divus is the author of a Latin translation of *The Odyssey* published in 1538 at the shop of the printer Christian Wechel ("in officina Wecheli"). (References like this one, so cryptic to early readers of the poem, have now been identified by Pound scholars and are compiled in Carol Terrell's *Companion to the Cantos*.) Pound is here assuring the ghost of Andreas Divus that he can lie quiet because Pound has revitalized his work for a twentieth-century audience just as Divus revitalized Homer for the sixteenth century by translating it into Latin. There is also the further parallel of Odysseus' revitalizing Tiresias (making him strong with blood) and the still further parallel of allowing Elpenor's spirit to lie quiet by keeping his memory alive through the proper ceremonial ritual.

Pound has "resurrected" Odysseus, and it is no accident that the pronoun referring to him shifts from first to third person at this point in the poem:

And he sailed, by Sirens and thence outward and away
And on to Circe.

(Cantos, 5)

The "I" of the first part of the canto has become a new Odysseus, thoroughly modern and able to sail off on his own. Pound concludes the first canto with a description of the golden crown of Aphrodite, the goddess of beauty and fertility, as well as with an image of the golden bough of Argicida, a name for Hermes, the messenger of the gods. These myths of the past are being renewed and delivered to the modern age. If there is a simple phrase that captures Pound's intent through almost all his work, it is the three words "Make it New," which he repeated again and again throughout his life.

To recapitulate, Canto I contains at least five strata of time and language existing simultaneously and interacting together: the ancient Greece of Homer, the slight echo of Rome (the Latin of Divus's edition), the strong cadence of seventh-century England, as reflected in the verse form and the Anglo-Saxon flavor of the language, the spirit of the Renaissance as it appears in the work of Andreas Divus that is Pound's immediate source, and finally Pound's own voice from the twentieth century bringing a modern consciousness to bear on the same ancient legend. For Pound, language contains its own history; this version of the poem is modern because it embodies many of the major layers of time that intervened between the poem's conception and our apprehension of it, an unquestionably extraordinary achievement. The first canto is a marvelous voyage of discovery for the reader approaching it for the first time. It illustrates exactly Pound's widely cited definition of literature: "news that stays news."

OTHER THEMES IN *THE CANTOS*. One of the most trenchant recent commentators on *The Cantos*, Leon Surette, has observed that the poem may be likened to a Gothic church, "built over many generations, under the direction of various master builders, and frequently with many changes of design."[24] Most important to remember about *The Cantos* is that it was written over a lifetime and embodies the shifting enthusiasms and enormous learning of that lifetime. It takes us through heaven and through hell, through China, ancient Greece and Rome, medieval Europe, Revolutionary America, fascist Italy, and all the other confusing complexities of the twentieth-century world. It is, in a sense, our first global poem, both multilingual and multicultural.

Pound's intention at the beginning seemed clear. According to W. B. Yeats, Pound told him that

There will be no plot, no chronicle of events, no logic of discourse, but two themes, the descent into Hades from Homer, a Metamorphosis from Ovid, and, mixed with these, medieval or modern historical characters.[25]

It is equally clear that Pound abandoned this dual theme of hell and transformation early and began to redesign the poem along the lines of his then-current reading and interests. He defined an epic as "a poem including history" and wanted the work to take in as much of a contemporaneous sense of history as possible. His own sense of history was essentially Emersonian: history is shaped by representative men, great leaders, who exert their will against the disintegrative processes that fracture societies, nations, and civilizations. One of the first of these to appear in the poem is Sigismundo Malatesta, an Italian Renaissance prince who was lord of Rimini during the fifteenth century. Although historians generally regard him as a corrupt tyrant and a murderer, Pound admired his generous patronage of the arts and his determination to leave a beautiful legacy, the Tempio Malatestiano in Rimini. The Malatesta Cantos (VIII–XI) chronicle his life imaginatively and attempt to ressuscitate Malatesta's historical reputation. In America's history, Pound viewed Jefferson and John Adams in this way, and throughout the Adams Cantos (LXII–LXXI), there are examples of the manner in which Jefferson and Adams turned the chaos of war and revolution into the order and progress of an emerging civilization.

The second of Pound's obsessions that begins to emerge early is his condemnation of usury, which he saw as the source of the world's economic problems. He set out to locate historically when in history human beings began profiting not from the production of goods or services but from money alone. This theme punctuates the poem throughout, culminating in the famous Usury Canto (XLV) in which Pound specifically defines usury as "a charge for the use of purchasing power, levied without regard to production" (230) and blames most of the woes of twentieth-century civilization on this practice. He is particularly outraged that usury is a sin against nature and destructive to artists. Using an archaic diction that underscores the antiquity of the practice, he exclaims,

> Usura rusteth the chisel
> It rusteth the craft and the craftsman
> It gnaweth the thread in the loom.
>
> (*Cantos*, 230)

Pound devoted much of *The Cantos* and much of his prose writing to trying to convince readers of the cancerous effect of usury, but shortly before his death he wrote:

re USURY:
I was out of focus, taking a symptom for a cause. The cause is AVARICE. (*SPr* 3)

This larger awareness, had it emerged earlier in his life, would have made his constant preoccupation with usury seem merely metaphoric rather than idiosyncratic.

A third theme in *The Cantos* is the discovery of a harmonious government—a rule of order that Pound felt had emerged at various epochs in human history. The beautiful Canto XIII—called the "Confucian Canto"—speaks of order as emerging from strength of character and is consistent with Pound's "great men" theory of history:

> If a man have not order within him
> He can not spread order about him;
> And if a man have not order within him
> His family will not act with due order;
> > And if the prince have not order within him
> He can not put order in his dominions.
> And Kung gave the words "order"
> and "brotherly deference"
> And said nothing of the "life after death."
>
> (*Cantos*, 59)

This emphasis on order, so philosophically supported in the early cantos, was to lead Pound down the path of fascism and to his arrest as a traitor following the Allied victory in World War II.

Pound, Fascism, and Anti-Semitism

No discussion of Pound's importance as a major twentieth-century American writer can be complete without acknowledgment of his political views, which are antithetical to some of the most fundamental values of a democratic society. Recently many scholars—notably William Chace, Cairns Craig, and Peter Nicholls—have begun to relate Pound's political views to his poetry and have underscored the inseparability of the two. That Pound was a fascist sympathizer and anti-Semite through most of his creative life is indisputable, but earlier readers of the poetry have argued that these beliefs do not infiltrate the poetry to any significant degree. While it is true that shortly before his death, Pound told Allen Ginsberg that anti-Semitism was his greatest error—a "suburban" prejudice he could never transcend—and remarked to both Ginsberg and others that his writing was filled with "stupidity and ignorance all the way through," these very remarks underscore the fact that Pound's work contains and expresses the pro-fascist, anti-Semitic identity he created for himself during his most productive years.

Irving Howe has argued that Pound's politics are not only not peripheral to the poem but that they are central to Pound's intent throughout. "Quantitatively," he reasons,

the percentage of anti-Semitic passages is small, but thematically they are closely related to the whole political drift of the poem, which at some points is explicitly Fascist and at other points supportive of the Fascist myth.[26]

The word *fascism* derives from the old Roman symbol of power and authority, the fasces, a bundle of sticks bound together by thongs with an ax head protruding from one end. One by one the sticks would be easy to break; bound together, they are indestructible and a potent weapon. Fascist ideology called for binding together all classes of a nation into a single organization with a single will. This aspect of the fascist myth was enormously appealing to Pound. Given his enthusiasm for great leaders—men who made a significant mark on the historical direction of their time—and given as well his love of Italy, a land that embodies the physical remains of a cultural tradition he sought to resurrect and extend, his virtual deification of Mussolini seems almost inevitable.

In *Patria Mia* (1912) he states the following as the first principle of his credo:

The arts come into prominence and there is what is called an 'age of art' when men of a certain catholicity of intelligence come into power. The great protector of the arts is as rare as the great artist, or even more so." (*SPr* 130)

Pound saw fascism, particularly in its Italian manifestation, as the culmination of historical processes designed to bring about an orderly society that would enable art and culture to prosper and flourish. He regarded the fascist potential to cope with the exigencies of national life in specific terms as greater than that of any other form of government. Pound clearly felt Mussolini's Italy was attempting to restore a sense of balance, order, and historical continuity through the application of intelligence to social problems and priorities. That history has shown this to be an extremely naive view of the nature and character of fascism is equally clear, but at the time he expressed these pro-fascist sentiments, Pound did not have the luxurious view of historical perspective.

When the fascist bubble burst, Pound found himself in the Detention Training Center at Pisa after broadcasting anti-American and anti-Semitic propaganda on Italian radio (he was to be incarcerated in a mental hospital for twelve years when he was returned to the United States at the end of the war). At Pisa he began to develop some of that perspective, and the nature and character of his poetry changed. Nowhere in *The Cantos* is the relationship between poetry and politics more cogent than in the Pisan poems, which chronicle the daily life of an artist bereft of political power or influence, alone in a cage. More than anywhere else in the poem, the reader here sees Pound's own personality breaking through the guises that carry the narrative of much of the earlier cantos. Instead of Odysseus, Malatesta, Adams, and the Chinese Emperors, we find the poignancy of Old "Ez" alone here, talking to cats and crickets. Like John Donne's *Devotions on Emergent Occasions*, the Pisan cantos are the meditations of a great poet who believes he is near the end of his life, trying to discover what he loves most and what remains when the remnants of human political and cultural life are taken from him.

From the first image in the Pisan sequence ("The enormous tragedy of the dream in the peasant's / bent shoulders"[*Cantos*, 425]), which depicts a spiritless humanity, burdened by hardship and bereft of ideals, Pound views the "progress" of civilization in the twentieth century as a catastrophic dissipation of constructive human energy. He sees himself as an emblem of that dissipation: "a man on whom the sun has gone down," repeating again and again the haunting words of Aubrey Beardsley, "beauty is difficult," clearly an understatment in the spartan confines of the detention center. And yet poetry enables him to survive and transcend his condition, which is that of twentieth-century humanity, devastated by two world wars, cut off from a cultural heritage. The conclusion of Canto LXXXI, which contains perhaps his noblest poetry, seems the only response to those who wonder how such an antiegalitarian figure could have achieved such literary prominence:

> What thou lovest well remains,
> > the rest is dross
> What thou lov'st well shall not be reft from thee
> What thou lov'st well is thy true heritage
> Whose world, or mine or theirs
> > or is it of none?
> First came the seen, then thus the palpable
> Elysium, though it were the halls of hell
> What thou lov'st well is thy true heritage
> What thou lov'st well shall not be reft from thee
>
> The ant's a centaur in his dragon world.
> Pull down thy vanity, it is not man
> Made courage, or made order, or made grace,
> Pull down thy vanity, I say pull down.
> Learn of the green world what can be thy place
> In scaled invention or true artistry,
> Pull down thy vanity,
> > Paquin pull down!
> The green casque has outdone your elegance.
> > (*Cantos*, 520–21)

· SIX ·

A World of Ideas, A World of Things: Wallace Stevens and William Carlos Williams

> What these two unlikely sons of Emerson and Whitman were really engaged in . . . was a struggle to determine the nature of reality and the imagination and the direction American poetry was to take in the twentieth century. In reality, this almost invisible war was one of the most significant dialogues into the nature and practice of American poetics.
>
> —Paul Mariani, *A Useable Past*

The counter effort to Eliot and Pound's intention to internationalize American poetry and reconnect it with its nonindigenous predecessors emerged from two unlikely sources. While there may be other pairs of twentieth-century poets with even more strikingly different temperaments than William Carlos Williams, (1883–1963), a pediatrician from Rutherford, New Jersey, and Wallace Stevens (1879–1955), an insurance lawyer from Hartford, Connecticut, none offers such a sharp and balanced contrast to the Europeanized and Orientalized poetics of Pound and Eliot. Though Williams's work is much more clearly in the American grain than that of Stevens, both sought to fashion a poetry from the physical world that surrounded them rather than from the literary worlds that preceded them. The two poets were friends—perhaps *acquaintances* is a better word—for most of their lives, but they were also extremely guarded toward one another. Both realized that each offered a different alternative to Pound and Eliot's brand of modernism, and as Williams's biographer notes, they "watched each other through gun-slit turrets for forty years."[1]

For Stevens, poetry was a kind of substitute religion and the poet a high priest of sorts, seeking to abstract essences from the world of daily experience that would enable him to recreate life on the level of what he called a "supreme fiction." "Metaphor," he wrote in "Adagia," a collection of aphorisms about poetry and art, "creates a new reality from which the original appears to be unreal."[2] Put another way, "Reality is a cliché from which we escape by metaphor" (*OP* 179). Poetry, in this view, enlivens the physical world by revealing its surprising correspondences. The poet becomes the maker of an exotic, lush, and sometimes voluptuous world inhabited by baboons, periwinkles, cockatoos, peacocks, blackbirds, green fans, red willows, firecats, midsummer blazes, jungle feathers, and even an "Emperor of Ice Cream." Reality, sifted through Stevens's imagination, emerges as intensified—a life of the mind that enhances the sometimes drab actualities of the physical world.

Williams's goals and intentions for poetry were less cerebral, and ultimately more revolutionary. It was his lifelong desire to invent a poetry rooted in American speech and experience, to convey a sense of felt life in his work by bringing poetry down from the pedestal of high art and locating it firmly in the familiar terrain of the poet's immediate environment. Far from heightening the experience of reality through exotic and highly refined language, Williams sought to express it directly, as artlessly as possible. Of course, he knew that it requires a great deal of art to achieve the effect of artlessness, and he was constantly troubled by critics and readers who saw his work as lacking poetic intensity. In response to an early book of Williams's verse, Stevens offered this assessment: "What strikes me most about the poems themselves is their casual character. . . . Personally I have a distaste for miscellany."[3] Williams wrote back offering a statement of his credo: "The imagination moves from one thing to another. . . . But the thing that stands eternally in the way of good writing is always one: the virtual impossibility of lifting to the imagination those things which lie under the direct scrutiny of the senses, close to the nose. It is this difficulty that sets a value upon all works of art and makes them a necessity" (Morse, 85–86). How to convey imaginatively the world directly before you, "close to the nose," became the imperative of Williams, his radical and distinctly American style emerging more and more assuredly with each successive book. Together Stevens and Williams provided an important dualistic model that enabled the next generation of American poets to convert a world of ideas and a world of things into a world of words.

Wallace Stevens

Stevens was born in Reading, Pennsylvania, on 2 October 1879; he was six years older than Pound and nine years older than Eliot. He attended Harvard and worked briefly as a reporter for the *New York Herald-Tribune* before entering the New York Law School in 1901. He was admitted to the New York State bar in 1904 and shortly after began a dual career as an insurance lawyer and poet, which absorbed his entire life. Ruefully, he once remarked, "I have no life. . . . except in poetry. . . . No doubt that would be true if my whole life was free for poetry" (Morse, 21). Of course his whole life was not—it is notoriously difficult to make a living as a poet in America—but his successful career with the Hartford Accident and Indemnity Company provided him with amenities that enabled him to work at his poetry without worrying about having to make a living from it. His first poems were published in 1914, and his first book of poems, *Harmonium*, appeared in 1923. The themes and concerns of Stevens's work throughout his life appear in this first book, and he tended to think of all of his work as a single, interconnected long poem. When *Collected Poems* was published in 1954, shortly before his death the following year, he had originally wanted to call it "The Whole of Harmonium."

In "Adagia," Stevens made many statements about the nature of poetry and art generally that illuminate his consistency of purpose. One of these points to the importance he attaches to poetry, particularly in a secular age:

The relation of art to life is of the first importance in a skeptical age since, in the absence of a belief in God, the mind turns to its own creations and examines them, not alone from the aesthetic point of view, but for what they reveal, for what they validate, for the support they give. (Morse, 23)

This statement is central to Stevens's conception of poetry as a this-worldly religion. No other subject engaged him more fully than the connection between the world as created by the artist to the world as experienced unimaginatively. Again and again in his poetry he contrasts the physicality and tangibility of the world with the rich and imaginative experience of that world within the human psyche:[4]

> Just as my fingers on these keys
> Make music, so the selfsame sounds
> On my spirit make a music, too.
>
>   ("Peter Quince at the Clavier," 8)

> Out of the window,
> I saw how the planets gathered
> Like the leaves themselves
> Turning in the wind.
> I saw how night came,
> Came striding like the color of the heavy hemlocks.
> I felt afraid
> And I remembered the cry of the peacocks.
>
>   ("Domination of Black," 15)

> I was of three minds
> Like a tree
> In which there are three blackbirds.
>
>   ("Thirteen Ways of Looking at a Blackbird," 20)

> One must have a mind of winter
> To regard the frost and the boughs
> Of the pine-trees crusted with snow
>
>   ("The Snow Man," 54)

Each of these examples, which could be multiplied many times in the Stevens canon, contrasts an external reality with a state of mind, and each of the poems they are extracted from explores the relationship between these two entities. In each of them, Stevens's idea that "the real world seen by an imaginative man may very well seem like an imaginative construct" (Morse, 52) is reinforced.

"Sea Surface Full of Clouds," a poem in five sections each consisting of six tercets, is a good example of Stevens's transformative imagination at work upon what is a very traditional, even clichéd, landscape. In a technique analogous to that of the French Impressionist painters, Stevens renders the same landscape in sharply different moods by altering only a few descriptive adjectives. Like Monet's water lilies or haystacks painted in different light and seasons, each variation conveys a thoroughly different mood. Each section begins with the same line, locating time and place: "In that November off Tehuantepec." The remainder of the section describes what the morning following the "slopping of the sea" all night "made one think of." It is easy to see the external-internal contrast here; a landscape is the world "out there," but an artist's rendering of it is distinctly his own. Although the imagery of each section is similar, images are radically transformed by the adjectives Stevens chooses to convey his sense of the experience. These adjectives are analogous to the colors on a painter's palette, each dab of the brush altering a viewer's impression of the finished product. In the first section "one thinks" of "rosy chocolate / And gilt umbrellas." This image becomes "chophouse chocolate / And sham umbrellas" in the second section, "porcelain chocolate / And pied umbrellas" in the third, "musky chocolate / and frail umbrellas" in the fourth, and "Chinese chocolate / And large umbrellas" in the fifth. In each case Stevens's imaginative choice transforms the remainder of the description. The green of the seascape is successively "Paradisal," "sham-like," "uncertain," "too-fluent," and "motley." While the ocean and its rhythmical motion is consistently described as a "machine," that machine is variously "perplexed," "tense," "tranced," "dry, and "obese," each of these terms rendering the natural world through human qualities, each of them a reminder of Stevens's control over the world he creates.

While this sort of reading of Stevens's poetry may seem overly technical, it is nearly impossible to read him without a heightened attention to technique. In this sense he is a poet's poet, constantly wrestling with questions central to his art and aesthetics. Reading him in large quantities creates something of a dizzying effect because his nuances are so subtle and rarefied they sometimes seem not to belong to this world. Yet in his strongest poems, his evoked world is truly exotic and palpable.

Consider "Sunday Morning," an early poem (1915) that some readers believe he never surpassed. Here Stevens contrasts the solemnity and otherworldliness of a Christian celebration of Sunday morning with its pagan counterpart, a true celebration of the sun. He makes the contrast vivid and highly visual by focusing the poem on a woman rising late one Sunday morning and feeling some guilt about not going to church. The bright colors and textures of the room around her darken as she thinks about "that old catastrophe," the crucifiction of Christ. The first stanza sets the scene almost cinematically as the reader moves from the surface of the description to the imagery contained within the woman's mind:

> Complacencies of the peignoir, and late
> Coffee and oranges in a sunny chair,
> And the green freedom of a cockatoo
> Upon a rug mingle to dissipate
> The holy hush of ancient sacrifice.
> She dreams a little, and she feels the dark
> Encroachment of that old catastrophe,
> As a calm darkens among water-lights.
> The pungent oranges and bright, green wings
> Seem things in some procession of the dead,
> Winding across wide water, without sound.
> The day is like wide water, without sound,
> Stilled for the passing of her dreaming feet
> Over the seas, to silent Palestine,
> Dominion of the blood and sepulchre.
>
> (5)

The bright colors associated with the here and now of the woman's life are set against the monochromatic darkness of Christianity; the green freedom of the present is contrasted with the "blood and sepulchre" of the ancient past. The second stanza raises the central question in the poem: Why should she give her bounty to the dead? Stevens compares the abundance and variety of the physical world around the woman with the ephemeral and chimerical "thought of heaven," the Christian promise of a life after death. Then, linking Christianity to classical myth by comparing the birth of Jove to the birth of Christ, Stevens projects a world stripped of humanity's necessity to worship something larger than itself. If we could accept the earth as the only paradise we will ever know, Stevens believes that

> The sky will be much friendlier then than now,
> A part of labor and a part of pain,

> And next in glory to enduring love,
> Not this dividing and indifferent blue.
>
> (6)

The woman expresses doubt about giving up the idea of an afterlife; life seems so transitory, and humanity has always longed for something more permanent. The narrator responds that there is no concept of heaven that has endured "As April's green endures; or will endure / Like her remembrance of awakened birds, / Or her desire for June and evening. Nature, the seasons, human memory, and desire: these are the enduring things of this world, not any "old chimera of the grave." Unsatisfied by this response, the woman still feels the need "of some imperishable bliss." The narrator's response to this persistent human desire is one of the most memorable moments in twentieth-century poetry:

> Death is the mother of beauty; hence from her,
> Alone, shall come fulfilment to our dreams
> And our desires.
>
> (7)

Some readers may object to the personification of death as woman and mother, but Stevens clearly means to exalt mortality here as the only thing that gives meaning and urgency to what would otherwise be the monotonous and unchanging days of our lives. He projects an "unchanging" paradise where fruit never falls from trees and rivers never find the seas toward which they flow.

Near its conclusion, the poem seems to burst its restraints, offering a pagan celebration of the sun, "not as a god, but as a god might be," as a substitute for the effete Christianity the poem has portrayed. The woman now appears ready to accept the uncertainties and ambiguities of the world we live in, "an old chaos of the sun," without constantly needing the reassurance of eternal verities.

The only eternal certainties in Stevens's work are the certainties of one day following another, the changing seasons, and the drama of birth and death. The poet can take pleasure in these things— the pleasures, as he puts it in the title of one of his playful poems, "of merely circulating." In that poem, Stevens relishes the cyclical quality of daily experience, the sense of recurrence and repetition that more and more seems to characterize life as one matures. He does not lament this lack of novelty but instead uses it to construct a poem in which a stanza of death imagery is sandwiched between two nursery rhyme–like stanzas that undercut the solemnity and finality of death. The poem begins in singsong fashion:

> The garden flew round with the angel,
> The angel flew round with the clouds,
> And the clouds flew round and the clouds flew round
> And the clouds flew round with the clouds.
>
> (96)

The repetition clearly has a comic effect: the garden, angel, and clouds involved in an endless chain of circularity. But the comedy is modulated by the second stanza where "skulls" and "black hoods" ominously intrude into the childlike tone of the poem:

> Is there any secret in skulls,
> The cattle skulls in the woods?
> Do the drummers in black hoods
> Rumble anything out of their drums?
>
> (97)

The changing rhyme scheme (from a b c b to d e e f) disrupts the regularity of the poem in the same way that death disrupts the pattern of our lives, and the rumbling, black-hooded drummers heralding death or execution seem doubly sinister next to the garden, angel, and clouds flying effortlessly around and around. In the final stanza, Stevens counters the death imagery with an image evoking birth, but he calls attention to its matter-of-factness rather than to any notion of birth as a miraculous event. In four lines he seems to accept "things as they are" with something more than resignation; he sounds almost gleeful about it:

> Mrs. Anderson's Swedish baby
> Might well have been German or Spanish,
> Yet that things go round and again go round
> Has rather a classical sound.
>
> (97)

The final couplet returns the reader to the circularity of the first stanza. With the poet, we have confronted death but come away relatively unscathed because he has domesticated it through language.

Stevens is often humorous; a sampling of some of his titles alone sounds like a catalog of comic routines: "Someone Puts a Pineapple Together"; "Man Carrying Thing"; "Frogs Eat Butterflies. Snakes Eat Frogs. Hogs Eat Snakes. Men Eat Hogs."; "A Rabbit as the King of Ghosts"; "The Revolutionists Stop for Orangeade"; and many others. But humor in Stevens is rarely an end in itself because he is essentially a philosophical poet whose central preoccupation is with epistemology: How do we discover the nature of reality? he asks again and again in his work, and for him reality and artistic depictions of it are sometimes interchangeable, sometimes hopelessly separate, sometimes loosely connected. Always, however, the poet is a "maker" whose "Blessed rage for order" ("The Idea of Order at Key West") sustains and ennobles life. And life, Stevens says, in "Men Made out of Words." "consists / Of propositions about life" (281). Here life and art seem interchangeable, for reality is made up of the propositions that describe and convey it.

But in much of his major work, poetry can never quite adequately convey the nature of reality because, as he writes in his marvelous long poem about the transformative powers of the imagination, 'The Man with the Blue Guitar,"

> Things as they are
> Are changed upon the blue guitar.
> (133)

The blue guitar, an image taken from Picasso's famous painting, is an emblem of the human imagination that paradoxically alters the world and reflects it precisely. "They" in the poem represents a society that demands from its artists a mirror image of the world as it is:

> And they said then, "But play, you must,
> A tune beyond us, yet ourselves,
>
> A tune upon the blue guitar
> Of things exactly as they are."
> (133)

This is an impossible charge since the artist can never duplicate reality exactly; the best that the man with the blue guitar can do is "patch it as I can" and make the world seem more beautiful and heroic:

> I cannot bring a world quite round,
> Although I patch it as I can
>
> I sing a hero's head, large eye
> And bearded bronze, but not a man,
>
> Although I patch him as I can
> And reach through him almost to man.
>
> (133)

Creating a heroic sculpture or poem (or painting or song or almost any other aesthetic object or event—for Stevens the artistic imagination is multiform) gets us almost to the nature of humanity but not quite. And just as the imagination can elevate and ennoble humanity, it can also convey its pain and suffering; in either case art about the world never adequately captures it.

Although the man with the blue guitar struggles to be honest and truthful about the world as he experiences it, it is always an imagined rather than a real world that he creates. Poetry is always poetry, never life itself (this idea contradicts his alternate notion of life consisting of propositions about life, but Stevens is sufficiently Emersonian to regard a foolish consistency as the hobgoblin of little minds) yet it is that most exalted or intensified sense of life that we can experience. Poetry can give us essences, or what Stevens called "abstractions." And these abstractions, in a secular age, replace religion by providing a sense of order, harmony, and tranquility. Poetry

> Exceeding music must take the place
> Of empty heaven and its hymns.
>
> (135)

But sometimes poetry and art seem inadequate to the challenge of supplanting religion in a secular world. They hardly seem to offer the solace and comfort that religion can. The very painting the poem alludes to depicts a dispirited musician, his body bent and contorted, washed over by an atmosphere of blueness. The narrator asks,

> Is this picture of Picasso's, this "hoard
> of destructions," a picture of ourselves,
>
> Now, an image of our society?
> Do I sit, deformed, a naked egg,
>
> Catching at Goodbye, harvest moon,
> Without seeing the harvest or the moon?
>   (140)

There is a kind of minimalism in "The Man with the Blue Guitar" that is unusual in Stevens's poetry. It is as if the world is truncated, stripped to its essentials. "The earth is not earth," he writes, "but a stone." Unlike the rapturous paganism of "Sunday Morning," the tone here is somber, almost funereal. As Helen Vendler has noted, "In *The Man with the Blue Guitar*, the gods are annihilated, and the third dimension which they represent is eliminated. A strict two-phase system is all that remains, as the mind alone confronts the world alone, without any sacred parental presences."[5] But the poem gathers imaginative momentum as the guitar player struggles to capture "things as they are" in ways that they have never before been captured. And in the final two stanzas the two-dimensional flatness of mind and world is expanded by the power of the imagination to make things new:

> Throw away the lights, the definitions,
> And say of what you see in the dark
>
> That it is this or that it is that,
> But do not use the rotted names.
>
> How should you walk in that space and know
> Nothing of the madness of space,
>
> Nothing of its jocular procreations?
>   (149)

The conclusion of "The Man with the Blue Guitar" unequivocally asserts the supremacy of the imagination to the hard realities of daily life. The poem's last lines are almost stately in their stark simplicity. They are, as one critic has observed, as "majestic and persuasive"[6] as anything Stevens had written to this point in his career.

> Here is the bread of time to come,
>
> Here is its actual stone. The bread
> Will be our bread, the stone will be
>
> Our bed and we shall sleep by night.
> We shall forget by day, except
>
> The moments when we choose to play
> The imagined pine, the imagined jay.
>   (150)

Because of Stevens's emphasis on the importance of the imagination, he is sometimes criticized for being little in touch with social issues and political realities. He lived through a depression and two world wars and wrote about them (the few times any current events enter his work) as remote events, not susceptible to the same sort of imaginative treatment that other human activities are. In fact, he argued that "the immense poetry of war and the poetry of a work of the imagination are two different things" (206). War replaces the imagination with "mere" consciousness and consciousness deals with fact, not imaginative reality. So it is not surprising that Stevens's one long poem dealing with World War II is called "Examination of the Hero in a Time of War." Stevens proposes in this poem to examine not the nature of heroism but the image of the hero as a figure that exalts and ennobles human life. The imagination produces the hero because "the hero is not a person" but rather a "feeling" embodied in a particular image:

> The hero is a feeling, a man seen
> As if the eye was an emotion,
> As if in seeing we saw our feeling
> In the object seen and saved that mystic
> Against the sight, the penetrating,
> Pure eye.
>   (204)

This tendency to turn actual people into imaginative constructs

that embody feelings is one of Stevens's least endearing qualities
and seems particularly pernicious when war, bloodshed, and human suffering are made the occasion for epistemological speculations of a particularly abstruse kind.

But the abstruseness of "Examination of a Hero" is modest next
to the elaborate philosophical discourse of one of Stevens's longest
poems, "Notes toward a Supreme Fiction." This extremely orderly
poem—three sections divided into ten subsections, each made of
of seven tercets—is presented as advice to an "ephebe" or ap-
prentice soldier who is gradually informed of the the nature of a
"supreme fiction," a concept that is particularly Stevensian and is
perhaps best defined as "the ultimate poem.'

Stevens says this ultimate poem must have three major qualities:
it must be abstract; it must change; and it must give pleasure.
These dicta are the headings of each of the poem's large sections.
The first section defines what Stevens means by "abstract", and
concludes that "the major abstraction is the idea of man." Poetry
must concern itself with humanity in its essences, and not with
individual human lives. This principle accounts for the impersonal,
objective quality of Stevens's verse, in some ways more impersonal
than that of Pound or Eliot. Second, since change is the most
essential quality of this world, the supreme fiction must embody
that change. As in "Sunday Morning," written nearly thirty years
earlier, a static, unchanging paradise is contrasted with the lush,
sensual, fecundity of this world:

> After a lustre of the moon, we say
> We have not the need of any paradise,
> We have not the need of any seducing hymn.
>
> It is true. Tonight the lilacs magnify
> The easy passion, the ever-ready love
> Of the lover that lies within us and we breathe
>
> An odor evoking nothing, absolute.
> We encounter in the dead middle of the night
> The purple odor, the abundant bloom.
>
> (221)

But what truly separates the "supreme fiction" from other diver-
sions is its capacity to give pleasure by ordering the world as a

harmonious, changing, constantly evolving entity, ever alive with the ability to provoke our wonder. In the last section, Stevens playfully addresses the earth as a "Fat girl, terrestrial" and asserts, "The fiction that results from feeling," though "irrational" is really more rational than the factual descriptions of reality that we get from science and philosophy. The purpose of poetry, Stevens wrote in "Adagia," "is to contribute to man's happiness" (*OP* 168).

Stevens's last poems, though concerned with the same questions that preoccupied him throughout his life, have a stoic, dark, and haunting air that sometimes cuts to the bone. The startling opening of "The Rock," for example, calls into question the physical tangibility of our being:

> It is an illusion that we were ever alive,
> Lived in the houses of mothers, arranged ourselves
> By our own motions in a freedom of air.
>
> Regard the freedom of seventy years ago.
> It is no longer air. The houses still stand,
> Though they are rigid in rigid emptiness.
>
> Even our shadows, their shadows, no longer remain,
> The lives these lived in the mind are at an end.
> They never were.
>
> (362)

In a short poem, 'As You Leave the Room," he wonders whether he has "lived a skeleton's life, / As a disbeliever in reality"(396), and in one of the last poems he wrote, "Of Mere Being," he speaks of the external world as an appendage to the mind, without human meaning or feeling. But Stevens's final vision remained true to the powerful poetic imagination that has always been able to imbue that appendage with an almost voluptuous vitality:

> The palm at the end of the mind,
> Beyond the last thought, rises
> In the bronze decor,
>
> A gold-feathered bird
> Sings in the palm, without human meaning,
> Without human feeling, a foreign song.

You know then that it is not the reason
That makes us happy or unhappy.
The bird sings. Its feathers shine.

The palm stands on the edge of space.
The wind moves slowly in the branches.
The bird's fire-fangled feathers dangle down.
(398).

William Carlos Williams

William Carlos Williams invented a poetry of heightened visual attention, rooted in a keen sense of place and expressed through the American idiom. In 1929, when the editors of the *Little Review* asked what he considered his strongest characteristic, he replied, "My sight. . . . I like best my ability to be drunk with a sudden realization of value in things others never notice."[7] Unlike Eliot and Pound who sought to internationalize American poetry, and unlike Stevens, who was concerned with elegant expression, Williams consistently tried to write down-to-earth poetry that grew from the perceptions of everyday experience.

Although he met Pound and H.D. at the University of Pennsylvania in the early 1900s where he was enrolled in medical school, he was probably more influenced by another acquaintance of that period, the painter Charles Demuth. Williams spent a great deal of time nurturing his friendships and associations with painters and photographers and was a charter member of the famed Stieglitz Circle, a group of friends associated with the photographer Alfred Stieglitz that included Demuth and other painters like Charles Sheeler and Marsden Hartley. For a while he considered becoming a painter himself, and a few of his early paintings have survived, including a likable "Self Portrait" that shows considerable painterly skill (reproduced in Tashjian, 19). "Had it not been that it was easier to transport a manuscript than a wet canvas," he wrote in the preface to his *Selected Essays*, "the balance might have been tilted the other way" (Tashjian, 18). Though he chose to write poetry rather than to paint pictures, he brought to the task a heightened visual attention that is evident everywhere in his work. He conceived of a poem as a "small machine made out of words" in which every part works with every other to produce an active, participatory work of art.

His famous poem, "The Red Wheelbarrow," much anthologized and overexplained, is nonetheless an excellent example of his poetry of attention. It shows his sharpness of visual perception—the way he looks at the world with a painter's eye. The simple and direct message of the poem is the importance of observing carefully, of opening our eyes to the physical world around us:[8]

> so much depends
> upon
>
> a red wheel
> barrow
>
> glazed with rain
> water
>
> beside the white
> chickens.
>
> (*CEP*, 277)

Apart from the first two lines, this little machine made of words is a nearly pure imagist poem that calls the reader's attention to a simple but precisely composed scene. The first two lines create a tension and tease us with an unsupported assertion—"so much depends / upon"—and the reader expects some important religious, scientific, or philosophical statement to follow. Instead there follows a simple painterly description of a bucolic scene. I say "painterly" because Williams constructs this poem almost as if it were a painting, isolating color, shape, object, texture, and relationship. Notice how the poem's scene unfolds, word by word—*red, wheel, barrow,* and so on—until the whole picture comes into view like a developing photograph. Once the picture comes into focus, the reader cannot help but refer back to the beginning of the poem and ask why it is that so much depends on these things. So much depends, Williams seems to be saying, on paying attention to the colors, shapes, textures, and relationships between the objects that are right in front of you, and what happened to be in front of him when he conceived this poem was a red wheelbarrow and some chickens. He took what was "close to the nose" and put it in a poem that invites the reader to do the same.

An even more painterly poem is "The Great Figure," which, like "The Red Wheelbarrow," gradually composes a single image, this time gathering sound and motion as it comes into clearer view:

Among the rain
and lights
I saw the figure 5
in gold
on a red
firetruck
moving
tense
unheeded
to gong clangs
siren howls
and wheels rumbling
through the dark city.
                              (*CEP*, 230)

Williams recorded the circumstances of this poem's creation:

Once on a hot July day coming back exhausted from the Post Graduate
Clinic, I dropped in as I sometimes did at Marsden's [Hartley] for a talk,
a little drink maybe and to see what he was doing. As I approached his
number I heard a great clatter of bells and the roar of a fire engine
passing the end of the street down Ninth Avenue. I turned just in time
to see a golden figure 5 on a red background flash by. The impression
was so sudden and forceful that I took a piece of paper out of my pocket
and wrote a short poem about it.[9]

"The Great Figure" is another of Williams's verbal paintings
focusing the reader's attention on Williams's immediate perceptions
of light, color, shape, motion, and sound. It removes a few details
from a dark, murky scene and frames those details, isolating a
moment in time and space before it disappears forever into the
darkness of the city. Charles Demuth was so struck by the poem
that he painted an interpretation of it, *I Saw the Figure Five in
Gold*.

In 1923 Williams published *Spring and All* (where "The Red
Wheelbarrow" first appeared), a remarkable little book combining
poetry, prose, autobiography, fiction, and criticism that summarized
his assessment of the state of modern poetry and defended his
own poetic principles against detractors who saw his work as a
kind of antipoetry because it lacked rhyme, conventional rhythm,

and other poetic devices. He constructs a mock attack on his work, speaking of it as "positively repellent." After the long harangue he responds simply, "Perhaps this noble apostrophe means something terrible to me, I am not certain, but for the moment I interpret it to say: 'You have robbed me. God, I am naked. What shall I do?' "[10]

To enter the "new world naked," as each child born into it does, becomes for him the task of the modern poet. He intends to confront experience directly and imaginatively without the intervention of convention and tradition. "Nearly all writing, up to the present," he argues,

> has been especially designed to keep up the barrier between sense and the vaporous fringe which distracts the attention from its agonized approaches to the moment. It has been always a search for the "beautiful illusion." Very well. I am not in search of "the beautiful illusion." (*Imaginations*, 89)

To abandon the search for the beautiful illusion in poetry meant stripping verse down to its essentials to convey the the hard, clear texture of actual experience. It also meant giving the imagination free rein, unhampered by the prohibitions of previous generations and also those of his more literarily oriented peers, Pound and Eliot.

Williams saw the human imagination as a kind of final step in the evolutionary process. It enables humanity to transform the mundane into the poetic, in the same way that spring transforms the dead earth into a fecund and miraculous garden. Yes, the world must be made new as Pound so often said, not by recovering and reinterpreting the classics or imitating European literary models but by re-creating actual experiences imaginatively. "I have maintained from the first," he wrote,

> that Eliot and Pound by virtue of their hypersensitivity (which is their greatness) were too quick to find a culture (the English continental) ready for their assertions. They ran from something else, something cruder but, at the same time, newer, more dangerous but heavy with rewards for the sensibility that could reap them.[11]

That sensibility was Williams's own, and its crude, new, and dangerous manifestations begin to emerge in *Spring and All*.

A World of Ideas, A World of Things

The first "poem" in the collection imitates the coming of spring in stark, precise mimicry, the words almost becoming the leaves, wind, and roots they describe. Spring here is an endless resurfacing of the earth's life, a constant challenge to winter and to the diseases that destroy and threaten life. Images of sickness, cold, waste, and death begin the poem—a kind of antihomage to the beginning of Eliot's *The Waste Land*—but they shortly become transformed by the "sluggish / dazed" entrance of spring:

> By the road to the contagious hospital
> under the surge of the blue
> mottled clouds driven from the
>
> northeast—a cold wind. Beyond, the
> waste of broad, muddy fields
> brown with dried weeds, standing and fallen
>
> patches of standing water
> the scattering of tall trees
>
> All along the road the reddish
> purplish, forked, upstanding, twiggy
> stuff of bushes and small trees
> with dead, brown leaves under them
> leafless vines—
>
> Lifeless in appearance, sluggish
> dazed spring approaches—
>
> (CEP 241)

Here is one of poetry's oldest themes, the rebirth of the year, treated originally by a simple observation of the roadside. Words like *surge* and *driven* animate the ominous scene in which each "thing," the residue of winter, seems to begin stirring.

In the poem's most famous lines, Williams seems to be speaking of the words themselves, as well as the objects they describe. Each poem is a kind of rebirth, each word like the buds of spring enters the new world naked:

> They enter the new world naked,
> cold, uncertain of all
> save that they enter. All about them
> the cold familiar wind—

> Now the grass, tomorrow
> the stiff curl of wildcarrot leaf
>
> One by one objects are defined—
> It quickens: clarity, outline of leaf
>
> But now the stark dignity of
> entrance—Still, the profound change
>
> has come upon them: rooted they
> grip down and begin to awaken.
>   (*CEP* 241–42)

Word by word, the poem awakens and stirs into being, undergoing the "profound change" of language to poetry. The death and rebirth of the year parallels the imaginative invigoration of language that Williams achieves by ignoring stale literary conventions and concentrating on a word-by-word re-creation of the world in front of him. "The imagination, drunk with prohibitions, has destroyed and recreated everything afresh in the likeness of that which it was. Now indeed men look about in amazement at each other with a full realization of the meaning of 'art' " (*Imaginations*, 93).

Spring and All continues to link the imitation of the natural cycle of life with the creative process. The imagination can be freed only when it is liberated from the constraints of "art" and "tradition" and makes the world over in its distinctive image. It must pay attention not to literary conventions but to the pulsing realities of life. "Composition," Williams wrote,

is in no essential an escape from life. In fact if it is so it is negligible to the point of insignificance. . . . Such names as Homer, the blind; Scheherazade, who lived under threat—Their compositions have as their excellence an identity with life since they are as actual, as sappy as the leaf of the tree which never moves from one spot." (*Imaginations*, 101)

And again, "The exaltation men feel before a work of art is the feeling of reality they draw from it. It sets them up, places a value upon experience—(said that half a dozen times already)" (*Imaginations*, 129). Williams went on to say that many more than half a dozen times throughout his career.

Although he disparaged tradition and high culture and exalted individual experience, Williams remained ambivalent about the barren cultural landscape that he believed characterized America. On the one hand, he insisted that American writers should write about American experience, and on the other he startlingly proposed (in a poem called 'To Elsie') that "The pure products of America / go crazy—"and wrote condescendingly of "mountain folk from Kentucky"

> and young slatterns, bathed
> in filth
> from Monday to Saturday
>
> to be tricked out that night
> with gauds
> from imaginations which have no
>
> peasant traditions to give them
> character.
>
> (CEP 270)

Like Eliot in the *The Waste Land*, he describes a loveless lovemaking, bereft of natural feeling and connection to the life cycle. The "young slatterns" described above

> . . . flutter and flaunt
> sheer rags—succumbing without
> emotion
> save numbed terror
>
> under some hedge of choke-cherry
> or viburnum—
> which they cannot express—
> (CEP 270-71)

Williams almost seems gleeful about his ability to name the choke-cherries and viburnum and contemptuous of the slatterns who are oblivious to the physicality of the landscape in which they are making love. But he also regrets our loss of a sense of place in America:

> as if the earth under our feet
> were
> an excrement of some sky

A World of Ideas, A World of Things

and we degraded prisoners
destined
to hunger until we eat filth.
(*CEP* 271–72)

PATERSON. To reconnect with that sense of place became the program of Williams's most ambitious work, *Paterson*, a long poem (254 pages) he began in the 1920s and worked on until his death in 1963. The poem is driven by Williams's search "to find an image large enough to embody the whole knowable world about me" (*Autobiography*, 391). He considered several possibilities but fixed on the city of Paterson, New Jersey, a river town neighboring his native Rutherford, as the ideal place. Perhaps recalling Stevens's early comments about this work having a random, miscellaneous character, Williams began to feel that his

isolated observations and experiences needed pulling together to gain profundity. I already had the river. Flossie [Williams's wife] is always astonished when she realizes that we live on a river, that we are a river town. New York City was far out of my perspective; I wanted, if I was to write in a larger way than of the birds and flowers, to write about the people close to me: to know in detail, minutely what I was talking about—to the whites of their eyes, to their very smells. (*Autobiography*, 391)

Like *The Cantos*, *Paterson* is a poem of epic proportions, written in a fragmented style, produced over a period of several decades, incorporating the life of the poet with the history of his environment. Pound's poem is much more bookish, remote, and pedantic than Williams's, but it clearly provided him with a model for his poetic ambitions. Also like *The Cantos*, the author diverged from the original conception of the poem as it became unable to contain his innovative imagination.

Paterson was originally conceived as a poem in four sections. "From the beginning," he wrote,

I decided there would be four books following the course of the river whose life seemed more and more to resemble my own life as I more and more thought of it: the river above the Falls, the catastrophe of the Falls itself, the river below the Falls, and the entrance at the end into the great sea. (Thirlwall, 254)

This schema was only loosely followed, but Williams did originally conceive the poem in four large sections. The first, "The Delineaments of the Giants," introduces the "elemental character of the place"—that is, its metaphoric and universal aspects. The second, "Sunday in the Park," presents what Williams calls "modern replicas," or the city as it exists on a particular day in the contemporary world. The third, "The Library," seeks a language to combine the elemental character of the city with its modern manifestations; finally, the fourth, "The Run to the Sea," links the city to time and eternity through the image of the river running out to the sea. Williams later added a fifth and fragments of a sixth section because he felt that the closed four-part structure could not incorporate the changes that occurred both within him and in the world since the poem's conception. In fact, *Paterson* is a poem organized around conflicting concepts more than it is an orderly progression. As one critic observes, the whole of the poem "is a conflict between Williams and his own experience of chaotic, pluralistic America, resulting in a number of polarizations: marriage/divorce, man and woman, convention and instinct, ideas and things, art and nature."[13]

Paterson was to be the ambitious summation of his poetic career, making "a start, / out of particulars" as he puts it in the poem's famous opening lines, making those particulars stand for general and universal values and experiences applicable to all human experience. Following the philosopher John Dewey, Williams believed that "the local is the only universal, upon that all art builds" (*Autobiography*, 391). And so to write a universal poem, he needed to begin with the specificity of the world he knew, paying careful attention to the impressions that world made on him. In the poem's first surprising image, the narrator compares himself to a dog:

> Sniffing the trees,
> just another dog
> among a lot of dogs.
> (*Paterson*, 11)

In the preface to *Paterson*, Williams creates the persona and formulates the concept that dominates the poem: he identifies man and city, combining his own identity as a physician with the physical urban landscape in a figure called "Dr. Paterson." This novel conception is the heart of the poem and Williams's unique metaphoric image of twentieth-century life: modern man is a city. The early lines of the poem delineate the birth of the metaphor, comparing it to the birth of a child:

> rolling up out of chaos,
> a nine months' wonder, the city
> the man, and identity—it can't be
> otherwise—an
> interpenetration both ways.
>
> (*Paterson*, 12)

If a man is like a city in his diversity, energy, chaos, and need for order, a city is also like a man: alive, capable of growth, stagnation, death, and rebirth. To say "man is a city," however, is too abstract a metaphor; Williams makes it both local and personal: "I am Paterson."

Williams imagines the city as a sleeping giant, delineated by the literal geography of the landscape that encases it: "Paterson lies in the valley under the Passaic Falls / its spent waters forming the outline of his back." (*Paterson*, 14). He likens the poet's discovery of language to unravel the vast undifferentiated flow of experience to the action of the falls, "combing" the flow of the river into straight lines:

> (What common language to unravel?
> . . combed into straight lines
> from that rafter of a rock's
> lip.)
>
> (*Paterson*, 15)

Here Williams extends and clarifies his central metaphor in terms that many contemporary readers may justifiably regard as sexist:

> A man like a city and a woman like a flower
> —who are in love. Two women. Three women.
> Innumerable women, each like a flower.
>
>   But
> only one man—like a city.
>
> (*Paterson*, 15)

It is clear from this passage and others like it in the poem that

Williams means "man" to refer not to humankind but specifically to men. This implicit sexism diminishes the metaphor because it suggests that men are much more complex and diverse than women, who are likened to flowers, traditional symbols of frailty and beauty. A similarly rigid dichotomy permeates all the books of *Paterson*, and while this dichotomy clearly points to a qualitative distinction between men and women that contemporary feminists rightly find offensive, it also merely reveals that Williams was very much a man of his time and shared traditional notions of gender roles.

But the uniqueness of *Paterson*, as well as one of its major difficulties for readers unfamiliar with Williams's personal history, is the inclusion of documents relating to his private life and philosophical beliefs within the context of the larger scheme. After expressing the metaphor of man as city and woman as flower, for example, he inserts an excerpt from a letter he received from a woman he later refers to as "Cress" but was actually Marcia Nardi, a poet who sought Williams's support for her work. He wrote an introduction to a group of her poems that appeared in the 1942 *New Directions Annual* but distanced himself from her personally when he felt she demanded more attention than he could give her. In sharp contrast to Williams's lofty literary and metaphorical view of woman as flower, Cress insists on her literal presence as an actual woman and castigates the poet who would use her metaphorically while remaining cool and aloof to her particular needs. "I know myself to be more the woman than the poet," she writes, "and to concern myself less with the publishers of poetry than with . . . living" (*Paterson*, 15).

A much longer (and more important) letter from Cress appears later in the poem (at the end of book 2), but this first prose insertion in *Paterson* signals a method for the work that animates it throughout, jostling it continuously away from literary self-consciousness and toward a continuing present moment. Unlike Eliot's notion of poetry as impersonal emotion, Williams's idea is to incorporate his ongoing life struggles in the work in order to heighten its sense of reality.

Although several major themes of *Paterson* emerge in "The Delineaments of the Giants," its most important concept is the separation of language from the actualities of American experience. Williams uses the figures of marriage and divorce to symbolize the past unity and present disunity of language and experience in American life. The further that language diverges from the physical realities of the world it is intended to describe, the more abstract and empty it becomes. Unlike the American Indian whose language is rooted in the particularities of place, modern urban man's language is out of touch with his physical habitat. For people of the modern city,

> The language, the language
> fails them
> They do not know the words
> or have not
> the courage to use them.
> (*Paterson*, 20)

And again,

> the language!
> —the language
> is divorced from their minds,
> the language . . . the language!
> (*Paterson*, 21)

Thus in place of the marriage of words and things characteristic of language in preurban civilizations, "Divorce is/the sign of knowledge in our time,/divorce! divorce! (*Paterson*, 28). Through *Paterson*, Williams attempts to reunite language and place, to discover an accurate and distinctive contemporary American speech.

"Sunday in the Park," book 2 of *Paterson*, begins a search for a new meter to accompany the search for a renewed language. Its headnote, from John Addington Symonds's *Studies of the Greek Poets* (possibly a bow in the direction of Eliot's erudition), asserts Symonds's belief that some of the classical poets sought "to bring the meter still more within the sphere of prose and common speech" (*Paterson*, 53). This is also obviously Williams's intention in *Paterson*. The metrical innovation that begins book 2 imitates the hesitancy and fragmented nature of ordinary speech and inserts as well the inner voice of the poet as he composes (literally "puts together") the objective landscape that exists apart from his consciousness of it:

A World of Ideas, A World of Things

Outside
> outside myself
>> there is a world,
he rumbled, subject to my incursions
—a world
> (to me) at rest,
>> which I approach
concretely—
> The scene's the Park
> upon the rock,
> female to the city

—upon whose body Paterson instructs his thoughts
(concretely).

(Paterson, 57)

The consciousness of the poet and the personification of *Paterson* are separate but intertwined entities. The city intrudes its insistent presence upon the narrator's awareness, but its presentation in the poem is "subject to [the narrator's] incursions." To create a concrete world, both the hard actualities of the real objective world and the transformative imagination of the artist are necessary. As Charles Doyle puts it, "Doctor Paterson and the city of Paterson are one, so the creating of a word-city is the poet's 'primary effort' to make himself" (Doyle, 87).

"Sunday in the Park," alternates descriptions of the external landscape with journeys within the narrator's consciousness. Williams wants to invent a new poetics for writing about the physical world, and at one point he celebrates the importance of inventiveness so that modern poetry can move forward:

> Without invention nothing is well spaced,
> unless the mind change, unless
> the stars are new measured, according
> to their relative positions, the
> line will not change, the necessity
> will not matriculate: unless there is
> a new mind there cannot be a new
> line, the old will go on
> repeating itself with recurring
> deadliness.

(Paterson, 65)

These lines articulate the central thrust of Williams's poetic aims;

like Pound, he sought to "make it new," but unlike Pound, he believed that life experience is a much greater teacher than book learning.

"Sunday in the Park" proposes a new poetic line derived from an actual afternoon's experience. In the three parts of this section, Dr. Paterson successively walks around the park climbing a small mountain to observe the surrounding city; watches a preacher named Klaus Ehrens deliver an exemplary sermon on the theme of destructive materialism, a sermon interrupted by the narrator's thoughts on American materialism generally, which he attributes to Alexander Hamilton's economic theories; and finally hikes down from the summit frustrated by his inability to marry the language to actual experience in the same way that the sounds, colors, textures, and forms of nature are wedded to their sources.

Metrically and rhythmically, the last part of "Sunday in the Park" is one of the most inventive sections of the poem. Williams experiments with a wide variety of metrical patterns—what he called the "variable foot." The section begins with short, mostly two-stress lines but the steady rhythm breaks into a more open, fragmented variable line after the narrator's evocation of spring in a rhymed couplet:

> But spring shall come and flowers will bloom
> and man must chatter of his doom . . .
>
> The descent beckons
>   as the ascent beckoned
>   Memory is a kind
> of accomplishment
>   a sort of renewal
>   even
> an initiation since the spaces it opens are new
> places.
>   (*Paterson*, 95–96)

The verse itself takes a downhill shape as the descent beckons and the narrator's trip down from the summit is both literal and figurative. Dr. Paterson is literally descending from the peak, but it is a descent "made up of despairs / and without accomplishment." Williams seems to be lamenting his inability to bring language as close to experience as he would like to. Metaphors of marriage, childbirth, and divorce permeate the section as Williams seeks to marry language and experience in order to give birth to a new American poem, but he faces the actuality of divorce—the disconnection between life and language that he dreads:

> Poet, poet! sing your song quickly! or
> not insects but pulpy words will blot out
> your kind.
> > He all but fails . . .
>
> And She—
> > Marry us! Marry us!
> > > Or! be dragged down, dragged
> > under and lost
> > She was married with empty words:
> > > > Better to
> > > > stumble at
> > > > the edge
> > > > to fall
> > > > fall
> > > > and be
> > > —divorced.
> > > > > (*Paterson*, 102)

This passage is almost a "concrete" poem—that is, the placement of words on the page solidifies and exemplifies their meaning.

"Sunday in the Park" concludes with a long letter from Cress that takes the reader much closer to an actual experience than Williams's poetry does, and his decision to include the document is testimony to the sense of failure that permeates much of this part of the poem. Cress castigates Williams for his hypocrisy. Although he talks a good game about connecting life and literature, she feels he avoids confronting real-life situations that are too emotionally charged and finds refuge in literary matters instead. For Cress life and literature are not merely connected; they are one and the same:

Only my writing (when I write) is myself: only that is the real me in any essential way. Not because I bring to literature and to life two different inconsistent sets of values, as you do. No, *I* don't do that; and I feel when anyone does do it, literature is turned into just so much intellectual excrement fit for the same stinking hole as any kind. (*Paterson*, 106)

This actual letter, which Williams received from Marcia Nardi, must have been difficult for him to read because it achieves so effortlessly what he struggled to attain in *Paterson:* a drama of actual life, written in clear, direct language, very much tied to particulars. As Paul Mariani notes, "Nardi's letter even contained many of the image clusters Williams had already employed in the poem. In fact that letter turned out to be, as Williams would explain years later, a found object paralleling Eliot's infamous use of footnotes at the end of the Waste Land."[14]

As if endangered by the intrusion of the real world, book 3 of *Paterson* retreats to "The Library" (the book's title) because

> A cool of books
> will sometimes lead the mind to libraries
> of a hot afternoon, if books can be found
> cool to the sense to lead the mind away.
>
> For there is a wind or ghost of a wind
> in all books echoing the life
> there a high wind that fills the tubes
> of the ear until we think we hear a wind,
> actual
>
> to lead the mind away.
> (*Paterson*, 118)

The idea that books can lead the mind away from its immediate concerns to a cooler world of intellectual solitude sounds more like Eliot or Pound than it does Williams, but the whole of book 3 "examines the question of whether . . . books offer anything the poet can use."[15] Williams seems to be addressing directly questions raised by Pound and Eliot throughout their careers. Both Europeanized Americans urged poets to study literary traditions closely and learn how to write poetry by borrowing and extending what poets of the past had achieved. Williams here argues that "the poet can't afford to think of himself as continuing the work of the past, as belonging to a 'tradition,' but must accept the fact that his own age makes entirely new demands, and go from this recognition to invent a form that will be appropriate to his own 'given' " (Sankey, 116).

The search for the "beautiful thing" (a phrase repeated again and again in book 3) must take the poet out of the library and back into the world of more intense human experience. While it is important for any writer to feel a sense of connection to the history of the place where he lives, he cannot turn away from the present too long because immersion in books diverts his attention from the physical, emotional, and aesthetic particulars of his own life. Dr. Paterson becomes burdened by the "roar of books" that almost drowns out the actual roar of the Passaic Falls. "The Library" concludes with his clear affirmation to turn away from the past and rivet his attention on the present moment. The Passaic Falls have been a key image throughout the poem, and Williams here specifies them as a symbol of past, present, and future. He again likens his own writing of poetry ("comb out the language") to the action of water, forming "lines" as it tumbles down over the falls:

> The past above, the future below
> and the present pouring down: the roar,
> the roar of the present, a speech—
> is, of necessity, my sole concern.
>
> .   .   .   .   .
>
>   I cannot stay here
> to spend my life looking into the past:
> the future's no answer. I must
> find my meaning and lay it, white,
> beside the sliding water: myself—
> comb out the language—or succumb
> —whatever the complexion. Let
> me out! (Well, go!) this rhetoric
> is real!
>
>   (*Paterson*, 173)

Book 4 of *Paterson*, orginally intended as the last book of the poem, is called "The Run to the Sea" and "describes symbolically the completion of the poem and the poet's 'death' " (Sankey, 167). It ends with a bang, not a whimper:

> This is the blast
> the eternal close

> the spiral
> the final somersault
> the end.
> (*Paterson*, 238)

But such a definitive ending seemed out of keeping with the idea of the poem as an open document containing flux. In an author's note to the complete edition of the poem, Williams wrote:

> [Since completing *Paterson, Four*] I have come to understand not only that many changes have occurred in me and the world, but I have been forced to recognize that there can be no end to such a story I have envisioned with the terms which I had laid down for myself. I had to take the world of Paterson into a new dimension if I wanted to give it imaginative validity. (*Paterson*, 3–4)

He completed a fifth section of the poem and part of a sixth, leaving it unfinished at his death, perhaps an appropriate kind of open-endedness for such a sprawling, life-affirming poem.

In the last years of his life, Williams, though suffering from the effects of a stroke and sporadic depression, continued to write strong, metrically distinctive, highly personal poems. *Pictures from Brueghel*, his last collection of poems, published in 1962, was awarded the Pulitzer Prize for poetry and gained for him the official recognition that had eluded him for most of his life. The long, last poem in that volume, "Asphodel, That Greeny Flower," is a deeply moving love poem to his wife, Flossie, written in the variable foot he discovered in book 2 of *Paterson* but taken to new lyrical heights. It is the poem of a sick, aging man asking his wife's forgiveness for his flaws and infidelities so that he might "die at peace in his bed" (Mariani, 670; see his excellent discussion of this poem, 670–78).

Williams made a major contribution to American Poetry; he taught a younger generation of poets to trust their experience and to write about the world they knew and felt. This is no small accomplishment given the intimidating presences of Pound and Eliot, with their emphases on turning away from American life and experience in order to internationalize American writing, which they regarded as largely parochial. Williams also offered an indigenous alternative to the elegant and stylish poems of Wallace

Stevens that lack the gritty feel of American life. In both his poetry and prose, Williams gives us writing that is thoroughly "In the American Grain," as the title of his book on pre-Columbian American history announces. His invention of the variable foot, his painterly eye, his incessant attention to the physical world, and his ear for the American idiom mark his work as distinctive and set a tone, style, and direction for a later generation of American poets.

· SEVEN ·

"The Visionary Company":
Hart Crane, E. E. Cummings,
and Robinson Jeffers

These fragments I have shored against my ruins.
            —T. S. Eliot, *The Waste Land*

And so it was I entered the broken world
to trace the visionary company of love . . .
            —Hart Crane, "The Broken Tower"

Do you see O my brothers and sisters?
It is not chaos or death—it is form, union, plan—
it is eternal life—it is Happiness.
            —Walt Whitman, "Song of Myself"

Stevens's faith in the power of the imagination and the art of
poetry and Williams's conviction that so much depends on the
objects within our world and our ability to present them in an
uncorrupted language constitute an important alternative to the
prophets who railed against the decline of Western culture. Even
Eliot turned from his arid wasteland to seek refuge and meaning
within the Anglican church. However, the darker vision found in
Eliot's earlier work remained a challenging obstacle to those poets
who, like Whitman before them, wished to present a vision of
"union" and "Happiness" and who, like Williams, insisted that
this vision confront the world and be in the American grain. Their
task would be to move beyond Eliot's *Waste Land* or Tate's "Ode
to the Confederate Dead" and its overpowering claim of the
"ravenous grave" and to devote their lives and their art to tran-
scending the modernist wasteland.[1] While acknowledging the illness of their time—the decline of beauty, truth, and love—these

poets form a visionary company that, along with Stevens and Williams, would offer yet another alternative to the wasteland. Hart Crane clearly sees his broken world but is not overpowered by it. Rather, he seeks the visionary, the transcendental world of love within the ruins, even if it lasts only for an instant. Crane, like Cummings and the romantic, mystic poets before and after him, would not resign himself to the inescapable limitations placed on human existence; his songs of love, secular and sacred, would provide a sharp counterpoint to the somber and bitter elegies of modernism. The romantic tradition, with its insistence on the ideal and the transcendent, so central to American poetry since Emerson and Whitman, would also be part of the modernist score; the music would not only descend but also ascend on the soaring notes of romantic singers. Among this visionary company would appear Hart Crane, E. E. Cummings, and Robinson Jeffers. Very different singers as they are, they, in their individual ways and in varying degrees, do find a path out of the wasteland and celebrate those moments of visionary insight so central to the romantic creed. In doing so, these poets emerge as key artists who keep alive the Emersonian-Whitmanesque tradition in the most difficult of times.

Hart Crane

Hart Crane (1899–1933), the only child of Clarence Arthur and Grace Hart Crane, was born in Garretsville, Ohio, in 1899. His early years were marked by the constant quarreling of his parents who separated temporarily in 1908, leaving Hart to live with his grandparents in Cleveland. He enrolled in 1913 at East High School and began writing poetry. In 1915 he and his mother journeyed to his maternal grandmother's plantation on the Isles of Pines in the West Indies, a site he would revisit and use as a setting for a number of his poems. In 1916, the year his parents divorced, Hart published his first poem, "C33" (the title is based on Oscar Wilde's cell number at Reading Gaol), in *Bruno's Weekly* and traveled to the West with his mother. After his parents' divorce, Crane, with the encouragement of Mrs. William Vaughn Moody, the widow of the American poet, headed to New York City to begin his career as a poet.[2]

These early years were undoubtedly painful ones for Crane. His parents had provided him with a loveless and disruptive model of modern marriage, a broken world. Throughout his life, Crane attempted to find, essentially with men, the love and security absent in his childhood. His homosexual encounters were primarily physical and transitory, but he did become involved for an extended period of time with a seaman who inspired his magnificent love poem, "Voyages." And in his last months, he fell in love with Peggy Baird (the former wife of Malcolm Cowley), who inspired a number of his Key West poems. In addition to this absence of love and stability in his early years, Crane's artistic inclinations werre also insufficiently nurtured. His father, who in 1908 had established a chain of retail stores, took some interest in his writings but did not provide the financial or emotional support that a young, highly sensitive, and insecure person needed. Hart did manage on his first journey to New York to meet with writers Alfred Kreymborg and Maxwell Bodenheim and to pursue his studies of poetry seriously; however, he was unable to support himself adequately and had to return to Cleveland. Rejected for the military draft, he moved from job to job and eventually joined his father's company. By 1921, however, he concluded that he could not serve two masters, business and poetry. He decided to break with his father and the world he represented and become a poet.

"Black Tambourine," his first major poem, was published in 1921. At this time, he returned again to the world of advertising and met William Somer and Ernest Nelson, both painter-lithographers, would-be artists who were also caught between their love of art and the need to make a living. Despite his progress in his art and craft and his new companions, Crane's personal life-style seemed self-destructive. He developed an ever-growing need for alcohol, and his sexual behavior struck most others as excessive. In 1923 he decided to move once again to New York City, where he was befriended by literary critic and author Gorham Munson. Again he attempted to support himself by doing ad work, but his working habits were poor, his earnings meager, and his drinking bouts, often with male partners, far too frequent. He moved about often and, as if it were divinely ordained, lived in the apartment that Roebling, the architect of the Brooklyn Bridge, occupied; here he would begin to design his own masterpiece, *The Bridge*. He also lived temporarily with Allen and Caroline Bird-Tate in Paterson, New York, a pastoral retreat, and traveled to the West Pines Plantation. This restlessness in part reflected his anguish and constant search for love and stability. Crane was unable to satisfy these needs and to shake his alcoholism and depression. In 1933, at the age of thirty-three, Crane, while returning from Mexico with Peggy Baird, jumped into the sea and ended his life. His suicide at such an early age is one of modern poetry's tragic tales.

In December 1926, Crane published *White Buildings*, his first volume of poetry; it contained twenty-eight poems written over nine years (1917–26). At the time it represented the reach and achievement of Crane's lyrical powers and established him as one of the most talented and interesting, if controversial and obscure, of the modernist poets. In many respects his debt to Eliot and Pound was very visible. From both he learned the importance of using, but going beyond, poets who preceded him—in Crane's case, Marlowe and the Elizabethans and the French symbolists. Crane also recognized the importance of craft and the specialness of a poetic language that could transcend the confines of scientific and logical language and present a higher, more truthful depiction of reality. From both, Pound especially, he learned that the commitment to poetry was total; all other interests and concerns had to be secondary to the study and practice of one's art. In one essential aspect, Crane differed significantly from Eliot: he did not want to dwell in his wasteland. In 1924, in a letter to Allen Tate, he indicated that he had "been facing [Eliot] for four years and saw that he was indeed a towering figure, however, he had discovered . . . a safe tangent to strike which . . . goes through him toward a different goal . . . he can be utilized to lead us to, intelligently point to, other positions and 'pastures new.' . . . I, for instance, would like to leave a few of his 'negations' behind me."[3] And in January 1923, he described to his friend Munson his "ecstatic goal": "I feel," Crane proclaims, "that Eliot ignores certain spiritual events and possibilities as real and powerful now as, say in the time of Blake. . . . After this perfection of death— nothing is possible in motion but a resurretion of some kind" (*Letters*, 115). It is ironic that Eliot in his later works, "Ash Wednesday" (1930) and the magnificant *Four Quartets* (1936–43), for example, would also transcend his "unreal city" and enter into a compelling mode of religious poetry. In the 1920s, however, Eliot represented the poetic force that challenged the visionary poet. As Jackson Pollock said of his relationship to the American regionalist and realist painter Thomas Benton, a developing artist needed a force to resist and work against. Benton played that role for Pollock, and Eliot played it for Hart Crane.

This movement from bleakness and death to light and resurrection thus becomes the central theme of Crane's lyrical poems. The poet as visionary finds himself in a world that constantly threatens to trap him in its death-in-life existence, its cold, mechanistic, and materialistic nature, and its temporal and spatial limitations—in short, Eliot's unreal city, the twentieth-century version of paradise lost. The poet's task is to struggle against this world, escape its confines and its illusions, and find his way to a new heavenly city, experience those ecstatic moments of arrival, and then find the means of expressing that experience so that it is captured forever in the words, images, and rhythms of language. It is, as William James claimed, a variety of religious experience, and the poetry expressing that experience becomes a form of religious poetry.

This mode of poetry is evident in "Legend," the first poem in *White Buildings*. In the initial two lines, Crane provides the reader with a haunting image of the phantom-like and inaudible nature of true reality, a reality that is extremely difficult to see, hear, and understand. Yet Crane, the poet-hero, is not ready either to repent or to compare his regrets for pursuing this ideal reality, for it is only in that realm where "Kisses are,— / The only worth all granting."[4] And the only means of acquiring love or kisses is to immerse oneself in the pain and suffering of this world. The poet is he who "Spends out himself again. / Twice and Twice / (Again the smoking souvenir, / Bleeding eidolon!) and yet again. / Until the bright logic is won / Unwhispering as a mirror / Is believed" (*CP* 3). Only after the poet "spends" (a word with both psychological and sexual connotations) himself outward where his soul (eidolon) again burns and bleeds again and yet again is that bright logic or mystical knowledge acquired and believed. That sacrifice, "drop by caustic drop," then forms "a perfect cry" and "Shall string some constant harmony,—." Thus out of the pain and joy, suffering and vision comes the lyrical poem—one of "constant harmony," a song that unifies the dissonant notes of existence.

This then becomes the paradigm, or the "Relentless caper," for all those "who step / The legend of their youth into the noon" (CP 3). It is a model for living intensely and undergoing relentlessly the pain of living in which innocence is left behind, and it is a model for poets who hope to capture the experience of resurrection, the cry of pain but also joy—that new pasture not realized in Eliot's early poetry. As the word *legend* connotes, it is a heroic and mythic venture, one of voyaging, traveling, a new map, and also, in the original sense of the word, the story of a saint's life— a saint who does not escape the world but rather transforms a world of ruins into a mystical realm of love and spiritualism.

In "Chaplinesque" Crane turns to another legend, this time a film star, Charlie Chaplin, to depict spiritual survival in an indifferent world (for Crane's extended reaction to Chaplin, see *Letters*, 68, 69). Collectively we make our "meek adjustments" to the modern world, Crane admits, but we also, because of our sympathy and love for others, "spend ourselves outward,"

> For we can still love, the world, who find
> A famished kitten on the step, and know
> Recesses for it from the fury of the street,
> Or warm torn elbow converts.
>
> (CP 11)

To preserve that kitten, symbolically the poetic and compassionate elements in this cold modern world, it is necessary to "sidestep," to "smirk," to "Dally the doom of that inevitable thumb [authority, death] / That slowly chafes its puckered index toward us," yet these "fine collapses" are only strategies for surviving the wasteland. What must not be evaded, as Hawthorne insists, is the human heart; as long as that "live[s] on" the poet can envision and experience a transformed and redeemed world for

> . . . we have seen
> The moon in lonely alleys make
> A grail of laughter of an empty ash can,
> And through all sound of gaiety and quest
> Have heard a kitten in the wilderness.
>
> (CP 11)

White Buildings, then, as the title implies, deals with those varying attempts to transform the modern world of gray skyscrapers into the whiteness of spiritual vision. At times during this quest, Crane is drawn "into hades almost," as he first escapes the naturalistic world and then journeys past the "city . . . With scalding unguents spread and smoking darts." However, by the conclusion of "Repose of Ruins," which portrays Crane's trip from the inferno to the city of God, he is able, as he enters the sea, to exclaim triumphantly: "At gulf gates . . . There beyond the dykes / I heard wind flaking sapphire, like this summer / And willows could not hold more steady sound" (*CP* 16). This "constant harmony," not heard in most other modernist poems, is scored a number of times in *White Buildings*. In "Lachrymae Christi" [Tears of Christ], for example, Crane presents a vivid counterimage to Eliot's wasteland. As spring comes to the land, Crane and his readers "recall / To music and retrieve what perjuries / Had galvanized the eyes." He then evokes his Christ / Dionysus deity to "Lift up in lilac-emerald breath the grail / Of earth again—" (*CP* 19–20).

As Crane confesses in "My Grandmother's Love Letters" he would question whether he could "carry back the music to its source" (*CP* 6) or would "stumble" with or without his wine as inspiration (see "Wine Menagerie," (*CP* 2, 3); however, the dominant motif in this volume is one of transformation and ecstasy. We hear this clearly in the two most ambitious poems in *White Buildings*, "The Marriage of Faustus and Helen" and "Voyages." In "Marriage," Crane employs the Faustus and Helen story as the mythic center of his own devotion and marriage to the ideal realm of beauty and poetry and as a testament to his faith that one can find love and beauty within the ruins of the modern world. Thematically this links Crane to H. D., who in "The Tribute" (*CP* 28–30) also envisioned the presence of beauty amid the squalor of the modern world. But whereas H.D.'s poem seems to be set in a mythical and emblematic world, Crane, like Williams, sets his quest for beauty within the American grain, the modern, urban city. In completing the poem, Crane felt he had answered Eliot and the nay sayers with a resounding, ecstatic "yes." Initially in "The Marriage" Crane recognizes the possibility of pastoral retreat; however, he insists on remaining within the modern world where he discovers Helen in the most unlikely of places, a transit car. She is seated across from him, her eyes "Still flickering," and he imagines that "There is some way, I think, to touch / Those hands of yours that count the nights / Stippled with pink and green advertisements." Rejecting the world of "stock quotations" and "stenographic smiles," he asks Helen to "Accept a lone eye riveted to your plane, / . . . One inconspicuous, glowing orb of praise" (*CP* 27–29).

Crane then demonstrates his new way of perceiving and praising beauty in what seem to be irreconcilable settings. Beauty is discovered, for example, on a tenement roof where a midnight-to-dawn dance is taking place to the beating rhythms of a black jazz band. Crane fuses this modern scene with the festivities and revels that take place on Mount Olympus and then invites us to "fall downstairs with me / With perfect grace and equanimity" and to partake of this new pagan world of music and celebration and reject the staid and puritan world that he himself left behind in Ohio, the world of "relatives serene and cool," for this new music has a "reassuring way" (*CP* 30–31). Despite her flaws, the drunken flapper at the party is our modern Helen, our earthly symbol of beauty.

Crane then faces his greatest challenge: he has to recognize and transcend the war that Pound and others so brilliantly and bitterly attacked. The military airman, the "Capped arbiter of beauty in this street," the symbol of humanity's frightful turn to a form of mechanistic warfare that threatened to obliterate all beauty, becomes Crane's guide as he flies through the memories of war to "unbind our throats of fear and pity." Once that catharsis is reached, we can transcend the bloody tragedies brought about by the "eternal gunman," move beyond despair, and thus regain hope and beauty.

> We did not ask for that [World War I], but have survived,
> And will persist to speak again before
> All stubble streets that have not curved
> To memory, or known the ominous lifted arm
> That lowers down the arc of Helen's brow
> To saturate with blessing and dismay.
>
> (*CP* 33)

Thus beauty and its healing powers prevail; its arc or rainbow still "saturate[s]"—with "blessing and dismay" as long as "The imagination spans beyond despair, / Outpacing bargain, vocable and prayer" (*CP* 33).

To curve, to arch, to span are key verbals in Crane's idiom. He is relentlessly attempting to discover or invent a means of voyaging from the secular to the spiritual realm. This becomes a very personal journey in "Voyages," a love poem based on Crane's intense, if short, relationship with Emil Apffer, a merchant seaman. The poem is perhaps, as R. W. B. Lewis feels, the most beautiful homosexual love poem in English, but that theme remains less central than the larger one of love found, lost, and justified.[5] "Voyages," in fact, emerges as one of the strongest love poems written in English, this in a period when Prufrock could not sing his love song, when love was absent or debased in the wasteland, and when Joseph Wood Krutch proclaimed in *The Modern Temper* that love, as a value, was dead.

The poem, consisting of six parts, some written originally as separate pieces, begins with a poster scene in which we see children or "striped urchins" in beach togs playing innocently and joyfully on the beach amid the threatening sounds and images of nature. Initially Crane takes the role of the preserver of innocence and youth as he imagines himself warning the children to avoid leaving the secure land for the mysteries and dangers of the sea, to avoid becoming the Melvillean mystic mariner who enters the unknown and uncharted waters of love and transcendence. Crane, however, quickly presents a counterargument that justifies the voyaging outward, the need as he indicated in "Legend" to spend "out himself" despite the inevitable pain. The sea then becomes a "wink of eternity"—a joyful glimpse of the boundless world of "rimless floods, unfettered leewardings." The sea also becomes the symbol of passionate and unrestrained love that both physically and spiritually beckons Crane and his lover. She is a spirit who "Laughing the wrapt inflections of our love" subjects "All but the pieties of lover's hands" to the "sceptred terror" of time (*CP* 36). For only in love is the power of time vanquished.

This transcendental voyage brings the two lovers to the lost paradise of San Salvador, where sea and meadow are joined. Here they "Complete the dark confessions her veins spell" (36), that is, their sexual and spiritual union. In a world distant from the taboos of Puritan America, a world both within and beyond time and matter, Crane fuses worlds irreconcilable as "sleep, death, desire, / Close round one instant in one floating flower" (CP 36), and then invokes the sea to "Bequeath us to no earthly shore until / Is answered in the vortex of our grave / The seal's wide spindrift gaze towards paradise" (CP 36). Crane has thus moved from a cautionary to an ecstatic voice that pleads for a sea journey that lasts until the lovers' death and their journey to paradise. Although the relationship is consummated and celebrated as both a religious and natural act and although the speaker pleads with Eros—"Permit me voyage, love, into your hands" (37)—separation is inevitable. Although the speaker initially suffers astonishment and despair—"In all the argosy of your bright hair I dreamed / Nothing so flagless as the piracy" (CP 39)—he seeks and finds deliverance. Once passions cool, he turns to the eternal world of poetry, his "Belle Isle," which will enable him to transcend the impermanent world of human love and thus justify his earlier voyage to San Salvador. This is a world where "rainbows twine continual hair— / Belle Isle, white echo of the oar!" The physical act of love (the oar), in poetry, is transformed into spiritual beauty (white echo) for

> The imaged Word, it is, that holds
> Hushed willows anchored in its glow.
> It is the unbetrayable reply
> Whose accent no farewell can know.
>
> (CP 41)

These, the last lines in *White Buildings*, are a testament to Crane's faith in visionary poetry and its ability to carry us beyond the soot and grime of the wasteland. Whereas Eliot's speakers retreat from life and its adventurous voyages—here one thinks of "Gerontion" (1920), "an old man driven by the trades / To a sleepy corner"—Crane's speakers take the "dangerous routes" and risk pain but achieve vision and song, which are counterpoints to Eliot's melancholy dirges.

Most would agree that Crane's most ambitious, if not most successful, effort in this quest was *The Bridge*, which he began in 1923 and published in 1930. In scope, intent, and range, the poem is often compared to Eliot's *The Waste Land* and Pound's *The Cantos*. "Very roughly," Crane states in 1923, *The Bridge* concerns a mystical synthesis of "America." History and fact, location, etc, all have to be transfigured into abstract form that would almost function independently of its subject matter. The initial impulse of our people will have to be gathered up toward the climax of the bridge, symbol of our constructive future, our unique identity, in which is included also our scientific hopes and achievements of the future. (*Letters*, 124)

From the start Crane realized that this "may be too impossible an ambition" (*Letters*, 124), but after "Faustus and Helen," he was prepared for a new and demanding voyage, one through time and space, in which he would rediscover the true identity of America and its people; then he would return with that valuable cargo and display his jewels to the assembled multitudes. That cargo would consist of mystic experiences, truths, and discoveries that countered the bleak trinkets of modern thought, materialism, and science and thus restore once again a belief in America as a new world, one built on love, unity, and beauty. If he succeeded, he believed there would be "such a waving of banners, such ascent of towers, such a dancing etc . . . will never before have been put down on paper" (*Letters*, 124–25).

It was indeed an ambitious project, and Crane's creative energies and faith at times diminished. In 1926, in a letter to Waldo Frank, he confessed despondently that "the bridge as a symbol today has no significance beyond an economical approach to shorter hours, quicker lunches, behaviorism, and toothpicks" (*Letters*, 261). Despite the storms, however, his passage was completed, and Crane produced a work that was initially attacked for the wrong reasons. Literary critics such as Allen Tate and Yvor Winters, for example, rejected the poem on grounds that Crane never intended to consider. To Crane, this was a subjective work, a synthesis brought about by his own intuitive genius and imagination, and if the poem failed to follow the conventions of an epic or failed to present an orderly, rational argument, that was of little import to him. His intent and design, as in "Faustus and Helen," was symphonic, one in which various materials, historic and contemporary, cultural and personal, would be blended or synthesized into a unified score celebrating the vision, imagination, and creative powers of the American spirit. The hero would be a collective one, a composite of all those who in the past manifested such a spirit, as well as the poet, Crane, who incorporates within his own body, mind, and imagination that historic spiritual vision and brings it forth for us to share, now and in the future. The poem would show us the danger of continuing along our present path and the joy of voyaging to a new world, of seeing America anew. In the traditions of other prophetic poets, Crane would lead us out of the twentieth-century wilderness, the desert or wasteland, and into the promised land. His journey could become our journey; his bridge, our bridge to the heavenly city and poetry; the music that spanned two shores, the temporal and the spiritual, would be our means of crossing.

As Richard Sugg indicates, Crane's symphony or suite after "To Brooklyn Bridge" seems to break into two major sections.[6] The first consists of "Ave Maria," "Powhatan's Daughter," and "Cutty Sark"; its subject matter is an imaginative journey into the past and across the body of the land (nature) in order to discover and reintegrate the true "initial impulses" of our people, which, if accomplished successfully, will enable the poet to see, without prejudiced and despairing eyes, nature and the modern world. Vision would ultimately inspire song or poetry, Crane's bridge or "threshold" to heaven. It is within poetry, our "harp and altar" that "we have seen night lifted in thine arms" (*CP* 46). But before he can sing, the poet must first absorb the holy vision of Columbus and rediscover the physical beauties of the earth as symbolized by Powhatan's daughter and the mystical Indian dance of Maquokeeta. Only then will he be able to avoid the fall suffered by the drunken sailor in "Cutty Sark" and be able to transform a brassy jukebox tune, "O. Stamboul Rose," into a white echo of "ATLANTIS ROSE." Returning home via the Brooklyn Bridge, he remembers and sings out the names of the old sailing ships, names suggesting the heroic quests of old (*Rainbow*, *Leander*, *Ariel*) and wonders where they might be in this age of the machine and whether he can retain his newly found vision.

Spiritual survival within this mechanistic age thus becomes the theme of the second half of *The Bridge*. In the "Cape Hatteras" section he again sees the ominous airplane, the ruler of the heavens and dispenser of death, as the symbol of modernism. In this "new realm of fact," Crane laments that we see humanity as "an atom in a shroud," an insignificant mortal cipher within an indifferent nature; to compensate for this, we foolishly turn to machines to prove our worth; hence we become "an engine in a cloud." To restore our "cancelled dreams" Crane calls upon Walt Whitman to replenish our spiritual vision, for his eyes still "Gleam from the great stones of each prison crypt," and they are "Confronting the Exchange." They are "bright with myth!" Crane then parodies our devotion to science and the dynamo, which, as Henry Adams recognized, had replaced the virgin as our prime symbol ("oilrinsed circles of blind ecstasy!") and our eventual use of the machine to shower destruction on humankind. Crane reminds the war pilot, the Falcon ace, the false modern hero that his true mission is not destruction but revelation: "Thou hast there in thy wrist a Sanskrit charge / To conjugate infinity's dim marge— / Anew!" (CP 89–92).

The model for this role is Walt Whitman, who advocates "a pact, new bound / Of living brotherhood!" Whitman, the wound dresser, can cure the "Ghoul-mound of man's perversity" for "Our Meistersinger" has "set breath in steel" and "flung the span on even wing / Of that great Bridge, our Myth, where I sing!" (CP 93–94). Hand in hand with Whitman, Crane is ready once again to face the trials of modernism. In "Three Songs" he again searches for love and beauty in the modern world. Although he is often left with imperfect choices—Eve or Magdelene, the virgin or the whore—he realizes it is necessary to love the flesh, even if it is corrupted, for it is the only means to things spiritual. In the third song, for example, there does exist a Mary figure who partakes of both the spirit and the flesh. This is a very temporary mood, however, for in "Quaker Hill," he acknowledges Whitman's vision of brotherhood, and love (Quaker Hill) has been replaced by selfishness and materialism. In a dismayed voice, Crane asks, "Where are my kinsmen and the Patriarch race?" (CP 105). And in the last section, which echoes both Emily Dickinson and Allen Tate, he reminds us of our mortal nature: "Leaf after autumnal leaf / break off, / descend— / descend—" (CP 106).

This descent into darkness continues and intensifies in "The Tunnel." Crane is literally and figuratively underground in this part of his journey back to Brooklyn. Psychologically he is facing that inner despair that especially confronts modernist artists. Some may never emerge from the tunnel, a metaphor for their desolate minds, but for Crane, as with most other mystics, the journey seems to represent a necessary part of the passage to light and salvation. As Blake in the inscription to this section indicates, one must pass "Right thro' the Gates of Wrath" (CP 107) to reach

Cathay or Paradise. Initially the section provides a series of grim images that capture his outlook: "The phonographs of hades in the brain / Are tunnels that re-wind themselves, and love / A burnt match skating in a urinal—" (CP 110). Like Poe, whom he addresses and whom he resembles in his search for Helen, or ideal beauty, he is obsessed with death and despair; however, once again he envisions, even here, a symbol of love in the form of an Italian mother who is sitting across from him, and as the train ascends, he feels, like Lazarus, the "lifting ground" and hears "—A sound of waters bending astride the sky / Unceasing with some Word that will not die. . . ! (CPP 112). Love, fertility, nature (water and sky) still speak to and inspire the poet. The journey through darkness is over, and the theme of inspiration and song begins to dominate as the "Hand of Fire / gatherest—" at the conclusion of "The Tunnel." He is now prepared to enter into the "pure fires," the creative world of the absolute.

Standing on the Brooklyn Bridge, the symbol of the spanning powers of the imagination, he is now prepared to discover Atlantis (section VIII) and echo back to the reader the music of paradise. As prophesized in "Cutty Sark," he records the music of the Atlantis Rose that arises from the harp like strings of the bridge. This is the music of Plato, "the knowledge of that which / relates to love in harmony and system" (CP 113). It is not music inspired by rum as in "Cutty Sark" and "Wine Menagerie" but by Emily Dickinson's liquor never brewed, the intoxicating stirrings of the imagination. The bridge, as harp, plays "As though a god were issue of the strings," and it plays a harmonious melody, "One arc synoptic of all tides below—". Its theme is 'Make thy love sure.' The poetic quest is completed; we find Jason among us, and Tyre, and Troy. To complete the circle, we again see the "Bridge, lifting night to cycloramic crest / Of deepest day" (CP 114–15). This imaginative music translates time "Into what multitudinous verb" and "recast[s] / In myriad syllables,—Psalm of Cathay!" the ultimate song of love, which becomes the "pardon for this history." This music is the "whitest Flower," the anemone, which Crane prays will "hold thy floating singer late." In Whitmanesque fashion, Crane leads us into the "Everpresence, beyond time," for "Now pity steeps the grass and rainbows ring / The serpent with the eagle in the leaves . . . ?" (CP 115, 117).

There has been a great deal of disagreement about the effectiveness of *The Bridge*. Waldo Frank, for example, in his introduction to *The Complete Poems of Hart Crane*, placed it first in the order of his works, as testament to its importance, and numerous critics have said Crane's reputation rested on its success or failure. Brom Weber, however, claimed that it should not dwarf his other poems; thus he arranged his edition chronologically. Crane's contemporaries, even if friendly in some regards, most often saw *The Bridge* as a noble effort that ultimately failed. To Crane, such critics misunderstood the poem and its intent and mistakenly asked him to "sum up the universe in one impressive little pellet" (*CP* 258). If Tate and company thought he was the last note in a dying romantic tradition, Crane argued strongly with Tate that there still existed a place for subjective vision. Not all wisdom, Crane insisted, was collective, logical, clear, or classical: "A great deal of romanticism may persist—of the sort to deserve serious consideration" (*CP* 257).

The absence of a clear narrative line or a consistent hero in *The Bridge* does weaken the unity of the poem, as critics have claimed. Crane, however, seemed more intent on bringing together, in collage-like fashion, a series of lyrical poems that collectively capture the emotional and spiritual struggle of the modern poet to create divine music in a secular and mechanistic age. Given this aim, it is not surprising that the emotional keys struck in this score are neither consistent nor linear. A more central question perhaps is the one asked of Pound's *The Cantos*. Does it cohere? What unifies or aesthetically fuses together somewhat separate materials in a long, modern poem? What are the elements of an autobiographical epic poem? Is it to be modeled only on Wordsworth's *Prelude*? The questions remain, attesting to the artistic challenges Crane faced in composing *The Bridge*.

Crane's defense of romanticism in many ways also proved prophetic. The visionary tradition of Blake and Whitman was not swept away by the neoclassical tendencies and tenets of modernism, and Crane would play an essential role in preserving that tradition. However, the difficulty of composing such an intense symphony as *The Bridge* took its toll on the poet's powers, and its ambiguous reception did little to reinspire him. Frequently critics point to his late poems in *Key West: An Island Sheaf*, collected and published posthumously, as an indication of his growing skepticism and waning creativity. The "Atlantis" section had been the first section of *The Bridge* to be written, and Crane could not, in his later years it seemed, make that journey to the West without intense struggle, if at all, which may have been, some speculate, the root cause of his alcoholism and chaotic life. Accordingly, readers often see in the *Key West* poems Crane's darker vision.

There is a good deal in these poems to support such a view. In the title poem, "Key West," for example, he tells us that his "salient faith" has taken him "Out of the valley, past the ample crib / To skies impartial, that do not disown me / Nor claim me" (*CP* 171). In addition to nature's indifference, Americans have abandoned "their initial impulse," and he wonders if his fate is to be the same: "Because these millions reap a dead conclusion / Need I presume the same fruit of my bone" (*CP* 171). He envisions a modern world caught in its "apish nightmares" and its "steel-strung stone" character. The last line of the poem captures the sense of despair and disillusionment that marks so much of modernistic literature: "There is no breath of friends and no more shore / Where gold has not been sold and conscience tinned" (*CP* 171).

As negative as this poem is, Crane, as in most of his other work, retains a touch of hope, a sense that one can survive, that water and wind, life and creativity are still possible: "O Steel and stone! But gold was scarcity before. / And here is water and a little wind" (*CP* 117). In fact, one way of examining the *Key West* poems is to see them as an individual's struggle to survive spiritually within a harsh natural setting that symbolizes our existential condition in the here and now. In some ways, this is Crane's version of *The Waste Land*. In contrast to *The Bridge*, social concerns are not central; in fact, they seem to be settled. The modern world is, at present, beyond redemption, so Crane's faith has brought him to a solitary confrontation with existence. Within this world there is water, which assures survival, but there is little wind or creative energy, little inspiration. Crane, the poet-prophet, is undergoing a test of faith, a stay within the wilderness to face what Thoreau called the essentials of existence.

Existence is not pleasant on the coral beaches of "O Carib Isle." Death or "Satan" seems omnipresent. Here only "The tarantula rattling at the lilly's foot / . . . No, nothing here / Below the palsy," only "Brutal necklaces of shells around each grave" (*CP*

156). The poet attempts to balance this scene of death by naming the living, fertile objects: "Tree names, flower names." However, his uninspired poetry cannot bridge the horror of the scene and charm this isle into life. He is no Prospero: "The wind that knots itself in one great death— / Coils and withdraws. So syllables want breath" (CP 156).

Metaphysical questions are then asked, as they are by Melville and Emily Dickinson, whom Crane spiritually aligns himself with in one of the stronger poems in this collection. "But where is the Captain of this doubloon isle / Without a turnstile?" "What man or What / Is Commissioner of mildew . . . [for] His Carib mathematics web the eyes' baked lenses!" (CP 156). Transcendental vision indeed seems impossible in the midst of this undeniable reality, so the poet yearns for release from this isle or this existence. One can sense Crane's attraction to the fate of the mad Bedlamite in "To Brooklyn Bridge" as he asks God to "render my ghost / Sieved upward, . . . Until it meets the blue's comedian host" (CP 156). He pleads that he "the pilgrim" not share the fate of the beached terrapins, hauled on to the wharf, who suffer "slow evisceration . . . their brine-caked eyes; / —Spiked, overturned; such thunder in their strain!" (CP 157).

The turtles strain for release, and Crane yearns with them. The poet, like the turtle, is caught in his shell, his physical being, his body, and it is Satan who has given him that "carbonic amulet / Sere of the sun exploded in the sea" (CP 157). It is only in the sea that one escapes the withering rays of the sun in this desert-like existence. Crane's poem is indeed a bridge back to another Pilgrim, Anne Bradstreet, as well as to Emily Dickinson, but also a bridge forward to Sylvia Plath, who would also yearn for her Ariel-like existence, free of her body and its torments.

In "Royal Palm," Crane longingly explores the stately palm and its "Green rustlings" as a symbol of his desire to rise above and beyond his physical existence, to be "Uneaten of the earth or aught earth holds." He too would like to be a "gracious anchorite," one who has retired from life and lives in religious seclusion, in a state of grace. Paradoxically the palm tree, a phallic symbol, abandons profane pleasures for "aetherial" or sacred pleasures. It ascends beyond "mortality" and seems to soar "suchwise through heaven too" (CP 167). These last lines, however, suggest that as tempting as the palm tree's transcendence may be, it may miss heaven also; by being so "aetherial," it may enter a realm beyond pleasure as we may conceptualize it. This troubles Crane and tempers his enthusiasm for the purely transcendent realm. As R. W. B. Lewis indicates in his discussion of the poem,[7] this royal, divine, palm is fruitless because it is "beyond that yield / Of sweat the jungle presses with hot love" (CP 167). The body, the physical, as Whitman asserted, remains our means, our only fruitful means of perceiving, desiring, achieving, the passage beyond things physical.

Crane in these poems, in fact, is only temporarily lost in the desert as he awaits rebirth as poet and prophet. Based on his own exhilarating experience of observing a hurricane at Pine Isles, he seizes upon this all-powerful event as a symbol of renewed, if wild, poetic inspiration. The "Air plant"—a species of bulbous tuft that grows on palm trees—serves as a symbol of the diminished poet without body or blood. He is "defenseless, thornless, sheds no blood, / Almost no shadow—but the air's thin talk" (CP 168). He is no redemptive Christ-Dionysus poet-hero, who makes the word flesh. But the storm that enlivens is on its way. "Angelic Dynamo ! . . By what conjunctions do the winds appoint / Its apotheosis, at last—the hurricane!" (CP 168). We see the divine nature of this storm, the sweeping away of stale breezes, the coming of divine and inspired winds in Crane's "The Hurricane": "Lo, Lord, Thou ridest! / Lord, Lord, thy swifting heart. / Nought stayeth, nought now bideth / But's smithereened apart!" (CP 169).

After the passing of the hurricane, we sense in "And Bees of Paradise" the sweeping away of doubt and despair; paradise and love have been regained. Inspired perhaps by his love for Peggy Baird, Crane now can see: "Sea gardens lifted rainbow-wise through eyes / I found" as well as "kindled skies . . . By the dove filled, and Bees of Paradise" (CP 172). Crane in the Key West poems continues to find paradise on earth and to reiterate his faith that love and beauty remain within our experiences. It is the poet's role to realize this vision and set it to song, to music.

He repeats this theme in "The Broken Tower," one of his most compelling poems. It is not the lofty music coming from the bell tower that inspires him but "she / Whose sweet mortality stirs latent power?" (CP 194). Crane "lift[s] down the eye" as sky "Unseals her earth, and lifts love in its shower" (CP 194). Thus, although Crane was tempted, as was Frost, to ride upward on his tree, the Royal Palm, he, like Frost, returned to earth because he did not know where love would go better. "And so it was I entered the broken world / To trace the visionary company of love" (CP 193).

If Crane is able to affirm his vision, he is less certain about his art. In the "Broken Tower" (1932), for example, he still questioned his poetic achievement: "My word I poured. But was it cognate, scored / Of that tribunal monarch of the air" (CP 193). Like Wordsworth and other romantics, Crane feels that spontaneity, the outpouring of inspired verse, is central, but he questions whether he has created for his modern audience the divine music of Blake and Whitman or the ideal music of Plato. Central to this question is the efficacy of Crane's diction and its density, which so often sends us to the dictionary to check primary and secondary meanings for any number of words in a single line. In addition, the denotative value of the word is often, as Crane explained to Harriet Monroe, who criticized his diction in "At Melville's Tomb" as being incomprehensible, not the major import of his diction. Rather he employs the cumulative connotative value of words to express that which is beyond the experiences and thoughts conveyed by logical language. Crane informs Monroe that

as a poet I may very possibly be more interested in the so called illogical impingements of the connotations of words on the consciousness (and their combinations and interplay in metaphor on this basis) than I am interested in the preservation of their logically rigid signification at the cost of limiting my subject matter and preceptions involved in the poem. (CP 234)

This "logic of metaphor" Crane claims is related to the romantic's belief that not all poetry is "rationalistic" in manner and that poetry has the right to be freed from logical restraints, "for there is much greater poetry of another order which will yield the reader very little when inspected under the limitation of such arbitrary concerns" (CP 236).

As any reader of Crane realizes, this creates great difficulty and often demands an immersion in Crane's idiom prior to an appreciation of his poetry. At times, as Crane openly stated, the lines often transcend understanding or precise paraphrase and create more of a psychological than intellectual impact. This technique and aesthetic disturbed many of Crane's contemporaries; however, most now would agree with Crane's insistence that this mode of poetry be available to the poet and that he or she not be forced within a single mode. As Crane indicated in his closing remarks to the editor of *Poetry* magazine, critics are free to judge the execution of one's technique but not the choice of poets to employ it.

As bold, innovative, and subjective as Crane's diction and resultant imagery are, it is surprising to note how frequently he employs the conventions of rhythm, rhyme, and sound patterns. While he could use free verse and blank verse very effectively, the surprising number of measured and rhymed lines is indeed very visible and indicates Crane's adherence to not only the models of Whitman but also those of Blake, Dickinson, and even at times Pope. As Eliot prescribed, Crane added his individual talent to a tradition. The problem seemed to be that his chosen tradition, the romantic tradition, was one his age judged defunct, a judgment that history has not borne out. In fact, as we reexamine Crane's vision and art, his score becomes more impressive; although written by a modern composer, it assured the continuance of the visionary mode of poetry.

E. E. Cummings

If Crane's status as a major modern poet is still questionable, the place of E. E. Cummings (1894–1962) in modern poetry is as, if not more, uncertain. Helen Vendler speaks of his "great aborted talent," his affirmation that "excludes too much pain," and his too stereotypical portraits; she accuses him of retreating into "the myth of the sensitive poet immersed in a greedy and unreceptive world." To Vendler, Cummings's penchant to divide the world into "most people" and the sensitive is a form of snobbery, an "affectation of superior wisdom." Most important, perhaps, to Vendler is Cummings's "murderous devaluation of intellect, "his guerilla war against intellect," which tops Wordsworth's and "takes on sinister potential." His poems, she claims, are often full of "slush about love and April." In short, "Cummings was happiest in ignorance." If his potential were to be realized, he would have had to pay more attention, Vendler believes, to "the ironic circumstances under which love is conducted"—that is, to employ more fully his wit.[8]

In large part, Vendler's attack seems to be aimed more at the counterculture values of the 1960s and to its youthful followers, but these later remarks, which elevate the values of irony and wit at the cost of presenting direct affirmative feelings, call to mind once again the more classical elements within the modernist tradition that would find (excluding, as Vendler does, the satiric poems) little to celebrate in cummings's lyric poetry. However, in defense of Cummings, critics such as Norman Friedman question what they feel to be a rigid, exclusive and narrow definition of poetry and insist on establishing a place for poets who do not embrace new critical tenets. Commenting on the critical disagreement over Cummings's status as poet, Friedman claims that

some of our reigning critics are bound by certain limiting conceptions as to what poetry should be and that these conceptions do not apply very comfortably to Cummings. To look in his work for the signs of a tragic vision, for an ambivalence of structure, for a studied use of verbal ambiguity, for the display of a metaphysical wit, for the employment of mythic fragments, for the climax of spiritual conversion—this is to look for things which are simply not there.[9]

What Cummings seems to do is to return to a form of poetry that is nearly pure in terms of sensibilities. He writes a type of lyric in which feeling is central, although often marked lightly by the wittiness of the argument; in contrast, in his satirical poems, wit and detachment dominate. Rather than fusing those sensibilities, as Eliot recommends, Cummings chooses to view and to employ them as nearly separate modes. If one believes with Eliot that the dissociation of sensibilities must be remedied, that poetry must be difficult, and that wit, intellect, and complexity constitute higher values in poetry than feeling, then Cummings can be seen as a failed poet who retreats to the simplistic music of earlier poets. Given Cummings's willingness to confront the dangers of twentieth-century life and his willingness to experiment with the visual, structural, and linguistic aspects of poetry, it is difficult to see Cummings as an anachronistic poet. What does stand out, however, as with Crane, is his insistence on writing lyric poetry that is much more passionate and intense than intellectual and detached, traits that tie both poets to romantic traditions. The fact that poets such as Crane and Cummings still have strong defenders and still command a large readership suggests that the New Critical approach to poetry, for good or ill, never completely or finally won its battles. The romantic, expressive lyric remained an important form and cummings played a central role in preserving that genre.

E. E. Cummings shared Hart Crane's belief in love and transcendence, as well as his refusal to be overcome by modernist values that threatened the mystery and joy of existence. In his first *Collected Poems* (1938), he brazenly staked out his territory as a human and poet:

> If most people were to be born twice they'd improbably call it dying—you and I are not snobs. We can never be born enough. We are human beings; for whom birth is a supremely welcome mystery, the mystery of growing. . . .[10]

Despite the unique diction and syntax, the echoes of New England individualism and romanticism are clear. Cummings, born and raised in Cambridge, Massachusetts, no doubt listened intently to his transcendental fathers who preached the virtues of nonconformity and praised the beauties and mysteries of nature, the ties that linked humans to the earth, and the spirit that circulated throughout. Cummings's parents were self-reliant, independent, witty, and loving humans who vividly modeled the ways of New England for their son. Mr. Cummings, a Unitarian minister and sociology professor at Harvard, is sketched with love in his son's *six non lectures* (1953), the Charles Eliot Norton lectures delivered by Cummings at Harvard. The father's wisdom, his many and varied abilities, his strength, individualism, love of life, and integrity are drawn with lively and appreciative strokes. In addition, his mother's bravery and determination after the bizarre death of his father in an auto accident clearly indicates her strength as well. Cummings's love and admiration for his parents is certainly a striking contrast to Crane's experience and no doubt contributed to his unshakable faith in the joys of existence. There is no "sundered parentage" here, no love withdrawn, no love withheld, and it accounts significantly for the paucity of pain and tragedy in his poetry. A lifetime of love, joy, and devotion was not a dream but a reality to the young Cummings, and he celebrated his parents' accomplishments in verse throughout his life.

"if there are any heavens my mother will (all by herself) have / one," he tells us, and within that heaven will be his father, "(deep like a rose / tall like a rose)," and his hands will "whisper / This is my beloved . . . (suddenly in sunlight / he will bow, / & the whole garden will bow)" (352). Similar praise is voiced in "my father moved through dooms of love"; "joy was his song and joy so pure / a heart of star by him could steer." "My father," he sings proudly, "moved through theys of we, / singing each new leaf out of each tree / (and every child was sure that spring / danced when she heard my father sing)" (520–21). The impact of his father as model and teacher is best captured in the last two lines of this poem: "because my father lived his soul / love is the whole and more than all" (521). These values, especially love, become the basis for much of Cummings's verse. We can see his life and his work as tributes to his parents' joy, love, and soul and as a lasting distaste for what he called "manunkind," a "busy monster" who merely "plays with the bigness of his littleness."

Cummings earned his B.A. and M.A. degrees at Harvard, where he became involved with a number of other student-poets. After graduation, he, along with a number of other young writers drawn to the conflict in Europe, volunteered to join the Norton Harjes Ambulance Corps in France. Given his background and temperament, it is not surprising that he and a close friend and writer, William Slater Brown, found themselves in trouble with a highly suspicious government that suspected them of being not sufficiently pro-French. The result was a three-month imprisonment, which became the basis for Cummings's prose work *The Enormous Room* (1922). As narrated in *six non lectures*, Cummings's father continuously pressed for his release and refused to sacrifice Brown to the authorities even if it meant his son's release. After the war, Cummings lived a bohemian existence, spending time in Paris and New York, extending his world beyond the boundaries of New England, while learning the craft of painting as well as writing. He, like Crane, refused to sacrifice his art to the necessity of making a living and lived a rather meager existence until a family inheritance provided him some financial security. As with Thoreau, art and the essentials of life were to be held above security, comfort, and the acquisition of money and status.

In contrast to Crane's all-too-brief career and relatively thin collection of writings, E. E. Cummings published poetry for four decades. His first volume, *Tulips and Chimneys*, appeared in 1923. His last, *73 Poems*, came out in 1963, shortly after his death. *Collected Poems* appeared in 1938; *Poems 1923–1954* in 1954; and *Complete Poems 1913–1962* in 1972, which includes twelve individual volumes of poems. In addition, he published essays, a novel, a travel book, plays, fairy tales, a libretto for a ballet, and a series of lectures; he considered himself to be a painter, and continued throughout his long career to be a provocative and innovative artist. His poetry is marked by a consistent vision and style. Rather than creating new themes and forms, he instead expanded or deepened themes or techniques that appeared early in his work.

Cummings endorsed Winfield Townley Scott's view of his work. In introducing Cummings to an audience at Brown University, Scott suggested that Cummings ought to be considered a New England poet, one who echoed Emerson in his intense pursuit of love and Thoreau in his scathing attack on American values and institutions. Scott concluded by stating that there were two sides to Cummings's verse, "love and rebellion" themes that linked Cummings to Emerson, Thoreau, Dickinson, and Robinson.[11]

Love and rebellion do indeed constitute Cummings's pervasive themes. The first poem in *Tulip and Chimneys* is an "Epithalamion" or marriage song composed for the wedding of his friends Scofield Thayer and Elaine Orr. In addition, poems such as "All in green went my love riding" mark Cummings as a twentieth-century troubadour poet who echoes the Elizabethan and Cavalier poets in his praise of love. However, he also strikes a more modern note in his keener recognition of the impermanence of the physical world but also, paradoxically, its lure. "Consider O / woman this / my body" (43), he advises his lover, though he has also "been true only to the noise of worms." Cummings is aware of "the passing of all shining things." Like the carpe diem poets who preceded him, he acknowledges the power of time and the transitory nature of existence; however, this does not usually result in the sense of urgency that we find in many seventeenth-century poets but rather a calm acceptance of the nature of things. Beyond the material world, cummings believes, resides the lasting world of love and spirit, the nothing "which lives." As in Crane, the transcendental tones and vision of Emerson, Thoreau, and Whitman can be heard and seen. Like Crane, he too refuses to reject the physical realm but instead chooses to celebrate the perpetual cycle of life and death and to embrace the joys of the body in the here and now. Although these joys may be temporary, they are, as in Whitman and Crane, the threshold to that "incorruptible nothing." The recognition of death's power does not, as in Prufrock, lead to an aborted love song but rather to a lifelong devotion to the singing of love songs in various forms and voices. We hear his celebration of the body in "i like my body when it is with your / body . . . i like the thrill / of under me you so quite new" (175). And we hear his transcendent vision of love in "stand with your lover on the ending earth" when the speaker concludes by contemplating for his love the consequences of a loveless existence:

> suppose we could not love, dear; imagine
>
> ourselves like living neither nor dead these
> (or many thousand hearts which don't and dream
> (743)

It is the brevity of existence that necessitates and elevates love to such heights, for without it the lovers are mere particles of "blind sand" at the mercy of time. To Cummings, "love is the every only God / who spoke this earth so glad and big" (526). Thus, Eros, the only God, unites the lovers and links them to the earth and sky, also part of love's creation, and the brightness of her eyes, like the brightness of the star, symbolizes a transcendent shining that will not pass away. To become lovers is to enter and become part of the eternal, the divine. As with Whitman and Crane, love is a visionary theme, and Cummings's faith in the divine nature of love and its centrality in our existence deepens and intensifies.

In 95 Poems (1958) he warns us that "unlove's the heavenless hell and homeless home" for it is "lovers alone wear sunlight"— and it is only within love that freedom exists. Within love, Cummings envisions that "april's day transcends november's year" (765). Cummings again proclaims that physical love, even if it is only a moment in time, is not an obstacle but rather a means to love and to love's creation. It is our dependence on the mind and its abstractions or creeds that blocks our discovery of love and eternity. It is only through the actual experience of love and the resultant song that lovers sing that November's wasteland is transcended and April is seen as the kindest month. As with Crane, then, we must be willing to take that voyage into the world of love. As Cummings indicates in one of his most accomplished songs of love, "rosetree, rosetree," 'giving (and giving / only) is living' and the rosetree gives its buds to "all." Eros is a world beyond the "prose mind," a world where "immensest / mysteries contradict / a deathful realm of fact /—by their precision / evolving vision." Here, Cummings proclaims, "gladness—unteaches / what despair preaches" (763–64).

Although Cummings refuses to acknowledge the death of love as a value and insists on experiencing its joys and singing its praises, he also feels that most people have lost their faith in love as well as their faith in the mysteries and beauties of nature and the sanctity of the individual. To attack these nay sayers and the faithless, Cummings turns to the other side of his poetic coin: the rebellious and satirical mode of poetry. Again Cummings's targets are quite consistent: any thought, behavior, rules, or form of authority that deny individuality, freedom, spontaneity, joy, spring, youth, and love. With Thoreau, he believes in a majority of one, and he also believes, as did Emerson, that to be a man, one must be a noncomformist. So throughout his life Cummings attacks rigid doctrines, social mores, the scientific method, the state, and its institutions.

In *Tulips and Chimneys*, for example, he lashes out at "prurient philosophers," "the naughty thumb of science," and doctrinaire religions for attempting to squeeze the earth and its mysteries into a formula; however, the earth survives and "answerest / them only with / spring" (46). In the "Cambridge ladies" sonnet, he attacks the genteel women "who live in furnished souls / are unbeautiful and have comfortable minds" and who keep themselves busy by believing in the dead, gossiping, and knitting for the Poles (70). In *Is 5* (1926), the assault is sharpened as he attacks the corrupting influence of advertising copy and patriotic cant on our language. As Williams insisted, modern language has lost its

vitality, and Cummings wittingly reveals this by parodying the
cant and commerical chatter of his time:

> believe me
> my country, 'tis of
>
> you, land of the Cluett
> Shirt Boston Garter and Spearmint
> Girl With the Wrigley Eyes (of you
> land of the Arrow Ide
> and Earl &
> Wilson
> Collars) of you i
> sing: land of Abraham Lincoln and Lydia E. Pinkham,
> land above all of Just Add Hot Water and Serve—
> from every B.V.D.
>
> let freedom ring.
>
> (230)

Cummings here also attacks the Mr. Vinals of this world, self-
appointed censors, moral guardians who would claim with others
that "Art is O World O Life / a formula" (230). In "next to of
course god America i / love you" he parodies in sardonic tones
the speech of a politician who relies on patriotic cant to justify
the senseless slaughter of young men in World War I:

> thy sons acclaim your glorious name by gorry
> by jingo by gee by gosh by gum
> why talk of beauty what could be more beaut-
> iful than these heroic happy dead
> who rushed like lions to the roaring slaughter
> they did not stop to think they died instead
>
> (268)

As in John Dos Passos's famous "Unknown Soldier" speech,
Cummings is quick to recognize that jingoistic language is used
to justify and fuel the war effort; he also recognizes that this
language can blind even one's family to the senselessness of war.
His speaker in "My Sweet Old Etcetera" is a wounded soldier,
who while dying bitterly remembers the thoughts and words of
first his aunt and then his parents who

. . . could and what
is more did tell you just
what everybody was fighting

for,

. . .

mother hoped that

i would die etcetera
bravely of course my father used
to become hoarse talking about how it was
a privilege and if only he
could . . .

(276)

Cummings, like many other rebellious writers of the 1920s and
1930s was initially drawn to the struggles of the Communists as
they placed their bodies and lives against the police and the state.
The "communists have (very) fine eyes" (275), he tells us in a
1926 poem; however, after his visit to Russia in 1931, he expressed
in *Eimi* (1931), a travel book, and in his poetry a new view of
the Russian experiment. Before the infamous Stalin trials and before
most sympathetic artists reached a similar conclusion, Cummings
concluded that Communist ideology was dogmatic, senseless, and
antithetical to freedom and life itself. In *No Thanks* (1935) he
satirically summed up his disdain:

Kumrads die because they're told)
Kumrads die before they're old

. . .

and Kumrads won't
believe in life) and death knows whie

. . .

every Kumrad is a bit
of quite unmitigated hate
(travelling in a futile groove
god knows why)
and so do i
(because they are afraid to love

(413)

In contrast, Cummings's heroes refuse to bend to an authority, ideology, or social order that impinges on their individuality and freedom. They include bohemian artists, such as Joe Gould, a Harvard graduate who refused to enter the everyday world of commerce and labor and lived on "air," devoting his life to the compilation of a never-ending oral history. To Cummings, "it's more . . . to be little joe gould)" (410). Unlike "most people" his heroes wish to and insist on "living" even if that means dying. One of the most striking examples is Cummings's song of praise for "Olaf, glad and big / whose warmest heart recoiled at war: / a conscientious object-or." Beaten and tortured at the behest of a "wellbelovéd colonel (trig / westpointer most succinctly bred)," he still refuses to embrace a nation at war: "I will not kiss your f.ing flag." The torture continues, but Olaf remains strong: "There is some some s. I will not eat." Olaf, on the president's command, is thrown into a dungeon to die because he, in the eyes of the state, was a "Yellowsonofabitch"; however, Cummings presents him as a Christian saint and brave hero:

> Christ (of His mercy infinite)
> i pray to see; and Olaf, too
>
> . . .
>
> unless statistics lie he was
> more brave than me: more blond than you.
>
> (339)

Lovers, as well as rebels, become heroes in Cummings's gallery. In *50 Poems* (1940), for example, Cummings presents a couple, named anyone and noone, who in contrast to the someones and everyones of this "pretty how town" lived, sang, danced, laughed, cried, and loved. But because they refused to conform to the town's mores and behavior, "Women and men (both little and small) / cared for anyone not at all." After anyone and noone died, the townspeople ignored them; however, in Cummings's eyes, they are not defeated in death but instead enter a more perfect existence:

> all by all and deep by deep
> and more by more they dream their sleep
> noone and anyone earth by april
> wish by spirit and if by yes.
>
> (515)

The words *deep, sleep, more, earth, april, spirit,* and *yes* attest to anyone's and noone's victory over death and a society in which "most people said their nevers" and "slept their dreams." In the later volumes Cummings often, as in this poem, fuses his belief in love and rebellion to create a model of behavior for his readers. So while it is true that his rebelliousness is in keeping with the New England Transcendentalists, his preference that this rebellion be shared by two lovers is an important variation on that theme. Thoreau's and Emerson's rebellions stress the single individual. Neither Thoreau at Walden nor Emerson on his walks in the occult woods is joined by a lover. Again, the Whitmanesque model is closer to Cummings's later vision.

Although it is true that Cummings's social and satirical poems lessen in number and intensity in his later volumes, it appears that this is due in large measure to a growing faith in the power of love. He still lashed out at America for proclaiming its belief in freedom while refusing to come to the aid of the Hungarian rebels (711) and attacked the "sub / human superstate" (803) in 73 Poems (1963), but these would become minor notes in his larger song of love and vision. His later quest, as evidenced in the final poem in his last volume, is to restore our full vision for "all worlds have half sight, seeing either with / life's eye . . . . or . . . death's." But

> Only whose vision can create the whole
>
> (being forever born a foolishwise
> proudhumble citizen of ecstasies
> more steep than climb can time with all his years)
>
> he's free into the beauty of the truth;
>
> and strolls the axis of the universe
> —love . . .
>
> (845)

The lines echo Whitman and surely establish cummings as being in the visionary company of Hart Crane. The last lines of Collected Poems, in fact, spoken lover to beloved, voice the poet's final testament of romantic faith;

> your lover (looking through both life and death)
> timelessly celebrates the merciful

wonder no world deny may or believe.

(845)

From the start, Cummings insisted on going his own way as a poet. While many other poets called for a new poetry, he often retained the diction, voice, themes, and forms of sixteenth- and seventeenth-century lyric poetry. He could write a love sonnet that lightly echoed the Elizabethans or Cavalier poets of old or employ rhyme and sound patterns in the melodic style of the troubadour poets. And as Crane observed in his essay on modern verse, Cummings, unlike his peers, often avoided the abstract, the intellectual, and the complex in his poetry, presenting what Crane called "impressions"—images of life in Paris, New York, or images of nature. More than most other poets, then, Cummings retained elements of past traditions. At the same time he proved to be one of the most innovative of poets. If he presented impressions, he often insisted that they be visually as well as verbally rendered on the page. His poems, in anticipation of the concrete poets, were another form of painting, as seen in such famous ideographic poems as the grasshopper poem (396) and "a leaf falls" (673), which in its visual arrangement reiterates the theme of oneness as it mimics the fall of the leaf on the page. Cummings was also quick to split words and lines when he felt the technique was advantageous to the visual value of the poem or when it best captured the way the poem should be read. Anticipating Charles Olson, Cummings realized the typewriter provided the poet with a means of extending the use of space in a poem and that space could play a central role in its composition if one were original, daring, and innovative.

He approached punctuation and syntax in a functional manner. Small, rather than capital letters, he felt, could intensify his themes; capital letters could work visually and thematically, as in the use of the capital letter O in poems depicting the moon. Irregular syntax could be used to balance two or more thoughts, to suspend the conclusion of the poem, or to provide a surprising and original flow to the poem. Cummings, like Crane, also developed his own structural logic and his own diction, converting parts of speech, enjambing words, or establishing a series of thematic words to convey his vision.

This unusual blend of the old and the innovative achieved Cummings's end, which was to establish his own unique voice and his own mode of singing. To some, it was too archaic and to others too innovative, but it was indisputably Cummings's own approach. Like Frost, another stubborn New Englander, he defined his territory and refused to budge. Cummings's territory, however, was not as traditional as Frost's in form or as stoic in theme. Rather than viewing poetry as "a stay against confusion," Cummings insisted, as had Thoreau before him, that it was a means of celebrating life and awakening his neighbors to the joys of existence.

Both Crane and Cummings, then, emerge as poets who offer a countervision to the loveless, meaningless world of the wasteland. Both would agree with Whitman that love is the "Kelson" of creation, that reality—the physical world—must be accepted and seen as the means to complete the passage to spirit, and that the function of the poet, in large part, is to keep that countervision alive. In addition, both poets refused to subject their own poetic principles and styles to the dominant aesthetic creeds of modernism. In doing so, they both assured the continuance and enrichment of the romantic strain of American poetry during a period in which the majority of poets and critics turned to classical tenets. Crane and Cummings compose a significant and arresting counterscore to the dominant music of modernist poetry.

Robinson Jeffers

The career of Robinson Jeffers, (1887–1962), like that of Cummings, was long and productive. His first volume of poems, *Flagons and Apples*, appeared in 1912; his last volume, *The Beginning and the End*, posthumously in 1963. During these fifty years, Jeffers produced twenty volumes of poetry, including two *Selected Poems* (1938 and 1965), the last published posthumously. He translated Euripides's *Medea* (1946), and an edition of his *Selected Letters* appeared in 1968. Throughout this time, Jeffers, like Cummings, forged his own vision and his own mode of existence and pitted his life and art against the currents of his time and country.

After moving to California and graduating from Occidental College in his teens, Jeffers tried his hand at studying medicine and forestry before turning to literature. During these early adult years, two events proved central to his life. First, he met Mrs. Una Call Kuster, whom he later married. Although he tried to resist his love for a married woman, his attraction to her was too strong, and after a number of separations, they were married in 1913. Their marriage survived a few disruptions and provided Jeffers with a solid foundation in a world that seemed to be drifting into chaos. The second refuge he found was the California coast off Carmel, where he lived in his famous rock house and tower and learned to love the beauty and indifferent power of nature and God. Here, he and Una raised twin boys, free for the most part from the disrupting events of a chaotic personal or public life. Although the Jefferses traveled and especially admired the scenes and landscapes of Ireland, their spirits were married to the rocks, the sea, and the natural life of Carmel. Whereas Cummings found his ideal themes in the pastoral scenes of New Hampshire, Jeffers was to discover his in the harsh but beautiful world of the Pacific coast. It was an environment that would forever remind him of the imperfections, frailties, and impermanence of humanity and the lasting and beautiful qualities of things inhuman and spiritual. This, in fact, would become his "Loved Subject," for the "mountain and ocean, rock, water and beasts and trees / Are the protagonists," he tells us in one of his last poems.[12]

To move or liberate his readers from their too inward gaze, their immersion in things human, Jeffers wrote a number of long narrative poems during the 1920s and 1930s that portray the consequences of excessive self-love and point to the need to adopt transhuman values, a philosophic view that he later called in-humanism. The first of these verse narratives, *Tamar* (1924), is set in contemporary California; its plot and characters, however, seem to arise from a Greek tragedy. The Caudwell family, polluted by the original sin of incest committed by the father and his sister, seems doomed from the start. Their lives, Jeffers implies, are "like a drunkard's last half dollar / Shoved on the polished bar," soon to be spent in a drunken frenzy.[13] Tamar, the leading character in this "baited trap" and symbol of unrestrained sex and passion, initiates the tragedy by committing incest with her brother Lee, thus repeating the act committed by their father and aunt before them. Her passion is further aroused by Will, a suitor, whom she loves intensely, if innocently. However, all innocence and restraint evaporates when she, dancing naked in the moonlight, partakes in a strange pagan ritual. Ruled by "the spirit of the place," she envisions the Indian ghosts of tribes past and offers her body to all that would enter it: ". . . now the desires of dead men and dead Gods and a dead / tribe / Used [her] for their common prey." Now her body is "wakening into wantonness." It is "Gone beast-like," "gone mad" (26).

Tamar's ultimate and last desire is to complete the cycle of incest begun by her father. She invites him into her circle so that she may have "her three lovers [brother, lover, and father] under one roof." Once under one roof, lust, murder (Will is murdered by the brother), and a raging fire that symbolizes Tamar's excessive passion consume the house and family. As the house burns, Tamar traps her brother within the flames, and the father cries out, "Christ have pity."

This tale of doom with its sexual perversions and violence did little to endear Jeffers to those who wished to see humanity as a species above the beasts, a species ruled by reason and ethical laws, not merely naturalistic pawns swayed by sexual drives and passions. Tamar's loss of innocence and entry into a life of lust and destruction seemed to be the inevitable result of heredity and the unleashing of the id. To followers of Irving Babbitt's neo-humanism, the tale was perverse and dangerous.

On numerous occasions in his letters, Jeffers sought to explain his intent in writing *Tamar* and employing the incest theme. In a letter to George West (22 January 1926) he defends his tale and theme by pointing out that sexual desire, of all the "primitive motives," is "the most poetized and dramatized" and that the family constitutes the most common of environments. Taken together they represent to Jeffers a universal situation that ought to "reach rather deeply into people's consciousness." He adds that our defenses against incest are strong, and hence the tale will not be a threat to audiences because it presents a theme that "isn't worn out." Most important, incest, to Jeffers, is a symbol of "immoderate racial introversion," that is, it represents humanity's excessive self-love, its narcissism, which keeps it from looking outward and seeing the transhuman beauty and power of the natural world. Most of us, Jeffers claims, waste time on "activities turned in on other people instead of outward on the world . . . . Too much human energy goes back into humanity."[14]

Later Jeffers viewed his use of the "racial incest" theme as a magical charm, a means of keeping personal tragedy away from his own house; he also claimed that the violation of deep-seated taboos best awakens a complacent audience; but his prime interest in the incest theme was "to uncenter the human mind from itself. There is no health for the individual whose attention is taken up with his own mind and processes; equally there is no health for the society that is always introverted on its own members" (*Letters*, 116). For Jeffers the quest is to escape that incestuous solipsistic trap and move outward.

In *Roan Stallion* (1925) and *The Tower beyond Tragedy* (1925), Jeffers presents two protagonists who attempt to move beyond racial incest and outward to nature and God, thus building on the theme first presented in *Tamar*. In *The Tower beyond Tragedy*, for example, Jeffers recasts the Electra–Orestes tale. Clytemnestra, the mother, emerges as Jeffers's symbol of racial self-love and power who is willing to murder her husband and children to achieve her own ends. Like Tamar, her passions and lusts are unrestrained as she pursues her own desires and power. To Cassandra, the captured Trojan prophetess, Clytemnestra's thirst for power is another human illusion, a tower without foundations. All such quests, she feels, are tottering towers, "drunkards" that will eventually topple. Rome, France, Spain, and England will fall she prophesies; then "When America has eaten Europe and takes tribute of Asia, when / the ends of the world grow aware of each other / And are dogs in one kennel, they will tear / The master of the hunt with the mouths of the pack" (114). Cassandra, repulsed by humanity, can ask only that she be freed from life: "Death, make me / stone, / Make me air to wander free between the stars and the peaks; / but cut humanity / Out of my being? that is the world that festers in me" (115).

Orestes, however, becomes Jeffers's hero. He rejects his sister's offer of incest and power and turns to the world of nature. There he will "not waste inward / Upon humanity, having found a fairer object" (137). For humanity "is all turned inward, all . . . desires incestuous." Orestes is able to "cut the meshes / And fly like a freed falcon . . ." to "the life of the brown forest / And the great life of the ancient peaks, the patience of stone," for he has "fallen in love outward" (138–39). We can, Jeffers dramatizes, choose to live as Electra, in a world of human desires, in a specific time and place, which is as Jeffers envisions it, inevitably tragic. Or we may live as Orestes, who has "climbed the tower beyond time, consciously, / and cast humanity, entered the earlier fountain" (140).

Jeffers's disillusionment with the promises of humanism and his turn to the world of nature and God is also portrayed in a lyrical fashion in his shorter poems. As with Orestes, Jeffers is quick to see and articulate the contrasts between the world of humans and that of nature. If we, as he tells us in "Natural Music," "listen without / Divisions of desire and terror," we will hear" the storm of the sick nations, the rage of the hunger-smitten / cities," but we will also hear the "old voice of the ocean" and voices—"Clean as a child's; or like some girl's breathing who dances alone / By the ocean-shore, dreaming of lovers" (77).

Rather than creating poems centered on self-love, Jeffers turns to nature for, as he explains in "Point Joe," "Permanent things are what is needful in a poem, things tem / porally / Of great dimension, things continually renewed or always / present . . . Fashionable and momentary things we need not see nor speak of" (78). Jeffers willingly leaves the world of transitory human quests and ambitions and enters instead the timeless world of sea, rock, and sky, the natural world he discovered in Carmel. The building of his house brought him closer to that world. Aided by a stonemason, he first constructed Tor house from the rocks and boulders at hand and then singlehandedly constructed his Hawk Tower, a forty-foot structure designed after Irish towers. After carrying, rolling, and then hoisting by block and tackle boulders that sometimes weighed up to four hundred pounds, Jeffers physically and spiritually embraced the primordial elements of nature. With these rocks, with Una and the twins, he would construct an existence that would go "beyond tragedy." This sanctuary was home to the Jefferses for the rest of their lives, and it became the subject of a number of his best lyrical pieces, which in many ways parallel the ruggedness of his home and environment.

His Tor house, Jeffers exclaims, is built of native granite rock, "primitive rock" and "the bones of the old mother." And "each stone / Baptized from that abysmal font / The sea and the secret earth gave bonds to affirm you" (82). In "To the Stone Cutters" Jeffers reiterates his belief that the marriage of nature and art provides the truest, if not perfect, mode of human endeavor.

Although the attempt of the Stone Cutters to fight time with marble is defeated, for "rock splits, records fall down," and although the poet also is defeated, "For man will be blotted out, the blithe earth die, the brave sun / Die blind and blacken to the heart: / Yet stones have stood for a thousand years, and pained thoughts / found / The honey of peace in old poems." (84).

So in "Continent's End," on the shores of Carmel, in accentual lines that echo the surf's rolling sounds, Jeffers, like Whitman before him, sees the sea as life's mother, for "The tides are in our veins . . . life is your / child"; like Whitman, Jeffers goes beyond this natural tie and envisions a union of poet, sea, and spirit that precedes physical life, for "there is in me / Older and harder than life and more impartial, the eye that / watched before there was ocean" (87).

It is within this impartial eternal spirit that creation's song is found, both the sea's and the poet's song:

> Mother, though my son's measure is like your surf-beat's ancient
>   rhythm I never learned it of you.
> Before there was any water there were tides of fire, both our
>   Tones flow from the older fountain.
>
> (88)

To Jeffers, "Christ and Gautama" and all human dreamers are "worshippers of oneness" (162) and dream of a God that is utterly "Alone, unencroached on, perfectly gorged, one God" (162). Thus "Fog," Thoreau's mystical mist, obscures and blots out the material realm and mercifully returns us to a world of spirit and oneness. This, to Jeffers, is the ultimate dream, the tower beyond tragedy that transcends death, time, violence, and chaos. The poet as prophet devours "The world with atonement for God's sake" and enters the oneness of existence ("Fog," 162).

Most people and nations, however, continue to pursue false dreams, and their strivings can, according to Jeffers, lead only to self-destruction. Ironically this, to Jeffers, is a blessing; it will further cleanse the earth of human stupidity and vanity. For example, in "Shine, Perishing Republic," he celebrates the coming demise of America as it "settles in the mold of its vulgarity, heav- / ily thickening to empire, / And protest, only a bubble in the molten mass, pops and sighs out, / and the mass hardens" (168).

While America perishes as a republic and becomes an empire, Jeffers remains distant, taking comfort from the fact that it, like all other empires and life itself, will perish; by becoming an empire so rapidly, America hastens its eventual demise. This empire will not be "stubbornly long"; it will resemble a shining meteor that speeds quickly through the heavens. Jeffers's advice to his twins is to remain apart, to "keep their distance from / the thickening center; corruption / Never has been compulsory, when the cities lie at the monster's / feet there are left the mountains. / And boys, [he concludes] be in nothing so moderate as in love of man, a clever / servant, insufferable master. / There is the trap that catches noblest spirits, that caught—they / say—God, when he walked on earth" (168).

Like the sharp-sighted hawks that soar high above the cliffs at Carmel, we must, Jeffers believes, be distant, aloof, impartial, and strong, and, above all, resist the trap of humanism. We must worship and emulate "The Rock and the Hawk," Jeffers's new religious symbols:

> . . . here is your emblem
> To hang in the future sky;
> Not the cross, not the hive,
>
> But this; bright power, dark peace;
> Fierce consciousness joined with final
> Disinterestedness;
>
> Life with calm death; the falcon's
> Realist eyes and act
> Married to the massive
>
> Mysticism of stone,
> Which failure cannot cast down
> Nor success make proud.
>
> (563)

Jeffers believes that it is too late for most humans to escape the trap. In "The Purse-Seine," for example, urban Americans are like frenetic sardines soon to be snared by the fishermen's nets:

> . . . We have geared the machines and locked all together
> into interdependence; we have built the great cities; now

There is no escape. We have gathered vast populations
    incapable of free survival, insulated
From the strong earth, each person in himself helpless, on   ❀
    all dependent. The circle is closed, and the net
Is being hauled in . . .
                                        (588–89)

To move beyond this human tragedy, or more precisely to rise
above it, we must love not humanity but "The Wild Swan" who
in its beauty and naturalness escapes the bullets of humanity:

Better bullets than yours would miss the white breast,
Better mirrors than yours would crack in the flame.
Does it matter whether you hate your . . . self? At least
Love your eyes that can see your mind that can
Hear the music, the thunder of the wings. Love the wild swan.
                                        (573)

In addition, as with Eastern thinkers, Jeffers envisions an apocalyptic ending that promises renewal. Thus "Shiva," like Blake's
tyger is, to Jeffers, a necessary part of existence. Shiva comes as
a Hawk in Jeffers's poem and one by one plucks from the sky
the virtues of our existence: peace, security, honesty, confidence,
liberty. "The prey she will take last is the wild white swan of
the beauty of / things. / Then she will be alone, pure destruction,
achieved and supreme, / . . . [However,] She will build a nest
of the swan's bones and hatch a new brood, / Hang new heavens
with new birds, all be renewed" (611).

As the 1930s came to a close, Jeffers recognized the growing
threat of totalitarianism and concluded that the masses would not
be able to resist. "We are easy to manage" he claims in "Ave
Caesar" (567). Shiva did indeed seem to rule the heavens as the
war clouds gathered over Europe and Asia. Jeffers thought America
should refuse to become entangled in Europe or Asia and instead
watch disinterestedly as the old empires tore themselves apart.
When Jeffers concluded that President Roosevelt was deceitfully
drawing the United States into the conflict, he came down from
his tower and railed against Roosevelt's policies, which he felt
would lead to tragic involvement in war. This becomes the basis
for Jeffers's first section of *The Double Axe* (1948), "The Love and
the Hate." Because of his political stance and fierce attacks on

Roosevelt, Jeffers's loss of status and acceptance, which in the previous decades had rivaled Eliot's, was inevitable. But disregarding the attack on Roosevelt, the work becomes a strong indictment of all war and the sophistry and hypocrisy employed in justifying wars, a theme that links Jeffers to cummings. The narrative evolves around Hoult, a dead soldier who wills himself back to life so that he can confront the adultery of his mother and the zealous patriotism of his father, acts that symbolize the betrayal of Hoult's parents and his countrymen. "It is the lies, it is the lies, it is the dirty / lies, / War-peddlers' lies and the people's imbecility / That raked me out of the grave."[15] Like Lazarus, Hoult rises from the dead, in this case to pronounce Jeffers's savage attack on our decision to enter the war: "if any / person / Begins to say we have to save England or rescue France / or avenge the Jews—Take him up and hang him. / He is pimping for war. If he says democracy, / Remember they pimped for war and they will again— / take him up and hang him. . . . we were sold to death / By liars and fools" (18–19).

As the narrative nears its end, Hoult asks "Why did you [mother] ever cast me out / of you / Into this butcher's dream?" (50). The mother, left at the conclusion of the narrative with a dead son, a slain husband (shot by Hoult), and a house consumed by flames, warns a detachment of black soldiers from Fort Ord:

> When they send you to fight in the third war, don't do it.
> Stay at home, love each other, you must love everyone,
> And apples will hang in every sycamore tree—
> No matter what they have done. Even my boy
> Was deceived for a time
> . . . kind, kind: we must be kind.
>
> (50–51)

Section 2, "The Inhumanist," introduces a wise prophet philosopher in the guise of the old caretaker of the Gore property who after the tragic events occupies the house and property. As Jeffers's spokesperson, he articulates the poet's theory of inhumanism and leads a solitary life in keeping with those principles. This section is more speculative and inward; the old man begins by contemplating the existence and nature of God. He concludes that there is little doubt that God does exist, that he is conscious, that he is "Not a ridiculous projection of human fears, need, dreams, / justice and love-lust" (53). Instead all life is joined by this singular energy called God: "One existence, one music, one organism, one life, one God!" (53). Although all of creation is alive, natural life differs from God in that it is mortal; "But only God's is immortal" (54). God's end seems to be beauty, the beauty of his creation; questions of happiness, goodness, and evil, which are human constructs, blind us to "the beauty of things" and their intrinsic value. Because humanity inevitably fouls the world with its self-love, its fears and terrors that have cursed it since its dark and terrifying origins in the primal world, we should embrace "the outer magnificence, the all but inhuman God" (83). Nor is it proper to partake in the slaying of either the body or spirit of other humans, even if they are a blight on God's creation, for this is God's long, evolved task, one embedeed in the natural evolution of creation. Jeffers has his prophet conclude, "I will grind no more axes."

Although he remains disengaged in his mountain retreat, he does become a singular voice in Jeffers's work in that he not only is able to transcend the trap of humanism but is also able to pass on his vision to future generations. He tells the children that they need not cry when born, for life is short, and when they are about to die, they need not grieve, for they are returning to their "better nature, the noble elements, / earth, air and water. That's the lost paradise / The poets remember" (105). He then sums up his religious beliefs for the children:

> There is one God, and the earth is his prophet.
> The beauty of things is the face of God: worship it;
> Give your hearts to it; labor to be like it.
>
> (105)

At the conclusion of this section, chaos and war break out once again; this time atomic weapons threaten human existence. To the old philosopher, it does not matter if humanity perishes; the earth and God will survive. They are absolutes; humankind is not. To Jeffers's sage, there are only two choices: the death of the species or a true reconciliation with existence in which we recognize our limited role within a vast and beautiful universe and see that we are but a single thread in the cloth of life.

This cosmic view of existence, which contrasts the beauty of life and the absolute power of God to the apish instincts and actions of humanity, continues to be Jeffers's theme in his last volume, *The Beginning and the End* (1963), a collection of shorter lyric poems that celebrate and extend the themes found in *Double Axe*. In "The Great Explosion" the universe with its expansions and contractions is seen as the heartbeat of God, "the root of all things," and this rhythm of expansion, contraction, diastole, and systole explains the creative, destruction cycle of life. "The great heart beating, pumping into our arteries His / terrible life. / He [God] is beautiful beyond belief . . . this is the God who does not / care and will never cease" (3–4). Humanity's mission, as Jeffers reveals in "The Beginning and the End," is "To find and feel; all animal experience / Is a part of God's life" (10) and to link the "animal stinking ghost-ridden darkness, the hu- / man soul. The mind of man" with the stars. Then, "Slowly, perhaps, man may grow into it—/ Do you think so?" (10) On the one hand humans are "villainous . . . beasts," "deformed apes"; however, their minds are more incalculable than "a comet's orbit or the dive of a hawk" (10).

Jeffers does leave us with a ray of light, a sense that we may be able to move to a vision of inhumanism that allows us to escape the world of tragedy and enter into the heart and mind of creation itself. To do that, humanity must renounce the glory of humanity and recognize the omnipotence of God and his visible creation. It is a stance that positions Jeffers as a prophet who fuses Calvinism and transcendentalism into a glorious vision. But this vision also contains a sense of terror and horror reminiscent of Jonathan Edwards. It is a vision of heaven and hell; which we shall inhabit remains to be seen. Jeffers's role as our modern-day Moses is to reveal the beauty and power of nature and God as well as our extinction, which may come about "rather quickly, if the great manners of death / dreamed up / In the laboratories work well" (50).

Jeffers's vision is much harsher than either Crane's or Cummings's; his image of humanity is bleak and his prognosis grim. Absent is Crane's and Cummings's discovery of love, beauty, and spirit within the modern and human world; even his vision of nature is more distant and aloof. In this respect, he seems more naturalistic and/or Calvinistic than romantic; however, his strong belief in the beauty of nature, his belief in nonconformity and individualism, and especially his belief in and yearning for the spiritual realm cast him as a romantic and a member of the visionary company.

We can, in fact, view his long narrative poems as twentieth-century versions of the romantic epic-narrative, more mythic than realistic, and his shorter poems as mystical lyrics celebrating the beauty and magnificence of transhuman existence. In many respects, he lived a Thoreauvian existence and wrote Whitmanesque lines; however, he could not envision humanity as a God in ruins. To Jeffers, and a number of other contemporary romantic poets, humanity would have to recognize and accept its limited place in creation.

Since Jeffers's death, a critical reevaluation of his work has taken place. Led by William Everson (Brother Antoninus), a leading poet of the San Francisco Renaissance, there is less concentration on Jeffers's use of violence and his political stance during the war and a more generous recognition of his cosmic, spiritual, and ecological vision.[16] Hostility is fading, as evidenced by the interest in the Jeffers centennial celebration (1987) held at the Tor House and the anticipation of the publication of his *Collected Poems*. Jeffers may once again be seen as one of the major modernist poets.

Crane, Cummings, and Jeffers form a strange company, but each presented a vision of life that went beyond shoring up a broken world with fragments. Each in his way, stylistically and thematically, provided a vision of life, as Jeffers stated, "beyond tragedy," a vision that transcended the ashes of Eliot's *The Waste Land* and echoed Whitman's song of unity. Eliot himself would find his way out of the lifeless and spiritless modern world in his later poetry. Younger poets, however, such as Theodore Roethke and Allen Ginsberg, would not follow his lead but rather that of this visionary company that in turn was led by the Meister Singer, Walt Whitman.

· EIGHT ·

Crosscurrents of Modernism:
The Fugitives and Objectivists

I stood in the rain, far from home at nightfall
By the Potomac, the great Dome lit the water
The city my blood had built I knew no more

—Allen Tate, "Aeneas at Washington"

For past objects have about them
past necessities

—William Carlos Williams, *Autobiography*

Classical Modernism: The Fugitives

Modernist literature is complex and diverse. It is like a river fed
by many divergent streams that enter at different points and with
different force and energy. The visionary poets, linked to Whitman,
became a major branch; however, they were not considered to be
the mainstream of modern literature. That honor belonged to the
classical rather than the romantic modernists. The classical modernists, taking their antiromantic cries and aesthetic values from
T. E. Hulme and T. S. Eliot, focus on human fallibility, the ironic
nature of existence, the decline of Western civilization, and the
value of tradition and art. They are conservative in philosophy,
politics, and aesthetics. Their allegiance is to the past and the
classical modes of art. In America, this current of modernism
essentially owes its existence and pervasive influence to a small
group of southern writers (John Crowe Ransom, Donald Davidson,
Allen Tate, and Robert Penn Warren) who were associated with
Vanderbilt University, as either faculty or students, during the
early 1920s. This group met with other Nashville, Tennessee,
citizens, exchanged and analyzed poems, and eventually published

a literary magazine, *Fugitive,* after which the group is named. In its nineteen issues (June 1922–December 1925), the *Fugitive* brought to its readers the tenets and models of classical modernism and became one of the most influential magazines of the twentieth century. Ransom, Tate, and Warren, building on Eliot's and Pound's work, quickly became national literary figures who shaped and institutionalized American literary values. They were outspoken cultural critics, assertive literary critics, influential teachers who fathered a new generation of poets, and critics who assured that classical modernism would experience a floodtide in American colleges during the years preceding and following World War II. They were indeed men of letters whose shadows still fall on our literary landscape.

JOHN CROWE RANSOM.   The senior figure in this group is John Crowe Ransom (1888–1974), a native of Tennessee and a graduate of Vanderbilt (1909), who returned to his alma mater after attending Christ Church College of Oxford University as a Rhodes Scholar and earning his B.A. degree in Letterae Humaniores in 1913. His academic career was interrupted by World War I; however, he continued working on his poetry, exchanging ideas with his friend, Donald Davidson, another poet. Shortly after resuming his position at Vanderbilt, he published his first book, *Poems about God* (1919). As a published poet, he became the leading member of the Fugitives, which included such young aspiring poets as Davidson, who was working on his M.A. degree, and two brilliant undergraduates: Allen Tate, who had impressed Ransom in his freshman writing class as an extremely well-read student, and Robert Penn Warren, Tate's roommate, who quickly fell under the sway of Ransom's influence.

Ransom, whose poetic output is slight and written almost exclusively during the period 1916–1927, is still considered by many to be the most important of the classical modernist poets because of his unique ability to capture the modern sensibility in the most artful of forms. This is especially true of the poems he published in the *Fugitive,* and that very fact assured the importance of the magazine. Following Hulme's advice, he discredited his earlier work on the grounds that the poems were aesthetically immature and too autobiographical, and he began to nurture the sense of distance and wit that mark his poetry.

Tate and others point to "Necrological," published in the *Fugitive* in 1922, as the poem that first illustrated Ransom's mature style. The poem, based on the story of Charles the Bold of Burgandy (1433–77), tells a tale of war and carnage viewed by a young Carmelite monk previously spared the realities of existence, who now must test his Christian tenets against the horrors of human violence and suffering. Love, sacrifice, and heroism seem far different in this world as the monk observes "a leman [mistress], who with her flame had warmed his tent, / For him enduring all men's pleasantries."[1] Now dead, clutching her slain warrior's knees, she is an emblem of worldly love whose sacrifice of reputation and life transcends the monk's love of God and his denial of physical pleasure. Once his unquestioned faith is severely tested by the enigmas and complexities of existence, the monk experiences spiritual and intellectual death:

> Then he sat upon a hill and bowed his head
> As under a riddle, and in a deep surmise
> So still that he likened himself unto those dead
> Whom the kites of Heaven solicited with sweet cries
> (10)

This loss of faith and certainty, conveyed paradoxically in decorous and charming linguistic and poetic forms usually associated with the poetry of chivalry and romance and treated with a wit that verges on black comedy, becomes the model for other Ransom poems. In "Bells for John Whiteside's Daughter," he once again dramatizes the enigmatic and shifting nature of existence. The speaker, a neighbor of the Whitesides, is reflecting on the totally unexpected death of John Whiteside's daughter. He remembers how he and others once gazed from their high window at the daughter's battle with the geese below as she "harried unto the pond / The lazy geese, like a snow cloud / Dripping their snow on the green grass," (11). Then "There was such speed in her little body, / And such lightness in her footfall" (11). But now "her brown study" is still. Although she did not hesitate, unlike Hamlet, to take "arms against her shadow," her "brown study" is now "Lying so primly propped" (11). At first the speaker is astonished that death came to such a lively and young creature.

The more he reflects, however, the more he is anguished and vexed by her death:

> But now go the bells, and we are ready,
> In one house we are sternly stopped
> To say we are vexed at her brown study,
> Lying so primly propped.

(11)

The poem reverberates with a number of striking contrasts that capture the paradoxical nature of human existence: life-death, past-present, memory-reality, astonishment-vexation, starkness-artifice (the brown study primly propped). The bells then, as John Donne exclaims, ring not only for Whiteside's daughter but, more important, for the speaker, as well as all others still alive, and the readers who are unable to solve the riddles of human existence. The fact that the "tireless heart" of the daughter has stopped has, in turn, "sternly stopped" either a comfortable or comforting vision of existence. To add to the paradoxical tone, Ransom plays his theme against the basic lightness and even gaiety of the poem's imagery and rhythms. Thus, we are both charmed and, to use Ransom's word, vexed by the poem. This resultant irony perhaps is Ransom's finest achievement. It brilliantly captures the enigmatic nature and complexity of existence; lightness and darkness, comedy and tragedy become one.

Ransom's three volumes of poetry contain not only a number of the most skillful and arresting modernist lyrics but also some of the most representative poems of the classical modernist temperament. His achievement was recognized when, after revising and editing his work in *Selected Poems* (1963 and 1969), he won the Bollingen Prize for Poetry in 1963 and the National Book Award in 1969.

Ransom's contribution to American literature is also evident in his role as social and literary critic, editor, and teacher. When the Scopes trial became a symbol of southern backwardness and cultural decline, Ransom, Davidson, Tate, Warren, and eight other southerners rallied to the South's defense and published *I'll Take My Stand* (1930). This collection of essays attacks the urban culture of the North, its materialism and rootlessness, its excessive belief in science and technology and, in contrast, praises the agrarian, traditional world of the South as a more humane, cultural, and satisfying mode of existence. As a literary critic, he articulated and illustrated the principles of formal or New Criticism, which claimed that too much attention had been given to such external factors as history, society, and biography in the study of literature and too little attention to the work itself. The text—its diction, imagery, rhythms, structures, its inner workings and relationships—should be, according to Ransom and his followers, the focus of literary criticism. Following Ransom's lead and critics such as T. S. Eliot, I. A. Richards, and William Empson, the advocates of this approach borrowed the title of Ransom's critical study (*New Criticism*, 1941) and employed their critical approach in the classroom, in textbooks, and in literary journals and established New Criticism as the leading literary theory until the 1960s. Allen Tate, R. P. Blackmur, Robert Penn Warren, and Cleanth Brooks, for example, in their criticism and teaching illustrated the centrality of the text, the specialness of poetic language that separated it and raised it above the language of science and philosophy, and, above all, the need to study the text closely.

In addition, Ransom edited two of the most influential modernist literature journals, the *Fugitive* and the *Kenyon Review*, the latter a journal that, under Ransom's leadership, published for over two decades many of the leading critical essays on modern verse. Ransom's influence as teacher was also significant. His students included Tate, Warren, Davidson, Cleanth Brooks, Randall Jarrell, Robert Lowell, and James Wright. And although each would go his own way, Ransom's poetry and criticism is embedded in the fabric of their work. Given his contributions, he is, in many respects, the founder of American classical modernism, and his influence certainly remained strong long after the heyday of the Fugitives. But there is also in Ransom a timidity and reluctance to go beyond what, although once avant-garde, had become the mainstream tradition of modern poetry. Content with polishing, refining, and institutionalizing earlier philosophic and aesthetic values, Ransom and his followers ironically can be seen as being antimodernist in their reluctance to make it new. Many of the poets of the new generation would, in fact, see Ransom and the New Critics as a significant obstacle to creative and innovative expression.

ALLEN TATE. Allen Tate (1899–1979), also played a leading role in the world of poetry and New Criticism. As the title of one of his works indicates, he, as well as Ransom and Warren, enacted the role of *The Man of Letters in the Modern World* (1955) who "recreate[s] for his age the image of man, and . . . propagate[s] standards by which other men may test that image, and distinguish the false from the true."[2] During his long career, he would present those images and standards in poems first appearing in the *Fugitive* in the early 1920s and continuing into the 1970s with his *The Swimmers and Other Selected Poems* (1970) and *Collected Poems: 1919–1976* (1977). In addition, he took a stand for the South in being one of the twelve contributors to the famous agrarian statement of 1930; he wrote two biographies, *Stonewall Jackson* (1928) and *Jefferson Davis* (1929); and he published *The Fathers*, a Civil War novel, in 1938. When he returned to Tennessee in 1944, he edited the influential *Sewanee Review* for two years. And he was a lively and provocative critic of modern literature and thought for more than four decades—generous and wise enough as he surveyed his essays in 1955 to admit that his ideas and beliefs had changed over the years. Tate writes, for example, that he no longer thinks "that men can achieve salvation by painting pictures or writing poetry, or by cleaving to an historical or social tradition [southern agrarianism]" (624). Although aesthetics and tradition gave way to a belief in Catholicism in 1950, Tate's faith in the values of art and a richer past remained strong themes throughout most of his poetic career.

We can see this in the title piece of his first volume of poems, *Mr. Pope* (1928), in which the physically deformed Pope becomes a symbol of man's ability to rise above imperfection and achieve artistic glory. However, modern man is cut off from the classical, formal, moral, and witty world of Pope's eighteenth century for

> he who dribbled couplets like a snake
> Coiled to a lithe precision in the sun
> Is missing. The jar [funeral urn] is empty; you may break
> It only to find that Mr. Pope is gone.[3]

Pope's wisdom, his "wit and rage," represented by the coiled snake, his lithe precision, his art, and his "strict" age are both missing and missed. We lack, Tate implies, aesthetic, moral, and cultural ties that bind us to a common culture and a humane existence.

Our separateness and isolation are effectively portrayed in "Last Days of Alice." Lewis Carroll's heroine has aged and declined as she sinks into reverie and self-absorption: "Alice grown lazy, mammoth but not fat, / Declines upon her lost and twilight age." To Alice, life is only self-reflection, an abstract image of our mental constructs. She "Gazes learnedly down her airy nose / At nothing, nothing, thinking all the day" (107). Caught in her narcissism and solipsism, she is alienated from the real world: "She cannot move unless her double move, / The All-Alice of the world's entity / Smashed in the anger of her hopeless love, / Love for herself" (107).

Alice's fate—to move from all to nothing, from reality to shadow or reflection, from life to abstract dream—is, to Tate, the modernist dilemma or fall, a fall that seemingly forever smashed our ties to existence. In five of the most haunting lines of modern poetry, Tate precisely etches our alientation:

> —We too back to the world shall never pass
> Through the shattered door, a dumb shade-harried
> crowd
> Being all infinite, function depth and mass
> Without figure, a mathematical shroud
>
> Hurled at the air—blessèd without sin!
>
> (108)

Here Faulkner's solipsistic characters come to mind—the Hightowers (*Light in August*) who exist only as shadows, abstractions lacking physical and earthly identities, cloaked only in "mathematical shrouds." Paradoxically Tate's mode of salvation lies in reenacting the Christian fall, one in which we subject ourselves to sin and evil and the imperfections of the flesh. Thus as supplicant, he pleads: "O God of our flesh, return us to Your wrath, / Let us be evil could we enter in / Your grace, and falter on the stony path!" (108)

In his essay "Narcissus as Narcissus," Tate would identify Alice's self-consciousness and self-love as a modern illness whose prime symptom is "the cut-off-ness of the modern 'intellectual man' from

the world" (598). Call it narcissism or solipsism, it "denotes the
failure of human personality to function objectively in nature and
society" (*Essays*, 595–96). A central means of dramatizing this
twentieth-century failure is to contrast a heroic past with a darker
present. "Aeneas at Washington," for example, begins with Aeneas's
description of the fall of Troy and his heroic acts and vision. Then
he was a "A true gentleman, valorous in arms, / Disinterested and
honourable" (5). But when Tate transports Aeneas to America's
capital, there is a dissipation of energy and purpose:

> Now I demand little . . .
> ....
> There was a time when the young eyes were slow,
> Their flame steady beyond the firstling fire,
> I stood in the rain, far from home at nightfall
> By the Potomac, the great Dome lit the water,
> The city my blood had built I knew no more
> While the screech-owl whistled his new delight
> Consecutively dark.
>
> (6)

Tate's greatest achievement in dramatizing our loss of faith in
and our passion for heroism is best exemplified in his famous
"Ode to the Confederate Dead." Often revised over a ten-year
period, it became an emblem of modernist pessimism. Tate's intent
in this poem is to dramatize the clash between solipsism, which
he defines in "Narcissus as Narcissus" as "a philosophical doctrine
which says that we create the world in the act of perceiving it,"
(595) and "active faith," a collective faith "not private, romantic
illusion" (599) in the nobility of the human spirit as manifested
in its chivalrous public deeds. The conflict arises in the mind of
a solitary man at the gate of a Confederate graveyard on a late
autumn afternoon, and it remains an internal debate between past
and present, between objective and subjective realities, between
faith and grim resignation and defeat.

Initially the speaker can only envision this late afternoon autumn
graveyard scene filled with its whirring, wind-driven leaves as a
"casual sacrament" of death, whose music sounds "the rumour
of mortality." As Tate states in the Narcissus essay, the speaker
is barely able to proclaim the traditional praise for the physical

and historical continuance of the Confederate dead and their sacrifices: "these memories grow / From the inexhaustible bodies that are not / Dead, but feed the grass row after rich row" (17). Caught in his own naturalistic vision of existence, the speaker presents images illustrating the ravages of time, eventually ending the first strophe with his blind crab image of the "Locked-in ego," signifying his inability to move beyond his solipsism and reconnect himself with the objective world: "You shift your sea space blindly / Heaving, turning like the blind crab" (17). Tate in the Narcissus essay explains that the crab has mobility and energy but "no direction and no purposeful world to use it in" (598). Lacking a sense of purpose, the speaker begins the first of his naturalistic refrains that speak to the failure of imagination and human insight: "Dazed by the wind / only the wind / The leaves flying plunge" (17).

The countertheme of active faith is advanced in the next strophe as the speaker momentarily recovers and is able to imagine the blowing leaves as heroic charging soldiers, who

> . . . know the unimportant shrift of death
> And praise the vision
> And praise the arrogant circumstance
> Of those who fall
> Rank upon rank, hurried beyond decision—
> Here by the sagging gate, stopped by the wall.
>
> (18)

These heroes of an "immoderate past," however, cannot become a permanent part of the modernist vision or poem. The speaker's awareness of mortality, his naturalistic views, ensure "they will not last" and "that the salt of their blood / Stiffens the saltier oblivion of the sea" (19). Nor can the modernist celebrate the perpetual cycle of existence, a central theme of romantic poets. "We shall say only the leaves / Flying, plunge and expire" for "Night is the beginning and the end" (19). Separated from both society and nature, we can engage only in "mute speculation," abstraction, and narcissism; thus "the jaguar leaps / For his own image." Our knowledge has been "Carried to the heart"; it has destroyed our relationship to life itself, and our most hopeful prospect is that "The ravenous grave" may become our theme, for it is "the grave who counts us all!" (19–20).

Traditionally an ode publicly celebrates, in stately and exalted lyrical verse, an aspect of human existence; Tate's ode is not celebrative, public, or exalted. It is a pessimistic, solitary, and, given its form and theme, grimly ironic dramatization of the modernist temper. At times its imagery is quite private and its allusions and arguments overly complex; however, it remains one of the most representative and compelling poems of the twentieth-century wasteland.

This Eliot-like vision can also be seen in "The Subway," a sonnet with a modernist setting, that in its octet likens the plunge into the subway to our fall from grace and our descent into the world of commerce, industry, and science—what Tate calls "the iron forestries of hell" (105). And even when he is above ground, the modernist is merely "a blind astronomer / Dazed," who sees only "worldless heavens . . . / In the cold revery of an idiot" (105). Unlike Crane's voyage, there is no redemptive journey for the modernist, no bridge back to nature, society, and heaven. He remains an "idiot," dazed by his "geometries" and "cold revery."

This descent into Hell is more religious and personal in Tate's later poems. In "The Swimmers," the title poem of the 1970 selected poems, Tate skillfully employs Dante's terza rima form to narrate a personal fall from grace and entry into the world of knowledge, sin, and guilt. Set in Montgomery County, Kentucky, in July 1911, the poem retells how Tate and four friends who are on a swimming expedition encounter the lynching of a black man. At the start of the poem Tate invokes his heart, and soul, his "fountain," to replenish the "spring of love and fear" and the "eye that looked and fled" that summer day. He then recounts his baptism into death, murder, and injustice: "I saw the Negro's body bend / And straighten, as a fish-line cast transverse / Yields to the current it must subtend" (40). Tate accompanies the body to town where "The faceless head lay still"; transfixed, he stands "Alone in the public clearing / This private thing was owned by all the town, / Though never claimed by us within my hearing" (41).

This brutal act becomes part of the community's heritage, part of its collective consciousness; however, it is never publicly claimed or proclaimed. It awaits expiation. The poem becomes Tate's scaffold on which he reveals his South's violent past and his own loss of innocence and childhood. The poem is surprising in its personal and nearly confessional tones. In addition, the relaxed and, at times, vernacular diction and the absence of classical allusions, and dense intellectual argument indicate Tate's willingness and ability to move beyond his earlier approaches. What remains constant, however, is the classical modernist image of human fallibility and the devotion to the craft of poetry. Like the fish line in "The Swimmers," Tate consistently yielded to that current.

ROBERT PENN WARREN. Robert Penn Warren (b. 1905) shares a number of traits with his fellow Fugitive poets. Born in Guthrie, Kentucky, he too was an active participant in the Vanderbilt group; he was an enthusiastic reader of Eliot (it is said that he painted scenes of *The Waste Land* to tack to his dormitory walls and that he could recite by heart every line of Eliot's poem). Under Ransom's and Tate's encouragement, he abandoned his scientific studies and turned to the study and writing of poetry. Still active today, his career spans over sixty years and includes the publication of sixteen volumes of verse, ten novels, a volume of short stories, a play, numerous historical and critical studies, and such influential textbooks as *Understanding Poetry* (1938), which, composed with Cleanth Brooks, became one of the chief means of introducing literature students to the close reading techniques and formalistic values of New Criticism.[4] While on the faculty at Louisiana State University with Brooks, he founded the *Southern Review*, a highly influential literary periodical. As with the other Fugitives, his interest in the South, its history and identity, remained an abiding theme. Following his critical study *John Brown: The Making of a Martyr* (1929), he wrote a conservative essay defending segregation in the South for *I'll Take My Stand* (1930) and then modified his views in a separate volume, *Segregation* (1956). Later works on the South include *The Legacy of the Civil War* (1961) and *Who Speaks for the Negro* (1965). His novel, *All The Kings Men* (1946), based on the career of Huey Long, is considered to be one of the central visions of the modern South. His awards are many; in 1986, he was selected the first official poet laureate of the United States.

Central to most of Warren's work is his vision of sin and the possibility of human progress or redemption. To Warren, the fall from innocence is inevitable, a central fiber in God's weaving of the creation; however, the question of our acknowledgment of that reality and the possibility of salvation are concerns that Warren puzzles over again and again. In an early poem he tells his lost brother, his pre-Adamic self perhaps, "A certain night has borne both you and me; / We are the children of an ancient band / Broken between the mountains and the sea."[5] Wandering in Eliot's wasteland, the speaker asks that his lost self "Renounce the night" as he has so that they may "meet / As weary nomads in this desert at last" (*SP* 300). This longing for unity and lost innocence and the desire to escape from the fallen world is one of the dominant notes in Warren's early verse. Often this theme is lo-calized, as in "The Kentucky Mountain Farm" series, but the myth of expulsion from the garden is ever-present. In "History among the Rocks," Warren envisages death and decay as an essential part of the natural and human realms of Kentucky. "There are many ways to die / Here" (*SP* 292), he tells us. Ironically "Under the shadow of ripe wheat" is "the copperhead, / Fanged as the sunlight" (*SP* 292). In addition, the hills house the bodies of the Civil War soldiers whose sacrifices, as in Tate's "Ode," now seem inexplicable, forgotten, and symbolic of a lost innocence: "Their reason [for dying] is hard to guess and a long time past: / The apple falls, falling in the quiet night" (*SP* 292).

The longing to return to the Garden, that lost state of innocence, or to escape from the wasteland are expressed often in these early poems. The speaker in "The Return: An Elegy," returning home for his mother's funeral, cries, "Turn backward turn backward O time in your flight / and make me a child again just for tonight" (*SP* 288), and in the oft-anthologized "Bearded Oaks," two lovers envision their momentary stay under the protecting oaks as a return to an ocean floor where they are divorced from the threat-ening world above and "The storm of noon." Beneath the sea "All our debate is voiceless here, / As all our rage, the rage of stone" (*SP* 274).

Any attempt to escape the realities of existence through time or space, however, as illustrated in "Mexico Is a Foreign Country: Four Studies in Naturalism," is futile. The journey to Mexico is first seen as one in which butterflies and their astonishing colors initially entice the protagonist who "robed in the pure / Idea" fled across the border; however, death remains a constant in Mexico also, although less stark. During a burial ceremony, the body of a young child is showered with colorful flower petals and "a pink cloth [is placed] on its face." Warren, however, remarks in a wry tone that "The pink cloth is useful to foil the flies, which are not few" (*SP* 263). And in the fourth poem in this series, "The Mango on the Mango Tree," the speaker envisions the mango as a symbol of God's inexplicable plan to divide man and nature. For this is "the Roman plan, / Divide and rule, mango and man" (*SP* 269). Whatever crime nature and humanity committed, each will pay "Drop by slow drop, day after day, / Until His monstrous, primal guilt be washed away" (*SP* 270). If only the word *pardon* or *forgive* could be said, "Then we might lift the Babel curse by which we live."

The vision is that of a fallen world, a wasteland in which humanity yearns for an innocent existence and mourns its fallen state but seems unable to do anything about its predicament. Based on the poems that followed, Warren seems to feel that our first step possibly to assuage, if not resolve, this condition is to acknowledge our heritage as humans, our tainted nature. In "Original Sin: A Short Story," for example, all attempts to escape what the speaker calls the "nightmare," with "its great head rattling like a gourd / And locks like seaweed strung on the stinking stone," are futile. Original sin "acts like the old hound that used to snuffle your door and moan" (*SP* 245). It reappears at Harvard Yard after he has left home; it remains forever, for "nothing is lost, ever lost." Surprising, it is not malevolent but an essential aspect of our existence, which we must embrace if we are to be whole again.

This need to acknowledge and accept our darker self is one of the dominant themes in Warren's longer narrative poems as well. In "The Ballad of Billie Potts" (*SP* 1943), Warren narrates a folk tale told to him when he was a child in Kentucky. The tale tells of the crimes of Big Billie Potts, an innkeeper, who with the aid of accomplices robs and murders his guests after they have left the inn. "Little Billy," their son, decides to make his parents proud and attempts to hold up one of the guests on his own, a crime that signals his fall from innocence and entry into his father's world. The stranger, however, is wise to Potts's scheme; he wounds Billie and sends him on his way home where "Pappy barred the door," gave him 'Two Hundred in gold', and sent him out West "to try his luck." Initially the West and time have seemingly created a new Billie Potts, a new Adam who has escaped the sins of his past and his father's ways: "For Time is innocence / For Time is West" (*SP* 231).

Time and space do not prove to be healing and redemptive, however. Instead, as Eliot indicated in the *Four Quartets*, the end is in the beginning, and every present moment or future moment is linked to the past. Billie feels he must return to his parents and to his past, for in his new vision of himself, he discovered "something was missing from the picture" (*SP* 233), something Billie tells us had been lost. When he arrives home, he hides his true identity from his parents in an attempt to be playful. But when his parents hear the jingling of coins in his pockets, they entice Billie to drink from a stream where they "set the hatchet in his head . . . went through his pockets and . . . buried him in the dark of the trees" (*SP* 234). Initially pleased with their efforts, the parents are horrified when they realize that they have killed their own son who finds in death his true identity, even if it is one of crime and punishment. At the conclusion of this tragicomedy we see Billie willingly accept his father, his original sinful nature, as he kneels "At the feet of the old man / Who is evil and ignorant and old" (*SP* 239).

Warren's imbedding of such complex moral and philosophic themes within a folklike style illustrates his ability to move beyond the metaphysical style of poetry that marks his earlier work. It also suggests his interest in reviving the narrative form in poetry. Previously he linked poems together under a common theme, locale or concern, but in "The Ballad of Billie Potts" he showed a strong interest in the narrative form, no doubt reinforced by his writing of novels. In *Brother to the Dragons* (1953) he displayed a new and remarkable ability to sustain a long narrative poem. Again the theme, as indicated by the title, acknowledges our violent, corrupt side. The action of the poem focuses on the brutal butchering of a black slave by Lilburn Lewis, a nephew of Thomas Jefferson. The slave's "crime" was that he broke a prized pitcher belonging to Lilburn's deceased mother; Lilburn's rage and sadism reveal a psychotic fixation on his mother, alive or dead. Eventually the crime is revealed, and Lilburn and his brother Isham, an accomplice, are indicted for murder. Prior to the trial, Lilburn and Isham arrange a suicide pact over their mother's grave. Lilburn is

slain by a bullet from his brother's gun; however, Isham is un-
harmed and flees but is caught and sentenced to hang. He once
again escapes and remains free until he is slain at the Battle of
New Orleans.

Warren's use of this grizzly historic tale captures the dark side
of human nature and the South's violent past; it also illustrates
the dangers of an excessive love of the past (Lilburn's love of his
mother) and an excessive adherence to a fixed idea that separates
oneself from one's wife (love and procreation) and community.
This inability to capture life within a single formula or idea is
also intensified in Warren's depiction of Thomas Jefferson, who
despite his strong belief in progress and reason is eventually forced
to acknowledge the grim deeds of his kin and, by extension,
humankind. R.P.W., a character who speaks for Warren, tells
Jefferson that the materials for this narrative are not appropriate
for a ballad because our hearts, he believes, are scarcely as innocent
as a ballad form suggests and because the action of a ballad cannot
account for the inexplicable action of the two brothers. "It is
explained, if explainable at all, by our most murderous / Com-
plicities, and our sad virtues, too . . . No, the form was not
adequate to the materials."[6] Jefferson agrees and confesses that
his world vision was also inadequate: "There is no form to hold
/ Reality and its insufferable intransigence. . . . I once tried to
contrive / a form I thought to hold the purity of man's hope. /
But I did not understand the nature of things" (BD 44). His previous
vision—that "we might take man's hand, strike shackle, lead him
forth / From his own monstrous nightmare—then his natural /
innocence / Would dance like sunlight over the delighted landscape" (BD 41)—has been smashed by the recognition that by the
ties of blood he is linked to Lilburn's crimes. Thus, he now lacks
"the absolute dream / and joy / That I once had" (BD 47) and
realizes that even love "Is but a mask to hide the brute face of
fact" (BD 47).

Just as Jefferson must acknowledge the brutality of existence,
so too must R.P.W. reassess his vision at the poem's conclusion.
Just prior to leaving Lilburn's gravesite, R.P.W. realizes, "Fulfillment is only in the degree of recognition / Of the common lot of
our kind. And that is the death of vanity, / And that is the
beginning of virtue" (BD 214).

Warren, like Hawthorne and Melville before him, endorses this
need to acknowledge our inevitable fall and our common identity

with all other humans and nature on the basis of that fall. Warren states that once we realize that

tragic experience is universal and a corollary of man's place in nature, he may return to a communion with man and nature. . . . Man eats of the fruit of the tree of knowledge and falls. But if he takes another bite, he may get at least a sort of redemption.[7]

In the poems that follow *Brother to Dragons*, Warren continued to pursue in a more personal and lyrical fashion "a sort of redemption" that follows the fall. He continued to bite the apple, to gain more knowledge, more moral awareness; in fact, he would claim that poetry is the best means to achieve moral awareness for "poetry—is knowledge. For . . . it gives the image of experience being brought to order and harmony. . . . The rhythm is, as it were, a myth of order, or fulfillment, an affirmation that our being may move in its totality toward meaning."[8]

Warren's affirmation can be seen in his *Promises* (1957), which received the Pulitzer Prize, the Edna St. Vincent Millay Award, and the National Book Award. It is a work that oscillates between his previous dark vision and the joys and promises of being a father who is able to envision a new generation and a new world. However, the arrival of his "Infant Boy at Mid Century" was none too soon:

You come in the year when promises are broken,
And petal fears the late, as fruit the early frost-fall;
When the young expect little, and the old endure total recall,
But discover no logic to justify what they had taken, or forsaken.[9]

Within this world of broken promises, a time "When the century dragged, like a great wheel stuck at dead center" (*NSP* 271), his new son, Gabriel, offers a sign of physical and spiritual revival. In "Lullaby: Smile in Sleep" Warren presents one of his most tender poems and a testimony to the value of fatherhood:

Watching you now sleep,
I feel the world's depleted force renew,
Feel the nerve expand and knit,
(*NSP* 277)

At times, however, Warren's vision is not so positive. In "The

Evening Hawk," he envies the soaring hawk "Who knows neither
time nor error," while he is left on earth to "hear / The earth
grind on its axis, or history / Drip in darkness like a leaking pipe
in the cellar" (*NSP* 167). In his later works, Warren spins out a
complex, charged dialectic that echoes Yeats's debate between
things physical and things spiritual. Warren, like Yeats, engages
his mind, heart, and soul as he debates the glories of the physical
and spiritual realms. Although this dialectic is never completely
resolved, it is interesting to note that in presenting his latest *New
and Selected Poems* (1985) Warren opened the volume with a poem
titled, "Three Darknesses." In the third section, the darkness is
the nighttime wait for a surgical procedure to take place in the
morning—"A dry run," Warren tells himself, for the inevitable
end. But while watching a television western, Warren contemplates
life once again and states in affirmative tones:

> You are sure that virtue will triumph. Far beyond
> All the world, the mountains lift. The snow peaks
> Float into moonlight. They float
> In that unnamable altitude of white light. God
> Loves the world. For what it is.
>
> (*NSP* 5)

Warren's movement from the dark and ironic side of classical
modernism with its penchant for formal and traditional lyrical
modes, as well as his ability to move beyond his southern roots,
helped to create an impressive work marked by growth and
evolution, wisdom and skill. He is the most expansive and experimental of the Fugitives. As George Garrett points out, he is
quick to go beyond the strictures of New Criticism.[10] His use of
the Kentucky vernacular and settings, his experiments with narrative forms, and his turn to personal and mystical lyrics in his
later years ensured that he would emerge as a strong force in
both modern and contemporary poetry.

The Objectivists: Making it New

The Fugitive poets proved to be a strong and lasting force in
modern American poetry. Their stress on the formal elements of
poetry, their impersonal, ironic, and witty mode of verse, and their

use of tradition and history, as well as their disdain for urban, industrial America, became important elements in the poetry of a significant number of younger poets, including Robert Lowell, Richard Wilbur, and John Hollander. In addition, their impact as editors, teachers, textbook writers, and cultural critics solidified and institutionalized the poetic values of New Criticism. They constituted a strong, if not the dominant, current of modern American verse.

There were also less visible and, for a time, less influential currents swirling about. One of the most interesting and influential of these movements was the objectivists, a loosely connected group of poets who were children of the twentieth century, came from Jewish backgrounds, and brought to American poetry an urban, ethnic, and class consciousness that contrasts sharply to the traditional Anglo-American vision of the fugitives. The four leading objectivists were Charles Reznikoff, Louis Zukofsky, George Oppen, and Carl Rakosi; a fifth poet, Lorine Niedecker, is included here because of her adoption of objectivist principles and her close ties to Zukofsky.

The so-called objectivist movement came about when Ezra Pound, who was impressed with Louis Zukofsky's criticism and poetry, convinced Harriet Monroe to invite Zukofsky to edit a special edition of *Poetry* in which would appear a younger generation of modernist poets. Monroe complied but insisted that the group of poets be identified as a movement and that Zukofsky explain the principles of the group in an introductory essay. Zukofsky agreed, pulled the term *objectivist*, Rakosi claims, "out of his hat," wrote his manifesto, and edited the February 1931 issue of *Poetry*.[11] Thus was born the objectivist movement. The issue proved to be controversial. Monroe denounced the obscurity of Zukofsky's essay, and letters to the editors condemned the poets for their obscurity, their nonpolitical stances, and their perceived attempts to advance Jewish nationalism. The next year the Oppens (George and Mary), under their To Publishers Press, housed in France, issued the *Objectivists' Anthology*, which included work by the four objectivist poets, Kenneth Rexroth (his first publications), as well as Pound and Eliot. In "Recencies in Poetry," Zukofsky once again identified what he considered the aims of objectivism. When the To Publishers Press ran into financial difficulty, it reorganized in the United States under the title of the Objectivist Press in the hope of establishing an affordable means of publishing the objectivists and the works of other modernists they admired.

Although each of the writers was quick to establish his own approach and style, some common traits appear in their work. The first is their interest in invention or process, the making of the poem, the poem as an autonomous object. Here they followed in the footsteps of Gertrude Stein, Ezra Pound, and William Carlos Williams. Williams, for example, defined the poem as a machine and in his *Autobiography* reminds readers that "the poem, like every other form of art, is an object."[12] Second, all shared an interest in moving from perception to what Pound called "the dance of the intellect" or mind. That is, the mind of the poet must engage the object being viewed, not merely report its presence. The poet thinks and feels with the object in sight. Third, the poet must confront what Zukofsky calls "the particulars" of his time and place; there is, as Oppen indicates, an empirical aspect to poetry. The poet recognizes the realities—social, political, cultural—of his time and is true or sincere in his presentations and reactions. *Sincerity*, in fact, becomes a key word in appraising both the content and the form of a poem. Neither should be contrived or false. Within this very broad and loose framework, the objectivists created a highly individual and inventive body of poetry.

CHARLES REZNIKOFF. Charles Reznikoff (1894–1976), the eldest of the objectivist poets, published twenty-five titles during his career as a writer; a two-volume collection, *Complete Poems*, edited by Seamus Cooney appeared shortly after his death. Following *Rhythms* (1918), he wrote verse plays, novels, and nonfiction prose dealing with both the history of American Jews and the nation while continuing to write poetry for nearly five decades. His poetry ranges from short haiku-like pieces in which he conveys a mood or feeling through a condensed type of imagery as in "Suburban River: Summer":

> The white gulls
> hover
> above the glistening river
> where the sewers empty
> their slow ripples.[13]

to longer narrative poems such as "Early History of a Writer," an urban American Jewish version of Wordsworth's *Prelude.*

His poetic values are precision, clarity, and testimony to what the poet actually sees, hears, and feels at a particular moment; this then creates sincerity, a vital element in Reznikoff's poetry. In keeping with Pound and the other imagists, the objectivists turn from Victorian sentiment. "We [the objectivists] were anti Tennysonian," Reznikoff writes;[14] however, it is also Reznikoff's training as a lawyer that drew him to testimony. Although he disliked the practice of law, he thought its study provided a poet with the means of being precise and the gift of bearing testimony in an empirical manner, without artificial rhetoric or false sentiment. To Reznikoff, "There is an analogy between testimony in the courts and the testimony of a poet."[15] Reznikoff, in fact, published four works in which he selects and arranges the words and rhythms of actual court records to create what he calls his version of Eliot's objective correlative wherein he captures the economic, social, and cultural identity of a given period of history. Three of these works, entitled *Testimony*, deal with antebellum and late-nineteenth-century American history (1885–1900) and were appropriately faulted for their lack of refinement, use of raw data, and unpoetic nature. Reznikoff claims, however, that the reader does receive through this technique a clear, precise, and empirical representation of the social, cultural, and economic disasters of a particular time and place. This approach is most compelling in his last work of testimony, *Holocaust* (1975), where he uses the records of the Nuremberg and the Eichmann trials to create a chilling understated "objective correlative" that captures the horrors of the Holocaust:

> They gathered some twenty *Hasidic* Jews from their homes,
> in the robes these wear,
> Wearing their prayer shawls, too,
> And holding prayer books in their hands.
> They were led up a hill.
> Here they were told to chant their prayers
> and raise their hands for help to God
> and, as they did so,
> the officers poured kerosene under them
> and set it on fire.[16]

The Jewish quest for spiritual survival as well as physical well-being is a dominant theme in the prose and verse of Reznikoff, not surprising since he was a Russian-American Jew who grew up in a Brooklyn ghetto and lived during the reign of Hitler. But one also sees in Reznikoff's verse a universal sympathy for all those who suffer isolation, spiritual, or economic poverty. He watches "Old men and boys search the wet garbage with fingers / and slip pieces in bags" (*CP* 29) or describes the unemployed "walking along the drive by twos and threes, / talking about jobs, / jobs they might get and jobs they had," (*CP* 173). In "Kaddish" he prays for safety for all persecuted humans: "upon Israel and upon all who meet with unfriendly glances, / sticks and stones and names—/ . . . who are pushed out of class-rooms and rushing trains, . . . / safety" (*CP* 185–86). To read Reznikoff is to read a poet's unflinching response, in the clear, precise and rhythmical language of poetry, to the world encountered, its momentary and personal incidents and its most historical and significant events.

LOUIS ZUKOFSKY. The poetic career of Louis Zukofsky (1904–78) is still being assessed.[17] For five decades he dazzled and baffled his readers with an array of highly inventive and idiosyncratic publications. Because he published his work in little magazines or in limited small press editions, it was difficult to gain access to his entire work to measure his accomplishments. It was not until Norton issued *All: The Collected Short Poems* (1965, 1966) and Doubleday reissued the privately printed 'A'-1–12 (1959) in 1967 that the literary and scholarly world at large was able to examine his work in some depth. In 1969, *Prepositions: The Collected Critical Essays*, appeared, presenting anew the aesthetic principles that inform his work and vision. In the same year his wife, Celia, published a much-needed bibliography of her husband's work. Finally in 1978, after Zukofsky's death, the University of California at Berkeley published 'A'1–24, a volume containing over 800 pages that in scope and intent is comparable to Pound's *The Cantos*. Hugh Kenner, in his homage to Zukofsky, considers *All*, 'A'1–24, *Prepositions*, and *Bottom: On Shakespeare* the central texts and concludes, "Readers . . . will still be elucidating all of them in the 22nd century."[18]

Not only was Zukofsky's work difficult to obtain; it was also diverse and highly inventive. In addition to his poetry, he has written a play *Arise, Arise* (written in 1936, published in 1962); short fiction, "It Was" and "Ferdinand," both written in the early 1940s but first published in the 1960s; a novel, *Little* (1967), that is based on his son's often frustrating experiences as a child prodigy and success as a young concert violinist; and two extremely unusual texts. The first of these is *Bottom: On Shakespeare* (1963), which Kenner considers" the most idiosyncratic of homages to the greatest master of English."[19] The second unusual text is the translation of *Catullus* (1969) by Louis and Celia, a unique venture in which Celia painstakingly measured out the rhythms, durations, and length of the original lines, which Louis then captured in English. It was a means of translating the music of the original into English, even if it obscured the meaning of the original or created a highly subjective and irregular form of English. Classicists were not pleased. In keeping with this unconventional approach, Zukofsky in 1970 published his *Autobiography*, a lean volume consisting of eighteen previously published songs now set to music by Celia and six terse, brief prose statements about his life. The work reiterates Zukofsky's belief that his entire life is located in his poetry and criticism written over a lifetime rather than in a narrative that necessarily excludes the bulk of his important writings. Although he has been accused of obscurity, it is all there, he tells us.

For many readers, however, obscurity remains a problem and creates bad verse. There are numerous passages, for example, where the word *impenetrable* seems inescapable, and as Marianne Moore in "Poetry" (1921) exclaims, "we / do not admire what / we cannot understand." Yet one can identify a number of significant and unique contributions Zukofsky brings to modernist poetry: his use of his urban, Jewish, lower-class roots, his extension of Poundian aesthetics, and his insistence on dealing with the social and historical events and forces of his time, as well as his domestic experiences as husband and father, for neither the public nor the private realm is ignored in Zukofsky's verse.

Zukofsky's background, as is true of most of the other objectivists, is a break from the traditional Anglo and most often middle-class background of American poets. His parents were Russian Jewish immigrants who lived in the slums of New York City, earned their living in the city's sweatshops, and spoke Yiddish. Louis, the only Zukofsky child born in the United States, remembers hearing Longfellow's *Hiawatha* being read in Yiddish. Within this culture, Zukofsky's wit, humor, intellect, and love of music, literature, and philosophy evolved. Although English became his primary language and he moved on to Columbia University where he earned B.A. and M.A. degrees and established lasting friendships with such people as Mark Van Doren, he never forgot his parents and their world. As Alfred Kazin documents in *Starting Out in the Thirties*, this was a time when writers from non-Anglo and working-class backgrounds were beginning to take their rightful place in the world of art and literature and thus enrich the culture and their sense of self-worth. Zukofsky and the other objectivists played a major role in opening the gates of the world of poetry to the next generation of poets who had similar backgrounds.

Zukofsky's interesting blend of Anglo and Jewish cultures appears early and often in his work. In "Poem Beginning 'The,' " first published in 1928 in Pound's literary magazine, *Exile*, Zukofsky, tongue in check, dutifully displays his knowledge of the Western canon of literature, as well as his knowledge of the latest modernist writers and techniques. The poem consists of 330 lines divided into six movements (a clear indication of Zukofsky's devotion to musical forms); each line is numbered on the left-hand side of the page, a satiric bow to the "Phi Beta" professors he mentions in the poem. In a preface, he lists the allusions in the poem and the numbered lines in which they appear. The list is impressive as it seemingly manages in a short space to equal or outdo Eliot's or Joyce's erudition and use of allusion. In addition, its associative and fragmented, collage-like structure displays Zukofsky's knowledge of and skill in employing modernist techniques. Yet as Harold Schimmel reveals, 60 of the 330 lines are taken from Yehoash's (pen name for S. Bloomgarden) *In the Web*, which is written in Yiddish verse and deals with bedouin life in Arabia.[20] Many of Zukofsky's themes here and in his later poetry, Schimmel claims, originate within his childhood experiences. Within the text of the poem, Zukofsky's devotion to his parents, especially his mother, is clear, and his Yiddish readings and experiences often are a counterpoint to the sterile wasteland of modernist literature and thought.

His determination to achieve success in the Anglo culture is nearly snarled in the following lines:

I'll read their Donne as mine,
And leopard in their spots
I'll do what says their Coleridge,
Twist red hot pokers into knots.
The villainy they teach me I will execute
And it shall go hard with them,
For I'll better the instruction,
Having learned so to speak, in their
                    colleges.[21]

In some ways this may explain Zukofsky's penchant for erudition, obscurity, and invention. Here is a young, poor, first-generation Jewish-American writer who attempts to out-Joyce Joyce in his first major poem and never after relents. But if this background suggests the need to achieve, it also suggests Zukofsky's allegiance to his own culture, which remains an important part of his work, and convinces him that "songs," as he tells his mother, "are joy, against nothingness joy." Therefore, "Sun, you great Sun, our comrade, / From eternity to eternity we remain true to you" (22).

Despite Ezra Pound's support of facism and anti-semitism, Zukofsky's close relationship with Pound lasted forty-five years. Although in total disagreement with Pound's politics (he advised Pound to listen to his own voice), he remained true to his mentor and literary father. Their relationship began with Pound's recognition and support of Zukofsky's early modernist poems, and it was Pound who provided Zukofsky with the basic elements of a modernist aesthetic. Pound's emphasis on the image, direct treatment, economy, the musical phrase rather than the measure of the metronome, and especially his belief that poetic language contains phanopoeia, melopoeia, and logopoeia provided Zukofsky with the foundation on which he built his poetic structure and critical theories. Whereas Williams often emphasizes phanopoeia, Zukofsky, following Pound, uses image as a starting point from which to move to logopoeia and melopoeia. In "To My Washstand," for example, he is initially very Williamsesque in his vivid recording of the simple but essential things of this world:

> To my wash-stand
> in which I wash
>   my left hand
> and my right hand

> To my wash-stand
> whose base is Greek
> whose shaft
> is marble and is fluted.
>
> (*All,* 59)

As Williams himself recognized, however, it is a mistake to approach Zukofsky as an imagist, a poet of pictures, for it misses Zukofsky's insistence on the value of thought and music to poetry, elements that engage fully the poet's emotions and intellect as the object is viewed.[22] As Pound insisted, the "musical phrase" and "the dance of the intellect" also need to be present if the imagistic poem is to enter the realm of art. Thus "To My Wash-stand" moves from image to thought and song. As the speaker mixes the hot and cold water from the two faucets, "comes a song":

> Comes a flow which
> if I have called a song
> is a song
> entirely in my head.
>
> (*All,* 59)

The form of the poem does not derive from the object in focus but from the poet engaged with the object, which as the poem evolves triggers the dance of the intellect and a flow of music. Zukofsky explained, "Writing occurs which is the detail, not mirage, of seeing, of thinking with the things as they exist, and of directing them along a line of melody."[23]

To Zukofsky, the poem becomes an object, hopefully an autonomous perfect melody, derived from "the direction of historic and contemporary particulars" (*P* 22), but its origins, as Pound and Zukofsky insist, are "within the veins and capillaries, if only in the intelligence" (*P* 23) of the poet who has to shape the multitudinous and often contradictory particulars of his experiences into a melody that is so true to the experience that it is forever captured in song.

This is an extremely ambitious and difficult task and one that Zukofsky tackles directly in "Mantis," the concluding poem in *55 Poems* (1941). The action of this poem centers on Zukofsky's discovery of a praying mantis in a New York subway stop. The insect begs to be acknowledged and to be "taken up," to be "saved" from an indifferent urban, capitalistic society. The speaker overcomes his initial repulsion and permits the mantis to light on his chest. The insect is then envisioned as an emblem of the poor and alienated individual who is either ignored or crushed by society. Even the poor reject the mantis out of shame, fright, or despair. But if the mantis can transform the speaker, it can also bring light to the oppressed, rekindle the spark of revolution, and create the energy to build a new world. Realizing this, the speaker tells the mantis:

> Android, loving beggar, dive to the poor
> . . . .
> Say, I am old as the globe, the moon, it
> Is my old shoe, yours, be free as the leaves.
>
> Fly mantis, on the poor, arise like leaves
> The armies of the poor, strength: stone on stone
> And build the new world in your eyes, Save it!
>
> (*All*, 74)

If the mantis's task is to save the world, the poet's task is to save this moment, this experience through language and music. The question of process and form become central; what form or structure will save this experience? Surprisingly, Zukofsky has chosen the sestina—a thirty-nine line poem consisting of six six-line stanzas and a three-line envoy; the initial six end words are repeated in differing order throughout the poem. Thus a highly traditional and formal structure is selected to capture a revolutionary experience. Zukofsky, who realizes this paradox and the fact that "Our world will not stand it, / the implications of a too regular form" (*All*, 77), provides an examination and rationale for his selection of the sestina in " 'Mantis,' An Interpretation," which immediately follows the poem itself. Here he writes that the poem is not merely an experiment in form, what he calls "wicker work," but rather the result of a natural, creative force that drew him to the sestina form. Key to this is the nature of the experience with its diverse, conflicting feelings and thought occurring in a simultaneous fashion: "Thoughts'—two or three or five or / Six thoughts' reflection (pulse's witness) of what was happening / All immediate, not moved by any transition" (*All*, 75). To Zukofsky, this was "the battle of diverse thoughts—/ The actual twisting / Of many and diverse thoughts" (*All*, 75). Six twisting thoughts naturally attract the poet to the sestina form, which is marked by its six twisting end words. That Zukofsky would create an interpretive poem dealing with process that is longer than the original poem is evidence in and of itself how interested he was in extending Pound's examination of process. It is this interest in the relationship between form and content that drew younger poets, such as Robert Creeley and Robert Duncan, to Zukofsky's work. Throughout his poetry and criticism, process—the making or creating of the poem— remains an essential theme. Zukofsky, then, as was the case with Pound, becomes the poet's poet.

"*A*," Zukofsky's magnum opus, also demonstrates his debt to Pound—in this case, *The Cantos*. Like *The Cantos*, *A* is written over a lifetime (fifty years) and attempts to order into art the public and private life of the poet. In his foreword to "*A*" 1–12, Zukofsky called the volume a "poem of a life /—and a time," and his objective, as before, was "not to fathom time but literally to sound / it as on an instrument and so to hear / again as much of what was and is together" (v).[24] The completed work "*A*"1–24 runs over 800 pages and is divided, as planned in 1926, into twenty-four movements of varying lengths, ranging from 4 words (*A–16*) to 242 pages (*A–24*). It employs traditional and modernist techniques, contains poetic and dramatic forms (*A–21*), as well as a masque (*A–24*), that draws its lines from Zukofsky's critical writings, his play, narratives, and poetry and is musically scored by Celia Zukofsky to Handel's *Harpsichord Pieces*. *A* is as erudite and obscure, in places, as *The Cantos* and no doubt will remain as controversial.

Given the scope, the range of emotions and thoughts and forms contained in *A*, it is impossible to examine such a text in detail; however, Zukofsky's preface offers a means of entering such an overwhelming volume. It is a sounding of a time and a life. Both the public and the private realms of Louis Zukofsky are explored throughout the work. He confronts his historical context, his immediate social and political context (the fall of Paris or John Kennedy's assassination, for example), and his private life, especially his life as husband and father. As he observed in Williams's personal epic, *Paterson*, and illustrated in his study of Henry

Adams's *Autobiography*, a single life can, if recorded and captured fully, recreate in words a particular time.

Zukofsky realized that in his attempt to capture "all" that exists between "The" and "A," the definite and indefinite articles of existence, he was only partially successful but that it was better to be partially successful than to lack the courage to try to capture all; "better a— / part / than / faint," he exclaims in "Finally a Valentine," the last poem in *All*, and thus he "has no / complaint" (*All*, 240).

Zukofsky's statement applies to modernist poetry generally, as well as to his own work. Given the discoveries of science, the tragedies of the time, and the seemingly insoluable human problems of the twentieth century, it was not a time for the fainthearted. It was a time for the courageous poet to face directly the bewildering particulars of a fragmented world, to retain his integrity as an artist, to move beyond convention and "to make it new." Louis Zukofsky, if only partially successful in his quest to confront and capture his time and place in new forms, became a model and inspiration for younger poets who wished to push beyond the classical modernist aesthetic.

GEORGE OPPEN. Sincerity certainly marks as well the life and work of George Oppen (1908–84), who along with Zukofsky has emerged as a central figure in the objectivist group. Oppen was born in New Rochelle, New York, moved to California when he was ten, and began his college studies at the University of Oregon. With the exception of a young literature instructor who gave him a copy of Conrad Aiken's anthology of modern verse, Oppen found college life unrewarding. He did, however, meet Mary Colby, his future wife and lifelong companion, who also wanted a more stimulating and open life than that offered at the university. After one semester, the two dropped out of college and hitchhiked across the country to New York City in search of the world of art and poetry. Oppen, rummaging through the offerings of a New York bookstore, came across a copy of *Exile* in which Zukofsky's "Poem, Beginning The" appeared. Later at a party he was introduced to Zukofsky and identified as the single reader of Zukofsky's poem. After a brief stay in New York, the Oppens travelled to Paris and started their To Publishers Press, which later became the Objectivist Press, with Zukofsky as editor and the Oppens as printers. Oppen published his first volume, *Discrete Series* (1934), with the press and in this slim book revealed his kinship with those who viewed the poem as an autonomous structure and object. In "Drawing," the last poem in the series, he writes:

> Written structure,
> Shape of art,
> More formal
> Than a field would be
> (existing in it)—.[25]

Objectivism, Oppen declares from the start, was about "the necessity for forming a poem properly, for achieving form."[26]

The volume as originally published presents each poem on a separate page, thereby emphasizing its autonomy and separateness even though it is part of a series. As Oppen reveals, "Not by growth / But the / Paper, turned, contains / This entire volume" (14). As in viewing a painting, we are dealing with the materials that make up an art object—a page on which words are placed to create a visual, aural, and mental construct. The series, as Oppen explains, is an attempt to capture in "imagist statements" the world about him and his relationship to it. "A discrete series [he tells us] is a series of terms each of which is empirically true. . . . I was attempting to construct a meaning by empirical statements, by imagist statements."[27]

The result is a series of cinematic fragments, capturing the images, feelings, and thoughts of the poet experiencing New York City. The volume begins with a typical Jamesian-like poem that contains one convoluted sentence in which Maude Blessingbourne, a character from a James short story, is reported to wish " 'to see / what really was going on,' " the boredom" . . . Of the world, weather-swept, with which / one shares the century" (3). The series then breaks from this Jamesian world and plunges us into the twentieth century, where we are confronted with the mechanistic nature of the modern urban world of New York City. The line moves quicker; it is terse and fragmented as it records the movement of elevators, refrigerators, cars, "20th century chic" boats, steam shovels, electric street cars, and tugboats. Most dominant is the car. "Nothing [Oppen claims] can equal in polish and obscured / origin that dark instrument / A car" (4). But the car darkens, obscures, and encloses its human inhabitants in a world of "false light." It and the other technological inventions separate us from reality. This, Oppen empirically claims through his images, is "What really was going on."

For the inhabitants of the modern world, there is little true light. Humans are "incapable of contact / Save in incidents" (8), and the "city ladies" whose "breasts / Pertain to lingerie" are told, "The fields are road-sides, / Rooms outlast you" (12–13). There is economic poverty as well as spiritual poverty: "By the elevated posts / And the movie sign. / A man sells post-cards" (13). Beneath the latest technological advance and the glitter of Hollywood illusions stands the impoverished man of the depression as ignored and separate, as in Zukofsky's "Mantis."

But Oppen juxtaposes his love and admiration for Mary and physical existence to the emptiness of the unreal world. "Your body in the sun. / You? A solid . . . your elbow on a car-edge / Incognito as summer / Among mechanics." (12). Mary or women seem to represent the real, the living, in a world of inanimate things. She is, Oppen exclaims, the "Plant, I breathe—" (9).

After *Discrete Series*, Oppen stopped writing poetry for twenty-five years. As he encountered the reality of the Great Depression and the absence of economic justice, he concluded he could no longer ignore the need for social action. He and Mary joined the Communist party and engaged in protest demonstrations, helped organize the unemployed and the homeless of New York City, and pressed for legislation to provide food and shelter for the needy. When the war broke out, Oppen enlisted to "fight the fascists"; but shortly after his return, the Oppens began to experience the reactionary policies of McCarthyism. The FBI began to harass them, and when it became clear that George would spend at least a year in jail for not cooperating with his interrogators, they fled to Mexico, where they lived for eight years (1950–58). At the end of this period of exile, Oppen again began to write.

In explaining this decision, Oppen cited not only the call for social action but also his belief that the poem could not and should not, as Marxist ideology claimed, become a weapon for social change. While poetry seemed to be a luxury one could not afford in the midst of a depression, one should not pretend, Oppen felt, that left-wing poetry was either art or effective social action. He was also aware that his experiences up to this point had not prepared him for the world he was facing and attempting to capture empirically in his verse. He recalls:

I gave up poetry because of the pressures of what for the moment I'll call conscience. But there were things I had to live through, some things I had to try out and it was more than politics, really; it was the whole experience of working in factories, of having a child and so on. . . . Hugh Kenner [correctly said] . . . "In brief, it took twenty-five years to write the next poem."[28]

In that poem, "Blood from the Stone," Oppen begins his renewed quest to realize the true nature of his and our existence as humans. We are given our time, our "Blood from a stone, life / From a stone dead dam, "The Planet's / Time" (33). And it is from this time we must define existence. If that time includes the 1930s and the depression, when one could see "A spectre / In every street," (31) or World War II, where one learned "To a body anything can happen, / Like a brick" (32), then it is from these experiences and not from some preconceived abstraction that one has to reach his vision of existence. Oppen is existential in this regard and insists throughout the rest of his work that we look at reality in all its complexity, its beauty and its horrors, and are true to that reality in both our reactions to and representations of it. Poetry thus becomes what Oppen calls a "test of truth," a "test of sincerity," "that moment, an actual time, when you believe something to be true, and you construct a meaning from those moments of conviction."[29] It begins with the "little hole in the eye," as Williams called it, which has "exposed us naked / To the world / And will not close." (81). The poet, as Zukofsky indicates, then is "interested in living with things as they exist"[30] or, as Oppen insists, being clear about one's existence.

In the next twenty years of his life (1958–78), Oppen published (beginning with *Materials* in 1962 and concluding with *Primitive* in 1978 six additional volumes of poetry and two *Collected Poems* (1973, 1975) in which he recorded his quest for clarity. He recognized the difficulty of this task, for the world often seemed impenetrable and words incapable of conveying his experiences. In "Of Being Numerous" (1968), his most admired work, he tells us he seeks "Clarity / In the sense of *transparence*, / I don't mean that much can be explained." (162). And in "Route," which appears in the same volume, he joyfully exclaims that "Clarity, clarity, surely clarity is the most beautiful / thing in the world," but he tempers his joy by reminding us that we are encountering "A limited, limiting clarity" (185). And although Oppen "never did have any motive of poetry / But to achieve clarity" (185), he is quick to recognize that the poet's materials, his words "cannot be wholly transparent. And that is the / 'heartlessness' of words." (186).

Although the mind and words cannot always penetrate and record reality, it is this world, in this air, this "bare sunlight where must be found / The lyric valuables" (29), for as Oppen quotes from Jacques Maritain, a modern theologian and philosopher, "We awake in the same moment to ourselves and to things" (16). Numerous Oppen poems and passages depict the sordidness rather than the "lyric valuables" of existence. In "The Source," he realized, "If the city has roots, they are in filth. / It is a slum. Even the sidewalk / Rasps under the feet." But within this world of "black brick / Tenement, a woman's body / Glows." (55). At times, Oppen achieves a sense of awe when witnessing the beauty of existence. In "Psalm," he presents an idyllic image of the "natural world." Here, "In the small beauty of the forest," are the wild deer:

> Their eyes
> Effortless, the soft lips
> Nuzzle and the alien small teeth
> Tear at the grass.
>
> (78)

Oppen focuses on the smallness of the scene, the smallness of his words, his nouns, his subjects, this small scene that provides inspiration and faith:

> The small nouns
> Crying faith
> In this in which the wild deer
> Startle, and stare out.
>
> (78)

Although these moments of "awe," as Oppen calls them, may

be temporary, for the deer do startle at the end of the poem, it is, to echo the title of this volume and the penultimate line of this poem, "this is which" we gain our "faith" that there is more to existence than the "fatal rock." Life is more, Oppen senses at moments such as this, than "The image of the engine / That stops. / We cannot live on that." (19).

The balance between alienation and belonging is always precarious in Oppen, especially in the modern, urban world. It is in the more natural world, where craftsmanship and community still seem in place, that Oppen feels most comfortable. In the woods and islands of Maine, where the Oppens spent their summers, they discovered a sense of connection to a real rather than glassed-in world. Here they see beauty and strength in the New England boats that skillfully cut through the ocean waves. Here "the carpenter's is a culture / Of fitting, of firm dimensions, / Of post and lintel." (41). And here they find people who practice the virtues of simplicity and faith. Boating to an island with a lobsterman and his wife, Oppen describes the "wife in the front seat / In a soft dress / Such as poor women wear" who expresses her belief in the spiritual nature of humanity:

> She took it that we came—
> I don't know how to say, she said—
>
> Not for anything we did, she said,
> Mildly, "from God". She said
>
> (202)

It is this type of island, not Crusoe's solitary island but one with "a public quality," that Oppen relishes: "What I like more than anything / Is to visit other islands . . ." (202). As with the small beauty of the forest, it is in these small and occasional moments in life that one senses meaning, unity, and value in life. Because Oppen encloses such moments within a very dark time frame, we sense his joy and awe more intensely, but always a sense of ambiguity remains. As Rachel Blau DuPlessis indicates, "These contradictions simply continue unresolved."[31]

Paradoxically, to be clear is to be contradictory, for that is the nature of existence. Although Oppen often found existence impenetrable, baffling, and discouraging, its complexity and ambiguity were arresting and a challenge to both the validity of his perceptions and the rightness of his poetic language and form. The last word in "Of Being Numerous" and "A Language of New York" perhaps best sums up Oppen's view of the mysteries of existence. The word, borrowed playfully from Whitman, is *curious*. Out of this curiosity came a canon that continues to grow in stature and along with Zukofsky's work ensures a lasting audience for objectivist poetry.

CARL RAKOSI. Like Reznikoff, Carl Rakosi (b. 1903) insists on being true to both the external world and his reaction to it. While he wishes to keep "objects as intact as possible, to keep their integrity intact, so there is this element of an adherence to the integrity of the object that makes it different from mere description," he also recognizes that what the poet "is experiencing in their [the objects] presence" is also central. Thus "the integrity of both the subject and the object" should be kept.[32] This adherence to the principles of sincerity and objectivism attracted Rakosi to the objectivist mode of poetry.

Although a midwesterner (he was raised in Kenosha, Wisconsin, after immigrating to the country with his Hungarian Jewish parents in 1910), Rakosi managed to establish contact with Zukofsky and became a contributor to the *Objectivists' Anthology*. He continued to write through most of the 1930s and published a collection, *Selected Poems*, in 1941. However, like Oppen, the social realities of the depression and his work as a social worker during this period convinced him that it was time to abandon poetry. In reviewing this decision, he concluded that "any young person with any integrity or intelligence had to become associated with some left-wing organization." Once he adopted the Marxist belief that literature was a weapon for "social change, for expressing the needs and desires of large masses of people" and concluded that he was not capable of writing in that mode, he stopped writing poetry for some twenty-odd years.[33] This conflict between the muse and social action is expressed in Rakosi's "And what were the poets doing then?":

> I have come to care
> for only laborers
> and poor people

and to feel ashamed
of poetry,
        sitting like Chopin
on its exquisite ass.[34]

So Rakoski joined the "unemployed, / against injustice" and remained silent until a young Englishman wrote to him in the early 1960s to tell him that he admired his poems and wanted to know if there were any more poems than the ones in his self-constructed bibliography. Excited by the fact that a new generation of readers might be interested in his work, Rakosi returned to poetry. In 1967 he published *Amulet,* his second volume of verse; he continued to write and publish and edited his *Collected Poems* in 1986. His determination to deal with the external world remains strong throughout his work. "I mean [he declares] to penetrate the particular / the way an owl waits / for a kangaroo rat" (204). In "The Vow" he promises: "Matter, / with this look / I wed thee / and become thy very attribute." (222) Of the objectivists, Rakosi is the most earthy and comical. He consistently lashes out against literary pretense, such as Pound's "personal need for supremacy, grandiosity," and Pound's need to become the epic poet.[35] And in "A Word With Conscience" he mockingly attacks his or any other poet's use of lofty and ethereal language: "Honest men / don't talk like that." (28)

Initially attracted to the artistic language of Stevens, Rakosi adopted a colloquial mode of diction and, in addition, adopted for his subjects many of the old, poor, and ignored people he had encountered as a social worker. He presents this portrait of a lonely old man:

> Like slag
>   the face,
> old,
> one who knows he has been banished,
> knows his place,
> expects no sympathy or interest.
>
>   (171)

But when the elderly man catches Rakosi's sympathetic look, they exchange smiles—silent recognition on the old man's part that Rakosi is "one of us!" (171)

In addition to his "peopled" poetry, Rakosi's collected poems deal with such commonplace objects as an avocado pit or a lobster, as well as the formal elements of poetry and U.S. history. His vision remains contemporary and includes such topics as the Vietnam War and rock, country, and punk music. Regardless of the topic, Rakosi is always sensitive to the arrangement of words and lines, the creation of rhythms, the desire to communicate, and the joys of wit. For these reasons, he continues to find new audiences.

LORINE NIEDECKER. Since her death Lorine Niedecker (1903–70) has also found a growing and highly appreciative audience. Although she is not directly associated with the objectivists, she has gladly acknowledged her debt to Louis Zukofsky, who introduced her to the principles and poetry of objectivism in the 1931 *Poetry* magazine issue and who later in his correspondence with Niedecker helped her achieve her own voice and style. It was Zukofsky, for example, who urged her to tighten her line and to condense her language, omitting punctuation when it was unnecessary, and it was Zukofsky who suggested that the poem begins in detail and then engages the poet's mind and feelings.[36] Like Zukofsky, she was totally committed to poetry. In her "Poet's Work" she tells us that her grandfather insisted that she learn a trade; so she "learned / to sit at desk / and condense / No layoff / from this / condensery" (141). Over the years, Niedecker faced many obstacles in establishing herself as a poet. Like Emily Dickinson, she traveled little, spending most of her life on Black Hawk Island, near Fort Atkinson, Wisconsin. When her mother lost her hearing, she was forced to leave Beloit College and help with the family chores. She had a short, unsuccessful marriage and later supported herself as a guide writer for the Works Project Administration, then as a radio scriptwriter, a proofreader for a local dairy publication, a landlord, and a cleaning woman. She was never interested in becoming comfortable; in fact, she lived a good portion of her life in a one-and-a-half-room cabin on Black Hawk Island. Poetry was her love, and she never lost sight of her true desire. In describing her job as a proofreader at the dairy association, she tells us, "I was Blondie, / I carried my bundles of hog feeder price lists / by Larry the Lug." Then after explaining she

"never got anywhere" because she never had "pull, favor, drag,"
(54), she wonders:

> What would they say if they knew
> I sit for two months on six lines
> of poetry?
>
> (55)

To Niedecker, as with Thoreau whom she admired, "Property
is poverty" (130), and she was content to live a simple life devoted
to her art. In her "Condensary," Niedecker, however, reveals she
was not isolated from life. Her work frequently alludes to historical
figures and events and is conscious of contemporary social events.
For example, in her early poem "Mother Geese," we find a strange
blend of surrealism and social realism as she comments on dis-
placed depression farmers in the language and rhythms of nursery
rhyme:

> The land of four o'clocks is here
> the five of us together
>   looking for our supper.
> Half past endive, quarter to beets,
> seven milks, ten cents cheese,
>   lost, our land, forever.
>
> (7)

Or she adopts the rhythms and language of the townsfolk to
attack a conservative stockowner who helps break unions:

> We know him—Law and Order League—
> fishing from our dock,
> testified against the pickets
> at the plant—owns stock.
>
> (28)

Because she observed and had experienced since childhood the
drudgery of a domestic woman's life, she includes numerous sharp
and cutting images of that life. As a child she remembers her
mother commanding, "Wash the floors, Lorine!— / wash clothes! /
Weed!" (81), and vividly captures the terrifying moment when

she, her mother, or any other woman finally assesses a life of chores and denial:

> I'm pillowed and padded, pale and puffing
> lifting household stuffing—
> carpets, dishes
> benches, fishes
> I've spent my life in nothing.
>
> (82)

Social and material rewards are always suspect in Niedecker's world. When she married for the second time in the early 1960s, she said she wanted "in the world's black night / . . . warmth / . . . At the close— / someone." Yet by the end of the poem, she concludes, "I married / and lived unburied. / I thought—" (176). It is the world of nature and poetry that Niedecker feels closest to. Again one thinks of Dickinson when reading such condensed and intimate songs to nature as this:

> My friend tree
> I sawed you down
> but I must attend
> an older friend
> the sun
>
> (20)

Niedecker realizes that there is another side to nature—that one could not always see the river, the air, and the soil as friends or close relatives. There was "another country," the wilderness, "the man" she calls it; this wilderness is the "prickly pear," "the violent storm," and "the torrent to raise the river / to float the wounded doe" (201). However, this destructive masculine, untamed side of nature is not the major motif in Niedecker's score. She seems most content within the natural world or sitting "in my own house / secure," watching the winter thawing of the river "thru window glass." watching the "Ice cakes / glide downstream / the wild swans / of our day" (91).

Despite the efforts of such poets as Zukofsky, Basil Bunting, Cid Corman, and Jonathan Williams, who praised and publicized her work, Niedecker remained an obscure figure most of her life. She was first published in literary magazines and by New Directions in the 1930s; issued her first volume of poems, *New Goose,* in 1946, which she kept a secret from her neighbors; published in Corman's *Origin Magazine* in the 1950s; and issued a second volume of poetry in 1961, *My Friend Tree.* It was only toward the end of her life that recognition and publication increased. One additional volume, *North Central* (1968), and two collections, *TCG* (1969) and *My Life by Water* (1970), appeared before her death; since then previously unpublished and new selected poems have appeared. Finally, *From this Condensary: The Complete Writings* (1985) was published; the collection contains, in addition to her previous volumes, three unpublished volumes of poetry, five plays written for radio, and three critical essays. The collection also illustrates Niedecker's constant revision of her earlier work. It is a canon that is and will continue to attract new readers. Again the comparison to Dickinson seems apt. As Robert Bertholf concludes in his Introduction, "Like Emily Dickinson, her only likely antecedent, she chose her way of life in order to fulfill her poetry" (xxvi, xxvii).

Niedecker and the objectivist poets chose an aesthetic and a life-style that carried them out of the mainstream of American poetry. Rather than codifying and institutionalizing modern poetry, they chose to continue to make it new. Their work was and remains obscure to most readers. However, the objectivist current of poetry, barely a ripple until the mid-1950s, would join forces with a renewed interest in Williams and the romantic mode of poetry and help form a new direction for contemporary American poetry.

· Notes and References ·

Chapter One

1. The "J" in the numbering system of Emily Dickinson's poems refers to Thomas H. Johnson, the editor and critic who attempted to bring order out of the chaotic state of her manuscripts in his landmark variorum edition, *The Poems of Emily Dickinson*, 3 vols. (Cambridge: Belknap Press of Harvard University Press, 1955). Johnson and his associate, Theodora Ward, were not unerring in their chronological placement of the poems, partly because their access to some of the manuscripts was restricted, but there is no Dickinson scholar who is not in their debt. A fascinating, if at times necessarily technical, account of the complex history and process of editing and ordering Dickinson's poems is R. W. Franklin, *The Editing of Emily Dickinson: A Reconsideration* (Madison: University of Wisconsin Press, 1967). A brief outline of the editing history appears in note 4 below.

2. As Albert J. Gelpi does in *Emily Dickinson: The Mind of the Poet* (Cambridge: Harvard University Press, 1966), 39–45.

3. According to Thomas H. Johnson's note in *Poems of Emily Dickinson*, 255, this poem was the fifth of only seven known to have been published during the poet's lifetime; with one minor variation, it appeared unsigned in the New York weekly *Round Table* of 12 March 1864 under the title "My Sabbath" (which may or may not have been of her choosing). Although most of Dickinson's poems were untitled and so are named by their first lines, she did often give titles to those that she sent to friends.

4. In the 1955 edition, the last line, reflecting the original manuscript, reads "From Manzanilla come!" The poem was another of the small handful of published poems; it appeared anonymously in the "Original Poetry" column of the *Springfield Daily Republican*, 4 May 1861, with the title "The May-Wine," and reflects the difficulty in determining a final form for many of Dickinson's poems. Apparently someone at the *Republican* altered three lines from her original manuscript to regularize the form. The last line in that version became "Come staggering toward the sun." In her own copying of the original for one of the fascicles (packets) in which she bound many of her poems, Dickinson changed the line to "Leaning against the—Sun—"; Mabel Loomis Todd and T. W. Higginson used that version in their editing of *The Poems of Emily Dickinson* (Boston: Roberts Brothers, 1890). Editorial difficulties have been compounded by

the enormous number of extant poems (close to 1,800); by the disarray in which Dickinson left her manuscripts; by the fact that they were in the possession of several different people; by the involvement of some of those people in a feud (with sister Lavinia and friend Mabel Loomis Todd, who had had an affair with Dickinson's brother Austin, on one side and Susan Gilbert Dickinson, Austin's wife and Emily's sometime confidante, on the other); and a number of editions published by well-meaning people including T. W, Higginson, Mabel Loomis Todd, Martha Dickinson Bianchi, Alfred Leete Hampson, and Millicent Todd Bingham, between Dickinson's death and Johnson's scholarly edition of 1955. Since Thomas H. Johnson's 1955 variorum edition, the most important event in the editing of Dickinson's poems has been the restoration of the fascicles and the addition of some unpublished poems by R. W. Franklin, ed., *The Manuscript Books of Emily Dickinson*, 2 vols. (Cambridge and London: Belknap Press of Harvard University Press, 1981). The work is a facsimile edition.

5. Both the comment to Abiah Root and the quote from J 1617 are in Gelpi, *Emily Dickinson: The Mind of the Poet*, 41, in his discussion of the Byronic quality of her poetry. As Gelpi points out, Lord Byron's influence on her is certain; there were sets of Byron in the library of the Dickinson home, and she alluded to his "genius" in a number of her letters. See Thomas H. Johnson and Theodora Ward, eds., *The Letters of Emily Dickinson*, 3 vols. (Cambridge: Harvard University Press, 1958), particularly 2: 369, 374, 393, 433; 3:903.

6. Stephen Crane, *War Is Kind* (New York: F. A. Stokes Co., 1899).

7. The lines from Melville and from Dickinson, J 1251, are both quoted by Gelpi, *Emily Dickinson: The Mind of the Poet*, 38.

8. Quoted in ibid., 40.

9. For example, John Cody, *After Great Pain: The Inner Life of Emily Dickinson* (Cambridge: Belknap Press of Harvard University Press, 1971), and Clark Griffith, *The Long Shadow: Emily Dickinson's Tragic Poetry* (Princeton: Princeton University Press, 1964).

10. Jay Leyda, *The Years and Hours of Emily Dickinson* (New Haven: Yale University Press, 1960), 2:179, 203. Quoted by Gelpi, *Emily Dickinson: The Mind of the Poet*, 7. The Amherst College history referred to is W. S. Tyler's *History of Amherst College during Its First Half Century, 1821–1871*. The "pillar" that the history referred to seems to have secretly stood on shaky legal or ethical ground. Barton Levi St. Armand, *Emily Dickinson and Her Culture: The Soul's Society* (Cambridge: Cambridge University Press, 1984), 307–10, presents a strong case for Edward Dickinson's misuse of considerable funds from the estate of his brother-in-law Mark Newman between 1852, when Newman died, and Dickinson's own death in 1874. Dickinson's private accounting shows him to have been much more interested in his own welfare than that of Newman's children, for whom,

as trustee of the estate, he was responsible. The effect of Dickinson's shady manipulation on his own demeanor makes for interesting speculation.

11. Both short quotations on the death of Dickinson's mother are from *The Letters of Emily Dickinson*, 3:752, 754–55, quoted by Richard B. Sewall, *The Life of Emily Dickinson* (New York: Farrar, Straus and Giroux, 1974), 1:89. Sewall also quotes from a letter that Dickinson wrote to Mrs. Holland pointing out eloquently that "Blow has followed blow, till the wandering terror of the Mind clutches what is left" (88). The death of her father in 1874 had not ceased to trouble her, and closer to her mother's death, two other men with whom she felt a spiritual intimacy had died—Samuel Bowles in 1878 and Charles Wadsworth in 1882.

12. Quoted by Sewall, *The Life of Emily Dickinson*, 2:90 from Millicent Todd Bingham, *Emily Dickinson's Home* (New York: Harper & Brothers, 1955), 414.

13. Credited by Griffith, *Long Shadow*, 178ff, but not by Sewall, *The Life of Emily Dickinson*, 1:65.

14. *The Letters of Emily Dickinson*, 1:94, quoted by Sewall, *The Life of Emily Dickinson*, 1:66.

15. Millicent Todd Bingham, *Emily Dickinson's Home*, 112, cited by Sewall, *The Life of Emily Dickinson*, 1:62.

16. Quoted by Gelpi, *Emily Dickinson: The Mind of the Poet*, 18, from *The Letters of Emily Dickinson*, 1:121. In the same place, Gelpi quotes the reference to Cromwell from the same volume of *Letters*, 470.

17. Leyda, *Years and Hours*, 2:83.

18. Ibid., 227.

19. Ibid., 288.

20. Ibid., 231–32.

21. Ibid., 1:136, quoted by Gelpi, *Emily Dickinson: The Mind of the Poet*, 32.

22. Gelpi, *Emily Dickinson: The Mind of the Poet*, 48, from *The Letters of Emily Dickinson*, 3:837, 2:502–3.

23. Her whistling in the dark through her fear of death is implied in her imagining her own death and/or funeral in many of her poems, for example, J 146, J 445, J 449, J 465, J 712, and J 1037; noted also by Gelpi, *Emily Dickinson: The Mind of the Poet*, 185.

24. Leyda, *Years and Hours*, 1:321.

25. Ibid., 2:227; quoted also by Gelpi, *Emily Dickinson: The Mind of the Poet*, 51. The quotation is taken from the account of Martha Dickinson Bianchi, *The Life and Letters of Emily Dickinson* (Boston: Houghton Mifflin, 1924).

26. Gelpi, *Emily Dickinson: The Mind of the Poet*, 51.

27. Ibid.

28. Leyda, *Years and Hours*, 2:109.

29. See Richard Wilbur's perceptive essay "Sumptuous Destitution" in Richard Wilbur, Louise Bogan, and Archibald MacLeish, *Emily Dickinson: Three Views* (Amherst: Amherst College Press, 1960), reprinted in Richard B. Sewall, ed., *Emily Dickinson: A Collection of Critical Essays* (Englewood Cliffs, N.J.: Prentice-Hall, 1963), 127–36.

30. William H. Shurr, *The Marriage of Emily Dickinson* (Lexington: University of Kentucky Press, 1983). The discussion and meaning of the fascicles that follows is based almost entirely on Shurr, to whom Dickinson criticism after 1983 must be greatly indebted. The present treatment can be little more than a precis and is no substitute for reading Shurr's persuasive argument.

31. See, for example, Donald E. Thackrey, "The Communication of the Word," in Sewall, *Emily Dickinson: A Collection*, 51–69, reprinted from his *Emily Dickinson's Approach to Poetry* (Lincoln: University of Nebraska Press, 1954).

32. See, for example, George F. Whicher, "American Humor," in ibid., reprinted from his *This Was a Poet* (New York: Charles Scribner's Sons, 1938).

33. Quoted by Shurr, *Marriage*, 124 (hereafter cited parenthetically in the text).

34. As Ruth Miller recognized as early as her *The Poetry of Emily Dickinson* (Middletown, Conn.: Wesleyan University Press, 1968), 248, quoted by Shurr, *Marriage*, p. 3. Working with a set of as yet defectively reassembled fascicles, Miller thought that she found a pattern in them that tended to work from yearning to some acceptance or determination.

35. R. W. Franklin, "The Emily Dickinson Fascicles," *Studies in Bibliography* 36 (1983): 17, quoted by Shurr, *Marriage*. Franklin believed that the fascicles, which he had now reconstructed accurately, were just a roughly chronological collection of poems to which Dickinson felt a particular attachment. Fascicle lists, Emily Dickinson's original arrangement of the poems in the bound booklets, listed now by Johnson numbers, are to be found in both Franklin's *Manuscript Books* and Shurr's *Marriage*, 199–209.

36. Shurr, *Marriage*, 7.

37. Ibid., 134–36.

38. Richard Wilbur "Sumptuous Destitution," in Sewall, *Emily Dickinson: A Collection of Critical Essays*, 293–94, also notes her seemingly perverse choice of Higginson, who never really comprehended Emily Dickinson or her work.

39. Leyda, *Years and Hours*, 352–53.

40. Dickinson, *Letters*, 2:374.

41. Shurr, *Marriage*, 41.

42. Ibid., 170–88, discusses "The Pregnancy Sequence" of her fascicle poems at length, in detail, and persuasively, as so touchy a subject requires.

Because a few discreet tiles of a mosaic cannot reveal the pattern and there is insufficient space to examine all the poems that constitute the design here, there is no point in trying to summarize the evidence of a few poems, but Shurr examines them all. The sexuality in Dickinson's poems can always be read as a metaphor for something else, primarily for her relationship to God. But sexuality is strongly revealed by a reading of the fascicle poems. Furthermore, it is difficult to evade the intimation of a pregnancy or its tragic aftermath in such poems as J 217 ("Father— I bring thee—not Myself—/ That were the little load—/ I bring thee the departed Heart / I had not strength to hold—") or J 491 ("While it and I lap one Air / Dwell in one Blood / Under one Sacrament / Show me Division can split or pare—").

43. Ibid., p. 196.

Chapter Two

1. Roy Harvey Pearce, *The Continuity of American Poetry* (Princeton: Princeton University Press, 1961), 253.

2. Eugene Field, *Second Birth of Verse* (New York: Scribner, 1893), 164.

3. Robert H. Walker, *The Poet and the Gilded Age: Social Themes in Late 19th Century American Verse* (Philadelphia: University of Pennsylvania Press, 1963), 36. Frederick Jackson Turner's view of the frontier is best encountered in his essay "The Significance of the Frontier in American History," in *The Early Writings of Frederick Jackson Turner, with a List of All His Works Compiled by Everett E. Edwards and an Introduction by Fulmer Mood* (Madison: University of Wisconsin Press, 1938).

4. A similar list is provided by Richard Crowder, "The Emergence of E. A. Robinson," *South Atlantic Quarterly* 45 (1946): 89, quoted and slightly expanded by Pearce, *Continuity of American Poetry*, p. 255. Donald M. Stauffer, *A Short History of American Poetry* (New York: E. P. Dutton, 1974), 194–220 reasonably calls the group "the Poets of the Twilight Years." He quotes Barrett Wendell, *A Literary History of America* (New York: Scribner's, 1900), who observed, "It is hard to resist the conclusion that whoever shall make a new library of American literature, thirty or forty years hence, will . . . find no place for many of our contemporaries momentarily preserved by our latest anthologists."

5. Lizette Woodward Reese, *The Selected Poems* (New York: George H. Doran Co., 1926), 17 (subsequent references to Reese's poems are from this volume and cited parenthetically in the text).

6. Noted, too, by Jean Wagner, *Black Poets of the United States from Paul Laurence Dunbar to Langston Hughes* (Urbana: University of Illinois Press, 1973), 91.

7. His poetry bears an even more marked resemblance to that of the French symbolists. If, as Stauffer, *Short History of American Poetry*, 217, points out, Crane was unacquainted with them, the resemblance is accidental. Daniel G. Hoffman, *The Poetry of Stephen Crane* (New York: Columbia University Press, 1951), 30–33, holds that the absence of French influence has not been proved but is probable, arguing that Crane's "intransigent sensibility" and "exposure to certain American influences pointing toward anti-heroic statement, ironic paradox, and a style purposely contrary to established models" would explain "the parallels" in his work" to the French poets' attitudes and technical resources." (Interestingly, those influences were at work in the poetry of Emily Dickinson). Hoffman's study is still the best on Crane's poetry, and the present discussion is, inevitably, based on it.

8. From John D. Barry, "A Note on Stephen Crane," *Bookman* 13 (April 1901): 448.

9. All quotations from Crane's poems are from Joseph Katz, *The Poems of Stephen Crane: A Critical Edition by Joseph Katz* (New York: Cooper Square Publishers, 1966). Like Emily Dickinson, Crane did not title his verses. They are identified here by first lines and, in parentheses, the abbreviated volume title (*BR* for *Black Riders* and *WIK* for *War Is Kind*) and the numbers that he gave them in both volumes.

10. Noted by Joseph Katz, "Introductions," *The Complete Poems of Stephen Crane* (Ithaca: Cornell University Press, 1966), note 50, xxxii–iii. As an example, Katz shows the correspondence between pp. 141–42 of *Maggie* (1893) and poem 57 of *Black Riders*.

11. Hoffman, *Poetry of Stephen Crane*, 278–79.

Chapter Three

1. This discussion owes a debt to Wallace L. Anderson, *Edwin Arlington Robinson: A Critical Introduction* (Cambridge: Harvard University Press, 1968), still perhaps the best overall view of Robinson.

2. "Luke Havergal" is, in fact, so interpreted by Ellsworth Barnard, *Edwin Arlington Robinson: A Critical Study* (New York: Macmillan, 1952), 38–39.

3. Louise Bogan, *Achievement in American Poetry* (Chicago: Henry Regnery Co., 1951, reprinted in Gateway ed., 1962), 17.

4. Quoted by Anderson, *Edwin Arlington Robinson*, 89.

5. Ibid., 92.

6. Ibid., 140.

7. Frost's magnanimity toward Robinson was typical of his treatment of students but not of other writers. The examples of less than magnanimous treatment of perceived rivals are manifold; for instance, according to Lawrance Thompson and R. H. Winnick, *Robert Frost: The Later Years*,

Notes and References

1938–63 (New York: Holt, Rinehart and Winston, 1976), 8–9, Frost deliberately distracted the audience at a poetry reading by Archibald MacLeish at a Bread Loaf conference of 1938 by rustling papers and pointing out in a stage whisper that "Archie's poems all have the same tune." As MacLeish approached the climax of his performance, the reading of the popular "You, Andrew Marvell," Frost reached his; at the back of the hall, Frost set fire to the papers and made a display of extinguishing the flames and dispelling the smoke.

8. Quoted by Louis Untemeyer, ed., *The Letters of Robert Frost to Louis Untemeyer* (New York: Holt, Rinehart and Winston, 1963), 387.

9. Lionel Trilling, "A Speech on Robert Frost: A Cultural Episode," *Partisan Review* 26 (Summer 1959): 445–52.

10. Ibid. Trilling gets the expression from Frost's biographer, Lawrance Thompson.

11. Robert Frost, "On Emerson," in *Selected Prose of Robert Frost*, ed. Hyde Cox and Edward Connery Lathem (New York: Collier Books, 1968), 118–19.

12. Lawrance Thompson, *Robert Frost: The Years of Triumph, 1915–1938* (New York: Holt, Rinehart and Winston, 1970), 495–96. It should be pointed out that much of the sense of Frost's character flaws that is pervasive in Frost biography and criticism is based on Thompson's view in his works on Frost. There is a more favorable revisionist perception of Frost in such studies as Stanley Burnshaw, *Robert Frost Himself* (New York: George Braziller, 1986). Burnshaw compares Thompson's misrepresentations of Frost to Rufus Griswold's calumnies against Edgar Allan Poe, and he has some success in arguing that Frost, while a difficult person, was far from the monster of Thompson's portrayal.

13. Ibid., 493–94. There were many reasons for Frost's self-blame. Lesley, for example, told Lawrance Thompson of a night when, as a little girl, she was awakened by her father who inexplicably demanded that she choose which parent he should shoot. He was holding a revolver. *Robert Frost: The Early Years, 1874–1915* (New York: Holt, Rinehart and Winston, 1966), pp. 308–9.

14. Thompson and Winnick, *Robert Frost: The Later Years, 1938–1963*, 6. Frost wrote one of his loveliest sonnets, "The Silken Tent" (originally "In Praise of Your Poise"), to convey his feelings to Kay Morrison, as Thompson and Winnick point out, 23–24.

15. Thompson, *Robert Frost: Years of Triumph*, 500, 505, 700–703. Frost's relevant comment on vengeance in the next paragraph is from Thompson, *Robert Frost: The Early Years*, 264.

16. Reprinted in *Selected Prose of Robert Frost*, 17–20. The following quotation appears on 19.

17. Ibid., 23–29.

18. Lawrance Thompson, *Robert Frost: The Early Years, 1874–1915* (New York: Holt, Rinehart and Winston, 1966), reports the incident, 173–89.

19. Robert Frost, *Complete Poems of Robert Frost* (New York: Holt, Rinehart and Winston, 1964), 13 (hereafter cited parenthetically in the text as *CP*).

20. Thompson, *Robert Frost: The Early Years,* 318.

21. Ibid., 597–98. Thompson states that Frost frequently asserted that the poem sprang from the marital difficulties of an Epping, New Hampshire, couple after the death of their child in 1895, but the Frosts' tragedy and relationship unmistakably undergirds the poem as well. Just as the wife in "Home Burial" says, "But the world's evil," so, according to Frost, did Elinor keep saying, following Elliott's death, "The world's evil." Furthermore, Frost told Thompson that he always had to omit "Home Burial" from his public readings because the poem was "too sad" for him to read to an audience.

22. Edward Connery Lathem, ed., *Interviews with Robert Frost* (New York: Holt, Rinehart and Winston, 1966), 49, quoted by Dorothy Judd Hall, *Robert Frost: Contours of Belief* (Athens: Ohio University Press 1984), 77. Hall deals incisively with Frost's Swedenborgianism, spiritual relationship to Emerson, and religious dimension.

23. Frost knew Pound, Eliot, and many of the other twentieth-century experimenters in poetry and their work, and, in his search for the place of the human being in the capricious cosmos, he sounds much like them in attitude. Technically, however, he was far more orthodox, offering the famous remark, for example, that writing poetry without rhyme is like playing tennis without a net. With the modernity of his vision on the one hand and the conservatism of his technique on the other, he embodies that epithet "transitional poet" probably more certainly than any other American poet of his time.

24. Quoted by Hyatt Waggoner, *American Poets from the Puritans to the Present* (New York: Dell Publishing Co., 1968), 458.

25. Noted, too, by Donald Barlow Stauffer, *A Short History of American Poetry* (New York: E. P. Dutton & Co., 1974), 285–86.

26. Alain Locke, "The New Negro," in Alain Locke, ed., *The New Negro: An Interpretation* (New York: Albert and Charles Boni, 1925).

27. *The New Caravan,* ed. Alfred Kreymborg, Lewis Mumford, and Paul Rosenfeld (New York: Norton, 1936), 633–54.

28. W. E. B. Du Bois, "On Our Bookshelf," *Crisis* 31 (1926): 239.

29. James Weldon Johnson, ed., *The Book of American Negro Poetry,* rev. ed. (New York: Harcourt, Brace, 1931), 220.

Chapter Four

1. David Perkins, *A History of Modern Poetry* (Cambridge: Harvard University Press, 1976), p. 293.

2. Richard Ellmann and Charles Feidelson, Jr., eds., *The Modern Tradition* (New York: Oxford University Press, 1965), vi–vii.

3. Stanley Coffman, Jr., *Imagism: A Chapter for the History of Modern Poetry* (New York: Octagon, 1972), p. 54 (hereafter cited parenthetically in the text).

4. T. E. Hulme, *Speculations* (New York: Harcourt Brace, 1924), 116 (hereafter cited parenthetically in the text).

5. Ian Dunlop, *The Shock of the New* (New York: American Heritage, 1972), 84 (hereafter cited parenthetically in the text).

6. Noel Stock, *The Life of Ezra Pound* (New York: Pantheon, 1970), 136 (hereafter cited parenthetically in the text).

7. Louis Untermeyer, ed., *The Complete Poetical Works of Amy Lowell* (Boston: Houghton Mifflin, n.d.), xxiii (hereafter cited parenthetically in the text).

8. S. Foster Damon, *Amy Lowell, A Chronicle* (Boston: Houghton Mifflin, 1935), 426 (hereafter cited parenthetically in the text).

9. Jean Gould, *American Woman Poets, Pioneers of Modern Poetry* (New York: Dodd Mead, 1980), 172 (hereafter cited parenthetically in the text).

10. L. M. Freibert, "Conflict and Creativity in the World of H.D.," *Journal of Women's Studies in Literature*, 1 no. 3 (Summer 1979): 258–71.

11. Hilda Doolittle, *Collected Poems, 1912-1944* (New York: New Directions, 1983), 55 (hereafter cited parenthetically in the text as H.D.).

12. Hilda Doolittle, *Tribute to Freud* (Boston: Godine, 1974), xxvii.

13. Janice Robinson, *H.D., The Life and Work of an American Poet* (Boston: Houghton Mifflin, 1982), 130.

14. Kingsley Widmer, *The Literary Rebel* (Carbondale: Southern Illinois University Press, 1965), 208.

15. David Antin, "Some Questions about Modernism," *Occident* n.s. 3 (Spring 1974): 31.

16. Richard Kostlanetz, ed., *The Yale Gertrude Stein* (New Haven: Yale University Press, 1980), xiii (hereafter cited parenthetically in the text).

17. Richard Bridgman, *Gertrude Stein in Pieces* (New York: Oxford University Press, 1970), 10.

18. James Mellow, *Charmed Circle* (New York: Praeger, 1974), 403 (hereafter cited parenthetically in the text).

19. Marjorie Perloff, *The Poetics of Indeterminacy* (Princeton: Princeton University Press, 1981), 77 (hereafter cited parenthetically in the text).

20. Gertrude Stein, *Lectures in America* (New York: Vintage, 1975), 166.

21. Robert Hass, *A Primer for the Gradual Understanding of Gertrude Stein* (Los Angeles: Black Sparrow, 1971), 49 (hereafter cited parenthetically in the text).

Notes and References

22. Charles Tomlinson, ed., *Marianne Moore, A Collection of Critical Essays* (Englewood Cliffs, N.J.: Prentice-Hall, 1969), 27 (hereafter cited parenthetically in the text).

23. Marianne Moore, *Poems* (London: Egoist Press, 1921).

24. Bonnie Costello, *Marianne Moore, Imaginary Possessions* (Cambridge: Harvard University Press, 1981), 14.

25. Marianne Moore, *Complete Poems* (New York: Macmillan, 1967), 134 (hereafter cited parenthetically in the text).

Chapter Five

1. Philip R. Headings, *T. S. Eliot*, rev. ed. (Boston: Twayne, 1982), 1–2 (hereafter cited parenthetically in the text).

2. Ezra Pound, *Selected Poems* (New York: New Directions, 1957), 47 (hereafter cited parenthetically in the text as *SP*).

3. Karl Shapiro, *Prose Keys to Modern Poetry* (New York: Harper & Row, 1962), 66 (hereafter cited parenthetically in the text).

4. Peter Ackroyd, *T. S. Eliot* (London: Abacus, 1985), 49 (hereafter cited parenthetically in the text).

5. T. S. Eliot, *To Criticize the Critic and Other Writings* (New York: Farrar, Straus & Giroux, 1965), 126.

6. T. S. Eliot, *The Complete Poems and Plays* (New York: Harcourt Brace & Co., 1952), 14 (hereafter cited parenthetically in the text).

7. T. S. Eliot, *The Waste Land. A Facsimile of the Original Drafts Including the Annotations of Ezra Pound*, ed. Valerie Eliot (New York: Harcourt Brace Jovanovich, 1971), 1.

8. Ronald Bush, *T. S. Eliot, A Study in Character and Style* (New York: Oxford University Press, 1984), 55 (hereafter cited parenthetically in the text).

9. D. D. Paige, ed., *The Letters of Ezra Pound* (New York: Harcourt Brace & Co., 1950), 169–72 (hereafter cited parenthetically in the text).

10. Lionel Trilling, "Commentary on *The Waste Land*," in *The Experience of Literature* (New York: Harcourt Brace Jovanovich, 1962), 939.

11. T. S. Eliot, *The Sacred Wood: Essays on Poetry and Criticism*, 6th ed. (London: Methuen & Co., 1948), 125.

12. James Miller Jr., *T. S. Eliot's Personal Waste Land* (University Park: Pennsylvania State University Press, 1977), 85.

13. B. C. Southam, *A Guide to the Selected Poems of T. S. Eliot* (New York: Harcourt, Brace and World, 1968), 87.

14. Helen Gardner, *The Waste Land, 1972* (Manchester: Manchester University Press, 1972), 19.

15. Caroline Behr, *T. S. Eliot, A Chronology of His Life and Works* (London: Macmillan, 1983), 35.

16. Helen Gardner, *The Composition of the Four Quartets* (London: Faber & Faber, 1978), 28 (hereafter cited parenthetically in the text as *CFQ*).

17. Burton Raffel, *Possum and Ole Ez in the Public Eye: Contemporaries and Peers on T. S. Eliot and Ezra Pound, 1892–1972* (Hamden, Conn.: Archon, 1985), 88 (hereafter cited parenthetically in the text).

18. Ezra Pound, *ABC of Reading* (Norfolk, Conn.: New Directions, n.d.), 17 (hereafter cited parenthetically in the text as *ABC*).

19. Ezra Pound, *Selected Prose, 1909–1965*, ed. William Cookson (New York: New Directions, 1973), 30 (hereafter cited in the text as *SPR*).

20. Ezra Pound, *The Cantos of Ezra Pound* (New York: New Directions, 1972), 659 (hereafter cited parenthetically in the text as *Cantos*).

21. Noel Stock, *The Life of Ezra Pound* (New York: Pantheon, 1970), 12 (hereafter cited parenthetically in the text).

22. Timothy Materer, *Vortex Pound, Eliot, and Lewis* (Ithaca, N.Y.: Cornell University Press, 1979), 24.

23. Carroll F. Terrell, *A Companion to the Cantos of Ezra Pound* (Berkeley: University of California Press, 1980), viii.

24. Leon Surette, *A Light from Eleusis: A Study of Ezra Pound's Cantos* (New York: Oxford University Press, 1979), 8.

25. William Butler Yeats, *A Vision* (New York: Macmillan, 1961), 4.

26. Irving Howe, *The Critical Point* (New York: Dell, 1973), 112.

Chapter Six

1. Paul Mariani, *A Usable Past, Essay on Modern and Contemporary Poetry* (Amherst: University of Massachusetts Press, 1984), 96.

2. Wallace Stevens, *Opus Posthumous* (New York: Alfred A. Knopf, 1951), 169 (hereafter cited parenthetically in the text as *OP*).

3. Samuel French Morse, *Wallace Stevens* (New York: Pegasus, 1970), 79 (hereafter cited parenthetically in the text).

4. All quotations from Wallace Stevens's poetry are from *The Palm at the End of the Mind* (New York: Vintage, 1972) and are cited parenthetically in the text.

5. Helen Vendler, *On Extended Wings: Wallace Stevens' Longer Poems* (Cambridge: Harvard University Press, 1969), 120.

6. Harold Bloom, *Wallace Stevens, Poems of Our Climate* (New Haven: Yale University Press, 1977), 135.

7. Dickran Tashjian, *William Carlos Williams and the American Scene* (Berkeley: University of California Press, 1978), 14 (hereafter cited parenthetically in the text).

8. Quotations from Williams's poetry are from *The Collected Earlier Poems* (New York: New Directions, 1951) (hereafter cited parenthetically in the text as *CEP*); *The Collected Later Poems* (New York: New Directions,

1963) (hereafter cited parenthetically in the text as *CLP*); *Paterson* (New York: New Directions, 1951) (hereafter cited parenthetically in the text by title).

9. William Carlos Williams, *The Autobiography of William Carlos Williams* (New York: New Directions, 1951), 172 (hereafter cited parenthetically in the text by title).

10. William Carlos Williams, *Imaginations* (New York: New Directions, 1970), 89 (hereafter cited parenthetically in the text).

11. John C. Thirlwall, ed., *The Selected Letters of William Carlos Williams* (New York: New Directions, 1984), 226 (hereafter cited parenthetically in the text).

12. Charles Doyle, *William Carlos Williams and the American Poem* (New York: St. Martins Press, 1982), 88 (hereafter cited parenthetically in the text).

13. Paul Mariani, *William Carlos Williams, A New World Naked* (New York: McGraw Hill, 1981), 475 (hereafter cited parenthetically in the text).

14. Benjamin Sankey, *A Reader's Guide to Paterson* (Berkeley: University of California Press, 1971), 116 (hereafter cited parenthetically in the text).

Chapter Seven

1. Allen Tate, *The Swimmer and Other Selected Poems* (New York: Charles Scribner's Sons, 1970), 19–20.

2. See John Unterecker, *Voyages: A Life of Hart Crane* (New York: Farrar, Straus and Giroux, 1969), for a detailed and illuminating depiction of Crane's stormy relationship with his parents, as well as an extensive study of Crane's life.

3. Hart Crane, *The Letters of Hart Crane*, ed. Brom Weber (Berkeley and Los Angeles: University of California Press, 1965), 90.

4. Hart Crane, *The Complete Poems and Selected Letters and Prose of Hart Crane*, ed. Brom Weber (Garden City, N.Y.: Anchor Books, Doubleday & Co., 1966), 3 (hereafter cited parenthetically in the text as *CP*).

5. R. W. B. Lewis, *The Poetry of Hart Crane: A Critical Study* (Princeton, N.J.: Princeton University Press, 1967), 168. See 148–79 for Lewis's full analysis of "Voyages."

6. Richard Sugg, *Hart Crane's The Bridge: A Description of Its Life* (Fairbanks: University of Alaska, 1977).

7. Lewis, *Poetry*, 400–401.

8. Helen Vendler, *Part of Nature, Part of Us: Modern American Poets* (Cambridge: Harvard University Press, 1980), 323–30.

9. Norman Friedman, *E. E. Cummings: The Art of His Poetry* (Baltimore: John Hopkins Press, 1960), p. 3.

10. E. E. Cummings, *Complete Poems: 1913–1962* (New York: Harcourt Brace Jovanovich, 1972), p. 461 (all subsequent references to Cummings's poetry are from this volume and are cited parenthetically in the text). Richard S. Kennedy in his biographical study notes that Cummings in 1922 had a very different collection in mind than the *Tulips and Chimneys* published by Thomas Seltzer in 1923, wherein only forty-one of the one hundred and fifty-two poems appeared and the original ordering of poems was lost as well. *The Collected Poems* (1972) includes the Seltzer edition; to capture what Kennedy calls the "remarkable" nature of the original volume see the Liveright edition of *Tulips and Chimneys* edited by George J. Firmage in 1972. See Kennedy's discussion in Richard S. Kennedy, *Dreams In the Mirror: A Biography of E. E. Cummings* (New York: Liveright Publishing Corporation, 1980), 233–53.

11. Charles Norman, *E. E. Cummings: A Biography* (New York: E. P. Dutton & Co., 1967), 219.

12. Robinson Jeffers, *The Beginning of the End and Other Poems* (New York: Random House, 1963), 50.

13. Robinson Jeffers, *The Selected Poetry of Robinson Jeffers* (New York: Random House, 1938), 3 (all subsequent references to Jeffers's poetry are from this volume through page 209 and are cited parenthetically in the text).

14. Robinson Jeffers, *The Selected Letters of Robinson Jeffers*, ed. Ann N. Ridgeway (Baltimore: John Hopkins Press, 1968), 59 (hereafter cited parenthetically in the text as *Letters*).

15. Robinson Jeffers, *The Double Axe and Other Poems* (New York: Liveright Publishing Corporation, 1977), 7.

16. See, for example, Brother Antoninus, *Robinson Jeffers: Fragments of an Older Fury* (Berkeley: Oyez Press, 1968), and James Karman, *Robinson Jeffers: Poet of California* (San Francisco: Chronicle Press, 1987).

Chapter Eight

1. John Crowe Ransom, *Selected Poems* (New York: Alfred A. Knopf, 1963), 9 (all subsequent references to Ransom's poetry are from this volume and are cited parenthetically in the text).

2. Allen Tate, *Essays of Four Decades* (Chicago: Swallow Press, 1968), 3 (hereafter cited parenthetically in the text).

3. Allen Tate, *The Swimmers and Other Selected Poems* (New York: Charles Scribner's Sons, 1970), 125 (all subsequent references to Tate's poetry are from this volume and are cited parenthetically in the text).

4. Cleanth Brooks, a colleague of Warren at Louisiana State University, also wrote *The Well Wrought Urn: Studies in the Structure of Poetry* (1947) and was coeditor of the *Southern Review* with Warren. He and Warren also collaborated on *Understanding Fiction* (1943).

Notes and References

5. Robert Penn Warren, *Selected Poems: New and Old 1923–1966* (New York: Random House, 1966), 299 (hereafter cited parenthetically in the text as *SP*).

6. Robert Penn Warren, *Brother to the Dragons* (New York: Random House, 1953), 43–44 (hereafter cited parenthetically in the text as *BD*).

7. John Lewis Longley, ed., *Robert Penn Warren, Collection of Critical Essays* (New York: New York University Press, 1965), 241–42.

8. Ibid., 244.

9. Robert Penn Warren, *New and Selected Poems: 1923–1985* (New York: Random House, 1985), 271 (hereafter cited parenthetically in the text as *NSP*).

10. Longley, *Robert Penn Warren*, 271.

11. L. S. Dembo, "The 'Objectivist' Poet: Four Interviews," *Contemporary Literature* 10 (Spring 1969): 179.

12. William Carlos Williams, *The Autobiography of William Carlos Williams* (New York: Random House, 1951), 265.

13. Charles Reznikoff, *The Complete Poems: Poems 1918–1936*, vol. 1, ed. Seamus Cooney (Santa Barbara: Black Sparrow Press, 1976), 112 (hereafter cited parenthetically in text as *CP*).

14. Dembo, " 'Objectivist' Poet," 97.

15. Ibid., 195.

16. Charles Reznikoff, *Holocaust* (Los Angeles: Black Sparrow Press, 1975), 40.

17. To Carroll F. Terrell, Zukofsky is "the greatest poet born in this century," but to M. L. Rosenthal there are two sides to Zukofsky: the "beautiful and the tiresome," the poet who creates wonderful lyrical passages, and the poet who gives us "hushed" impenetrable and self-indulgent passages. See Carroll F. Terrell, Introduction to *Louis Zukofsky: Man and Poet* (Orono, Maine: National Poetry Foundation, 1979), 15, and M. R. Rosenthal, "Zukofsky: 'All My Hushed Sources,' " in *Louis Zukofsky: Man and Poet*, 233.

18. Hugh Kenner, "Louis Zukofsky: All the Words," *Paideuma, Special Issue on Remembrance of Louis Zukofsky* 7, no. 3 (Winter 1978): 389.

19. Ibid.

20. Harold Schimmel, "*Zuk, Yehoash, David Rex*" in *Louis Zukofsky: Man and Poet*, 237.

21. Louis Zukofsky, *All: The Collected Short Poems, 1923–1964* (New York: W. W. Norton & Co., 1971) (hereafter cited parenthetically in the text as *All*).

22. William Carlos Williams, "Louis Zukofsky," *Agenda: Louis Zukofsky: Special Edition* 3, no. 6 (December 1964): 1–4.

23. Louis Zukofsky, "An Objective," in *Prepositions: The Collected Critical Essays* (London: Rapp & Carroll, 1967), 19 (hereafter cited parenthetically in the text as *P*).

24. Louis Zukofsky, Foreword to *'A' 1–12* (Garden City, N.Y.: Doubleday, 1967).

25. George Oppen, *The Collected Poems of George Oppen* (New York: New Directions Book, 1975), 14 (all subsequent references to Oppen's poetry are from this volume and are cited parenthetically in the text).

26. Dembo, " 'Objectivist' Poet," 160.

27. Ibid., 161.

28. Ibid., 174.

29. Ibid., 161.

30. Ibid., 205.

31. Rachel Blau Du Plessis, "Objectivist Poetics and Political Vision: A Study of Oppen and Pound," in *George Oppen: Man and Poet*, ed. Burton Hatten (Orono, Maine: National Poetry Foundation, 1981), 146.

32. Dembo, " 'Objectivist' Poet," 186.

33. Ibid., 179.

34. Carl Rakosi, *The Collected Poems of Carl Rakosi* (Orono, Maine: National Poetry Foundation, 1986), 299 (hereafter cited parenthetically in the text).

35. Dembo, " 'Objectivist' Poet," 181.

36. Lorine Niedecker, *From this Condensary: The Complete Writing of Lorine Niedecker*, ed. Robert J. Bertholf (Winston-Salem, N.C.: Jargon Society, 1985), 141. See Berthoff's "Introduction." All references to Niedecker's poetry are from this volume and are cited parenthetically in the text.

· Selected Bibliography ·

PRIMARY WORKS

Crane, Hart. *The Complete Poems and Selected Letters and Prose of Hart Crane*. Ed. Brom Weber. New York: Liveright Publishing Corporation, 1966.

———. *The Letters of Hart Crane*. Ed. Brom Weber. Berkeley and Los Angeles: University of California Press, 1965.

Crane, Stephen. *The Poems of Stephen Crane: A Critical Edition by Joseph Katz*. New York: Cooper Square Publishers, 1966.

Cullen, Countee. *On These I Stand: An Anthology of the Best Poems of Countee Cullen Selected by Himself and Including Six New Poems Never Before Published*. New York: Harper & Row Publishers, 1947.

Cummings, E. E. *Complete Poems: 1913–1962*. New York: Harcourt Brace Jovanovich, 1972.

———. *six non lectures*. Cambridge: Harvard University Press, 1953.

Dickinson, Emily. *The Complete Poems of Emily Dickinson*. Ed. Thomas H. Johnson. Boston: Little, Brown, 1960.

———. *The Letters of Emily Dickinson*. Ed. Thomas H. Johnson and Theodora Ward. Cambridge: Harvard University Press, 1958.

———. *The Manuscript Books of Emily Dickinson*. Ed. R. W. Franklin. Cambridge: Belknap Press of Harvard University Press, 1981.

———. *The Poems of Emily Dickinson*. Ed. Thomas H. Johnson. 3 vols. Cambridge: Belknap Press of Harvard University Press, 1955.

Doolittle, Hilda. *Helen in Egypt*. New York: Grove Press, 1961.

———. *Collected Poems, 1912–1944*. New York: New Directions, 1983.

———. *Tribute to Freud*. Boston: Godine, 1974.

Eliot, T. S. *To Criticize the Critic and Other Writings*. New York: Farrar, Straus & Giroux, 1965.

———. *The Complete Poems and Plays*. New York: Harcourt Brace & Co., 1952.

———. *The Sacred Wood: Essays on Poetry and Criticism*. London: Methuen & Co., 1948.

———. *The Waste Land. A Facsimile of the Original Drafts Including the Annotations of Ezra Pound*. Ed. Valerie Eliot. New York: Harcourt Brace Jovanovich, 1971.

Bibliography

Ellman, Richard, and Robert O'Clair, eds. *The Norton Anthology of Modern Poetry*. New York: W. W. Norton & Co., 1973, 1988.

Frost, Robert. *Complete Poems of Robert Frost*. New York: Holt, Rinehart and Winston, 1964.

———. *Selected Prose of Robert Frost*. Ed. Hyde Cox and Edward Connery Lathem. New York: Collier Books, 1968.

———. *The Letters of Robert Frost to Louis Untermeyer*. Ed. Louis Untermeyer. New York: Holt, Rinehart and Winston, 1963.

Guiney, Louise Imogen. *Happy Ending: The Collected Lyrics of Louise Imogen Guiney*. Boston: Houghton Mifflin, 1927.

Hughes, Langston. *Selected Poems*. New York: Alfred A. Knopf, 1969.

Jeffers, Robinson. *The Beginning of the End and Other Poems*. New York: Random House, 1963.

———. *The Double Axe and Other Poems*. New York: Liveright Publishing Corporation, 1977.

———. *The Selected Letters of Robinson Jeffers*. Ed. Ann M. Ridgeway. Baltimore: John Hopkins Press, 1968.

———. *The Selected Poetry*. New York: Random House, 1938.

Kostlanetz, Richard, ed. *The Yale Gertrude Stein*. New Haven: Yale University Press, 1980.

Locke, Alain. *The New Negro: An Interpretation*. New York: Albert and Charles Boni, 1925.

Lowell, Amy. *The Complete Poetical Works of Amy Lowell*. Ed. Louis Untermeyer. Boston: Houghton Mifflin, n.d.

McKay, Claude. *Selected Poems*. New York: Harcourt Brace Jovanovich, 1969.

Masters, Edgar Lee. *Spoon River Anthology, New Edition with New Poems*. New York: Macmillan, 1961.

McKay, Claude. *Selected Poems*. New York: Harcourt Brace Jovanovich, 1969.

Masters, Edgar Lee. *Spoon River Anthology, New Edition with New Poems,* New York: Macmillan, 1961.

Millay, Edna St. Vincent. *Collected Poems*. Ed. Norma Millay. New York: Harper & Row, 1956.

Moody, William Vaughn. *The Poems and Plays of William Vaughn Moody, with an Introduction by John M. Manly*. Vol. 1. New York: AMS Press, 1969.

Moore, Marianne. *Complete Poems*. New York: Macmillan, 1967.

———. *Poems*. London: Egoist Press, 1921.

Niedecker, Lorine. *From This Condensary: The Complete Writing of Lorine Niedecker*. Ed. Robert J. Bertholf. Winston Salem, N. C.: Jargon Society, 1985.

Oppen, George. *The Collected Poems of George Oppen*. New York: New Directions, 1975.

Bibliography

Oppen, Mary. *Meaning a Life: An Autobiography.* Santa Barbara: Black Sparrow Press, 1978.

Pound, Ezra. *The Cantos of Ezra Pound.* New York: New Directions, 1972.

———. *The Letters of Ezra Pound.* Ed. D. D. Paige. New York: Harcourt Brace & Co., 1950.

———. *Selected Poems.* New York: New Directions, 1957.

———. *Selected Prose, 1909–1965.* Ed. William Cookson. New York: New Directions, 1973.

Rakosi, Carl. *The Collected Poems of Carl Rakosi.* Orono, Maine: National Poetry Foundation, 1986.

Ransom, John Crowe. *Selected Poems.* New York: Alfred A. Knopf, 1963.

Reese, Lizette Woodward. *The Selected Poems.* New York: George H. Doran Co., 1926.

Reznikoff, Charles. *Holocaust.* Los Angeles: Black Sparrow Press, 1975.

———. *The Complete Poems.* Vol. 1. Ed. Seamus Cooney. Santa Barbara: Black Sparrow Press, 1976.

Robinson, Edwin Arlington. *Collected Poems.* New York: Macmillan, 1928.

Sandburg, Carl. *The Complete Poems of Carl Sandburg.* Rev. and expanded ed. New York: Harcourt Brace Jovanovich, 1970.

Stein, Gertrude. *Lectures in America.* New York: Vintage, 1975.

Stevens, Wallace. *The Palm at the End of the Mind.* New York: Vintage, 1972.

———. *Opus Posthumous.* New York: Alfred A. Knopf, 1957.

Tate, Allen. *Collected Poems, 1919–1976.* New York: Farrar, Straus & Giroux, 1977.

———. *Essays of Four Decades.* Chicago: Swallow Press, 1968.

———. *The Swimmers and Other Selected Poems.* New York: Charles Scribner's Sons, 1970.

Teasdale, Sara. *Collected Poems of Sara Teasdale.* New York: Macmillan, 1966.

Toomer, Jean. *Cane: With an Introduction by Darwin T. Turner.* New York: Liveright, 1975.

Warren, Robert Penn. *Brother to the Dragons.* New York: Random House, 1953.

———. *New and Selected Poems: 1923–1985.* New York: Random House, 1985.

———. *Selected Poems: New and Old, 1923–1966.* New York: Random House, 1966.

Williams, William Carlos. *The Autobiography of William Carlos Williams.* New York: Random House, 1951.

———. *The Collected Earlier Poems.* New York: New Directions, 1951.

———. *The Collected Later Poems.* Rev. ed. New York: New Directions, 1963.

———. *Imaginations.* New York: New Directions, 1970.

————. *Paterson.* New York: New Directions, 1951.

————. *Pictures from Brueghel and Other Poems.* New York: New Directions, 1962.

————. *The Selected Letters of William Carlos Williams.* Ed. John C. Thirlwell. New York: New Directions, 1984.

Yeats, W. B. *A Vision.* New York: Macmillan, 1961.

Zukofsky, Louis. *A.* Berkeley and Los Angeles: University of California Press, 1978.

————. *All: The Collected Short Poems 1923–1964.* New York: W. W. Norton & Co., 1971.

————. "An Objective." In *Prepositions: The Collected Critical Essays.* London: Rapp & Carroll, 1967.

————. Foreword to *'A' 1–12.* Garden City, N.Y.: Doubleday, 1967.

SECONDARY WORKS

Ackroyd, Peter. *T. S. Eliot.* London: Abacus, 1985.

Anderson, Allen, Gay Wilson. *Carl Sandburg.* University of Minnesota Pamphlets on American Writers, no. 101. Minneapolis: University of Minnesota Press, 1972.

Anderson, Wallace L. *Edwin Arlington Robinson: A Critical Introduction.* Cambridge: Harvard University Press, 1968.

Antin, David. "Some Questions about Modernism." *Occident* n.s. 3 (Spring 1974): 7–38.

Baker, Houston A. *A Many-Colored Coat of Dreams: The Poetry of Countee Cullen.* Detroit: Broadside Press, 1974.

Barksdale, Richard K. *Langston Hughes: The Poet and His Critics.* Chicago: American Library Association, 1967.

Barnard, Ellsworth. *Edwin Arlington Robinson: A Critical Study.* New York: Macmillan, 1952.

Bedient, Calvin. *He Do the Police in Different Voices, The Waste Land and Its Protagonist.* Chicago: University of Chicago Press, 1986.

Behr, Caroline. *T. S. Eliot, A Chronology of His Life and Works.* London: Macmillan, 1983.

Berry, Faith. *Langston Hughes: Before and beyond Harlem.* Westport, Conn.: Lawrence Hill and Co., 1983.

Bianchi, Martha Dickinson. *The Life and Letters of Emily Dickinson.* Boston: Houghton Mifflin, 1924.

Bingham, Millicent Todd. *Emily Dickinson's Home.* New York: Harper and Brothers, 1955.

Bloom, Harold. *Wallace Stevens, Poems of Our Climate.* New Haven: Yale University Press, 1977.

Bibliography

Bogan, Louise. *Achievement in American Poetry*. Chicago: Henry Regnery Co., 1951, reprinted in Gateway ed., 1962.

Bradbury, John M. *The Fugitives: A Critical Account*. Chapel Hill: University of North Carolina Press, 1958.

Breslin, James E. B. *William Carlos Williams, An American Artist*. New ed. Chicago: University of Chicago Press, 1985.

Bridgman, Richard. *Gertrude Stein in Pieces*. New York: Oxford University Press, 1970.

Brower, Reuben A. *The Poetry of Robert Frost: Constellations of Intention*. New York: Oxford University Press, 1963.

Burnshaw, Stanley. *Robert Frost Himself*. New York: George Braziller, 1986.

Bush, Ronald. *T. S. Eliot, A Study in Character and Style*. New York: Oxford University Press, 1984.

Callahan, North. *Carl Sandburg: His Life and Works*. University Park: Pennsylvania State University Press, 1987.

Chace, William M. *The Political Identities of Ezra Pound and T. S. Eliot*. Stanford: Stanford University Press, 1973.

Chase, Richard. *Emily Dickinson*. New York: Dell, 1965.

Cody, John. *After Great Pain: The Inner Life of Emily Dickinson*. Cambridge: Belknap Press of Harvard University Press, 1971.

Coffman, Jr., Stanley. *Imagism: A Chapter for the History of Modern Poetry*. New York: Octagon, 1972.

Cooper, Wayne F. *Claude McKay, Rebel Sojourner in the Harlem Renaissance: A Biography*. Baton Rouge: Louisiana State University Press, 1987.

Costello, Bonnie. *Marianne Moore, Imaginary Possessions*. Cambridge: Harvard University Press, 1981.

Craig, Cairns. *Yeats, Eliot, Pound and the Politics of Poetry*. Pittsburgh: University of Pittsburgh Press, 1982.

Damon, S. Foster. *Amy Lowell, A Chronicle*. Boston: Houghton Mifflin, 1935.

Davis, Arthur P. *From the Dark Tower: Afro-American Writers, 1900–1960*. Washington, D.C.: Howard University Press, 1974.

Dembo, L. S. "The 'Objectivist' Poet: Four Interviews." *Contemporary Literature* 10, no. 2 (Spring 1969): 155–219.

Deutsch, Babette. *Poetry in our Time*. 2d ed. Garden City, N.Y.: Doubleday, 1963.

Dijkstra, Bram. *The Hieroglyphics of a New Speech: Cubism, Stieglitz and the Early Poetry of William Carlos Williams*. Princeton: Princeton University Press, 1969.

Doyle, Charles. *William Carlos Williams and the American Poem*. New York: St. Martin's Press, 1982.

Dunlop, Ian. *The Shock of the New*. New York: American Heritage, 1972.

Bibliography

DuPlessis, Rachel Blau. "Objectivist Poetics and Political Vision: A Study of Oppen and Pound." In *George Oppen: Man and Poet,* Ed. Burton Hatten. Orono, Maine: National Poetry Foundation, 1981.

Ellmann, Richard, and Charles Feidelson, Jr., eds. *The Modern Tradition.* New York: Oxford University Press, 1965.

Franklin, R. W. *The Editing of Emily Dickinson: A Reconsideration.* Madison: University of Wisconsin Press, 1967.

Freibert, L. M. "Conflict and Creativity in the World of H. D." *Journal of Women's Studies in Literature* 1, no. 3 (Summer 1979): 258–71.

Friedman, Norman. *E. E. Cummings: The Art of His Poetry.* Baltimore: John Hopkins Press, 1960.

————. *E. E. Cummings: A Collection of Critical Essays.* Englewood Cliffs, N.J.: Prentice Hall, 1972.

Gardner, Helen. *The Composition of the Four Quartets.* London: Faber & Faber, 1978.

————. *The Waste Land 1972.* Manchester: Manchester University Press, 1972.

Gelpi, Albert J. *Emily Dickinson: The Mind of the Poet.* Cambridge: Harvard University Press, 1966.

Gibson, Donald B. *Modern Black Poets: A Collection of Critical Essays.* Englewood Cliffs, N.J.: Prentice-Hall, 1973.

Gilbert, Sandra M. *The Madwoman in the Attic: The Woman Writer and the Nineteenth-Century Literary Imagination.* New Haven: Yale University Press, 1979.

Gould, Jean. *American Women Poets, Pioneers of Modern Poetry.* New York: Dodd, Mead, 1980.

Griffith, Clark. *The Long Shadow: Emily Dickinson's Tragic Poetry.* Princeton: Princeton University Press, 1964.

Hall, Dorothy Judd. *Robert Frost: Contours of Belief.* Athens: Ohio University Press, 1984.

Hallwas, John E., and Dennis J. Reader, eds. *The Vision of This Land: Studies of Vachel Lindsay, Edgar Lee Masters, and Carl Sandburg.* Macomb: Western Illinois University, 1976.

Hass, Robert. *A Primer for the Gradual Understanding of Gertrude Stein.* Los Angeles: Black Sparrow Press, 1971.

Headings, Philip R. *T. S. Eliot.* Rev. ed. Boston: Twayne Publishers, 1982.

Hoffman, Daniel G. *The Poetry of Stephen Crane.* New York: Columbia University Press, 1951.

Hoffman, Michael. *Gertrude Stein.* Boston: Twayne Publishers, 1976.

Howe, Irving. *The Critical Point.* New York: Dell, 1973.

Hulme, T. E. *Speculations.* New York: Harcourt Brace, 1924.

Johnson, James Weldon, ed. *The Book of American Negro Poetry.* Rev. ed. New York: Harcourt, Brace, 1931.

Bibliography

Juhasz, Suzanne, ed. *Feminine Critics Read Emily Dickinson.* Bloomington: Indiana University Press, 1983.

———. *The Undiscovered Continent: Emily Dickinson and the Space of the Mind.* Bloomington: Indiana University Press, 1983.

Kennedy, Richard S. *Dreams In the Mirror: A Biography of E. E. Cummings.* New York: Liveright Publishing Corporation, 1980.

Kenner, Hugh. "Louis Zukofsky: All the Words." *Paideuma: Special Issue on Remembrance of Louis Zukofsky* 7, no. 3 (Winter 1978): 386–89.

———. *The Pound Era.* Berkeley: University of California Press, 1971.

Kirk, Russell. *Eliot and His Age: T. S. Eliot's Moral Imagination.* New York: Random House, 1971.

Lewis, David Levering. *When Harlem Was in Vogue.* New York: Alfred A. Knopf, 1981.

Lewis, R. W. B. *The Poetry of Hart Crane: A Critical Study.* Princeton, N.J.: Princeton University Press, 1967.

Leyda, Jay. *The Years and Hours of Emily Dickinson.* 2 vols. New Haven: Yale University Press, 1960.

Longley, John Lewis, ed. *Robert Penn Warren: Collection of Critical Essays.* New York: New York University Press, 1965.

Mariani, Paul. *William Carlos Williams, A New World Naked.* New York: McGraw-Hill, 1981.

———. *A Usable Past, Essays on Modern and Contemporary Poetry.* Amherst: University of Massachusetts Press, 1984.

McKay, Nellie Y. *Jean Toomer, Artist: A Study of His Literary Life and Work, 1894–1936.* Chapel Hill: University of North Carolina Press, 1984.

Massa, Ann. *Vachel Lindsay: Fieldworker for the American Dream.* Bloomington: Indiana University Press, 1970.

Mellow, James. *Charmed Circle.* New York: Praeger, 1974.

Miller, James, Jr. *T. S. Eliot's Personal Waste Land.* University Park: Pennsylvania State University Press, 1977.

Miller, Ruth. *The Poetry of Emily Dickinson.* Middletown, Conn.: Wesleyan University Press, 1968.

Morse, Samuel French. *Wallace Stevens.* New York: Pegasus, 1970.

Nicholls, Peter. *Ezra Pound: Politics, Economics and Writing.* London: Macmillan, 1984.

Norman, Charles. *E. E. Cummings: A Biography.* New York: E. P. Dutton & Co., 1967.

O'Daniel, Therman B., ed. *Langston Hughes, Black Genius.* New York: William Morrow, 1971.

Onwuchekwa, Jemie. *Langston Hughes: An Introduction to the Poetry.* New York: Columbia University Press, 1976.

Ostriker, Alicia Suskin. *Stealing the Language: The Emergence of Women's Poetry in America.* Boston: Beacon Press, 1986.

Bibliography

Pearce, Roy Harvey. *The Continuity of American Poetry*. Princeton: Princeton University Press, 1961.

Perkins, David. *A History of Modern Poetry*. Cambridge: Harvard University Press, 1976.

Perloff, Marjorie. *The Poetics of Indeterminacy, Rimbaud to Cage*. Princeton: Princeton University Press, 1981.

Primeau, Ronald. *Beyond Spoon River: The Legacy of Edgar Lee Masters*. Austin: University of Texas Press, 1981.

Quinn, Vincent. *Hilda Doolittle*. Boston: Twayne Publishers, 1967.

Raffel, Burton. *Possum and Ole Ez in the Public Eye: Contemporaries and Peers of T. S. Eliot and Ezra Pound, 1892–1972*. Hamden, Conn.: Archon, 1985.

Rampersad, Arnold. *The Life of Langston Hughes*. Vol. 1: 1902–1941. New York: Oxford University Press, 1986.

Rich, Adrienne. "Vesuvius at Home: The *Power of Emily Dickinson*." In *On Lies, Secrets and Silence*. New York: W. W. Norton & Co., 1979.

Robinson, Janice. *H. D., The Life and Work of an American Poet*. Boston: Houghton Mifflin, 1982.

Ruggles, Eleanor. *The West-Going Heart: A Life of Vachel Lindsay*. New York: W. W. Norton & Co., 1959.

St. Armand, Barton Levi. *Emily Dickinson and Her Culture: The Soul's Society*. Cambridge: Cambridge University Press, 1984.

Sankey, Benjamin. *A Reader's Guide to Paterson*. Berkeley: University of California Press, 1971.

Schimmel, Harold. "Zuk Yehoash David Rex." In *Louis Zukofsky: Man and Poet*. Ed. Carroll F. Terrell. Orono, Maine: National Poetry Foundation, 1979.

Sewall, Richard B., ed. *Emily Dickinson: A Collection of Critical Essays*. Twentieth Century Views. Englewood Cliffs, N.J.: Prentice-Hall, 1963.

———. *The Life of Emily Dickinson*. 2 vols. New York: Farrar, Straus and Giroux, 1974.

Shapiro, Karl. *Prose Keys to Modern Poetry*. New York: Harper & Row, 1962.

Shucard, Alan R. *Countee Cullen*. Boston: Twayne Publishers, 1984.

Shurr, William H. *The Marriage of Emily Dickinson*. Lexington: University of Kentucky Press, 1983.

Southam, B. C. *A Guide to the Selected Poems of T. S. Eliot*. New York: Harcourt, Brace & World, 1968.

Spears, Monroe. *Dionysus and the City: Modernism in Twentieth Century Poetry*. Oxford: Oxford University Press, 1970.

Stauffer, Donald M. *A Short History of American Poetry*. New York: E. P. Dutton & Co., 1974.

Stock, Noel. *The Life of Ezra Pound*. New York: Pantheon, 1970.

Sugg, Richard. *Hart Crane's The Bridge: A Description of Its Life.* Fairbanks: University of Alaska, 1977.

Surette, Leon. *A Light from Eleusis: A Study of Ezra Pound's Cantos.* New York: Oxford University Press, 1979.

Tashjian, Dickran. *W. C. Williams and the American Scene, 1920–1940.* Berkeley: University of California Press, 1978.

Terrell, Carroll F. *A Companion to the Cantos of Ezra Pound.* Berkeley: University of California Press, 1980.

Thompson, Lawrence. *Robert Frost: The Early Years, 1874–1915.* New York: Holt, Rinehart and Winston, 1966.

———. *Robert Frost: The Years of Triumph, 1915–1938.* New York: Holt, Rinehart and Winston, 1970.

Thompson, Lawrence, and R. H. Winnick. *Robert Frost: The Later Years, 1938–43.* New York: Holt, Rinehart and Winston, 1976.

Tomlinson, Charles, ed. *Marianne Moore, A Collection of Critical Essays.* Englewood Cliffs, N.J.: Prentice-Hall, 1969.

Trilling, Lionel, "A Speech on Robert Frost: A Cultural Episode." *Partisan Review* 26 (Summer 1959): 445–52.

———. "Commentary of The Waste Land." In *The Experience of Literature.* New York: Holt, Rinehart & Winston, 1967.

Unterrecker, John. *Voyages: A Life of Hart Crane.* New York: Farrar, Straus and Giroux, 1969.

Vendler, Helen. *On Extended Wings: Wallace Stevens' Longer Poems.* Cambridge: Harvard University Press, 1969.

———. *Part of Nature, Part of Us: Modern American Poets.* Cambridge: Harvard University Press, 1980.

Waggoner, Hayatt H. *American Poets from the Puritans to the Present.* New York: Dell, 1968.

Wagner, Jean. *Black Poets of the United States from Paul Laurence Dunbar to Langston Hughes.* Trans. Kenneth Douglas. Urbana: University of Illinois Press, 1973.

Walker, Jayne. *The Making of a Modernist: Gertrude Stein.* Amherst: Massachusetts University Press, 1984.

Walker, Robert H. *The Poet and the Gilded Age: Social Themes in Late 19th Century American Verse.* Philadelphia: University of Pennsylvania Press, 1963.

Whicher, George F. *This Was a Poet.* New York: Charles Scribner's Sons, 1938.

Widmer, Kingsley. *The Literary Rebel.* Carbondale: Southern Illinois University Press, 1965.

Williams, William Carlos. "Louis Zukofsky." *Agenda: Louis Zukofsky: Special Edition* 13, no. 6 (December 1964): 1–4.

Wrenn, John H., and Margaret M. Wrenn. *Edgar Lee Masters.* Boston: Twayne Publishers, 1983.

· Index ·

Index

Index

Index

210–11); *Flagons and Apples*, 202; "Fog," 207; "The Great Explosion," 212; "Love Subject," 203; "Natural Music," 206; "Point Joe," 206; "The Purse-Seine," 208–9; *Roan Stallion*, 205; "The Rock and the Hawk," 208; *Selected Letters*, 202; *Selected Poems (1938 and 1965)*, 202; "Shine, Perishing Republic," 207–8; "Shiva," 209; "The Tower Beyond Tragedy," 205–6; *Tamar*, 203; "To the Stone Cutters," 206–7

Johnson, James Weldon, 56, 60, 63

Johnson, Thomas H., 18

Joyce, James, 126, 236, 237

Juhasz, Suzanne, 18

Kazin, Alfred: *Starting Out in the Thirties*, 236

Keats, John, 61

Kennedy, President John F., 50, 240

Kenner, Hugh, 95, 244

Kenyon Review, the, 218

King, Stanley, 43

Kirk, Russell, 95

Kreymborg, Alfred, 173

Krutch, Joseph Wood: *The Modern Temper*, 179

Lawrence, D. H., 78

Lazarus, Emma, 25; "The New Colossus," 25; *Songs of a Semite*, 25

Lewis, R. W. B., 179, 188

Lewis, Sinclair, 52

Lewis, Wyndham, 125, 126; *Time and Western Man*, 126

Lind, Jenny, 7

Lindsay, Vachel, 23, 32, 53–54, 63; "The Congo," 53, 54; "Bryan, Bryan, Bryan, Bryan," 53; "General William Booth Enters into Heaven," 53; "The Santa Fe Trail," 53; "Simon Legree:—A Negro Sermon," 54

Locke, Alain, 55, 56, 60

Lodge, George Cabot, 24–25; *Cain, a Drama*, 24; *Herakles*, 24

Longfellow, Henry Wadsworth, 21, 33, 44, 50; *Hiawatha*, 235

Lord, Judge Otis P., 16

Lowell, Amy, 62, 66, 70–77, 125; "The Basket," 73–75; "A Critical Fable," 76; *A Dome of Many-Coloured Glass*, 72; *Fir Flower Tablets*, 77; "Patterns," 74–75; *Pictures of the Floating World*, 77; *Sword Blades and Poppy Seeds*, 72; *Tendencies in American Poetry*, 75–76

Lowell, James Russell, 21

Lowell, Robert, 231

Lyon, Mary, 9

MacDowell Colony, 36

Manifest Destiny, 19

Masters, Edgar Lee, 23, 32, 52–53; *Spoon River Anthology*, 52–53, 95

Mariani, Paul: *A Useable Past*, 138, 167

Maritain, Jacques, 245

Martz, Louis, 82

Marvell, Andrew, 108

Marx, Karl, 65–66, 68

McKay, Claude, 56–57; "America," 57; *Banana Bottom*, 57; *Banjo*, 57; "Baptism," 57; *Constab Ballads*, 56; *Harlem: Negro Metropolis*, 57; *Harlem Shadows*, 57; *Home to Harlem*, 57; "If We Must Die," 57; *A Long Way from Home*, 57; "The Lynching," 57; "The White City," 57; "To the White Fiends," 57

McLow, Jackson, 85

Melville, Herman, 3, 4, 179, 187, 228

Mifflin, Lloyd, 21

Millay, Edna St. Vincent, 50, 54, 55, 229; "Poem and Prayer for an Invading Army," 54; "Renascence," 54

Miller, Joaquin, 21

Mistral, Gabriela, 64

Modernism, 65–93, 214–52

Monet, Claude, *Sunrise, An Impression*, 68, 142

Monroe, Harriet, 45, 50, 51, 53, 54, 71, 72, 77, 89, 99, 189–90, 231; "Symposium on Marianne Moore," 89

Moody, William Vaughan, 21, 22–25, 34, 50; "The Bracelet of Grass," 24; *The Death of Eve*, 24; *The Fire-Bringer*, 24; "Gloucester Moors," 23; *The Masque of Judgment*, 24, 34; "Ode in a Time of Hesitation," 23–24

Moore, Marianne, 66, 88–94, 126; *Complete Poems*, 89, 91; "The Mind Is an Enchanted Thing," 90–91; *Observations*, 89; *Poems*, 89;

Index

"Poetry," 89–90, 94, 235; "The Steeplejack," 91–93
Morrison, Kay and Theodore, 43
Moulton, Louise Chandler, 21
Mount Holyoke Female Seminary, 9
Munson, Gorham, 173, 174

Nardi, Marcia, 162, 167
Nelson, Ernest, 173
New Criticism, the, 218, 219, 224, 230, 231
New Negro Renaissance, the. See Harlem Renaissance
Newton, Benjamin F., 15–16
Nicholls, Peter, 135
Niedecker, Lorine, 231, 249–52; "Condensary," 250; From this Condensary: The Complete Writings, 252; "Mother Geese," 250; "My Friend Tree," 252; My Life by Water, 252; New Goose, 252; North Central, 252; "Poet's Work," 249; TCG, 252
Norcross, Frances, 7, 8, 13, 15
Norcross, Louise, 7, 8, 13, 15

Objectivists, the, 230–52
Objectivist Anthology, 231, 247
Objectivist Press (formerly To the Publisher Press), 231–32, 241
Olson, Charles, 201
Oppen, George, 231, 241–47; exile in Mexico, 243–44; "Blood from the Stone," 244; Collected Poems, 244; Discrete Series, 242–43; "Drawing," 242; "A Language of New York," 247; Materials, 244; "Of Being Numerous," 244–45, 247; Primitive, 244; "Psalm," 245–46; "Route," 244; "The Source," 245
Ostriker, Alicia, 18
Over-Soul, the, 1–2

Pearce, Roy Harvey, 20
Poe, Edgar Allan, 3, 11, 18, 31, 41, 53, 54
Poetry (magazine), 45, 50, 51, 54, 70, 77, 89, 99, 190, 231
Pollock, Jackson, 175
Pope, Alexander, 190
Pound, Ezra, 20, 45, 51, 62, 66, 67, 68, 70–71, 72, 73, 76, 77, 78, 79, 95–96, 98, 102–3, 120–37, 138, 150, 152, 155, 167, 169, 174, 178, 215, 231, 232, 233, 235, 236, 237, 238,

240, 248; The ABC of Reading, 121–22; A Lume Spento, 123; "Ancient Music," 126; "At a Station in the Metro," 71; "Ballad of the Goodly Frere," 126; The Cantos, 122, 126–34, 159, 180, 185, 240; A Draft of XVI Cantos for the Beginning of a Poem of Some Length, 126–27; Drafts and Fragments of Cantos, 127; "Exultations," 123; "Homage to Sextus Propertius," 126; fascism and anti-semitism, 135–37; "How I Began," 124; "How to Read," 121; "Hugh Selwyn Mauberly," 125; "I Gather the Lambs of Osiris," 122; "Na Audiart," 126; Personae, 123; The Pisan Cantos, 81, 128; "Portrait D'une Femme," 126; A Quinzane for This Yule, 123; "The Seafarer," 126, 129; "Sestina Altaforte," 124; "The Spirit of Romances," 123–24
Prynne, Hester, 18
Puritanism, 4, 5, 9, 10, 20, 47–48, 49

Quinn, John, 69, 102, 125

Rakoski, Carl, 231, 247–49; Amulet, 248; Collected Poems, 248; Selected Poems, 247; "The Vow," 248; "A Word with Conscience," 248
Ransom, John Crowe, 214, 215–18, 219; "Bells for John Whiteside's Daughter," 216–17; I'll Take My Stand, 217; "Necrological," 216; New Criticism, 218; Poems about God, 215; Selected Poems, 217
Reese, Lizette Woodworth, 21, 25–26; "After Disaster," 26; "The Dust," 26; "Lord, Oft I Come," 25; "In Praise of Common Things," 25
Rexroth, Kenneth, 84, 231
Reznikoff, Charles, 231, 232–34, 247; Complete Poems, 232; "Early History of a Writer," 233; Holocaust, 233; "Kaddish," 234; Rhythms, 232; "Suburban River: "Summer," 232; Testimony, 233
Rich, Adrienne, 18
Richards, Henry, 35
Richards, I. A., 218
Richards, Laura E., 35
Riley, James Whitcomb, 21
Robinson, Edwin Arlington, 19, 22, 27–28, 32–40, 41, 195; the

Index

Index

· *About the Authors* ·

Alan Shucard received his Ph.D. from the University of Arizona and is professor of English at the University of Wisconsin-Parkside. His published works include articles and reviews on American, Afro-American, and Commonwealth literature and *American Poetry: The Puritans through Walt Whitman, Countee Cullen,* and two collections of poems, *The Gorgon Bag* and *The Louse on the Head of a Yawning Lord.*

Fred Moramarco teaches literature at San Diego State University and has written widely on modern and contemporary American poetry for many literary periodicals, including *American Poetry Review, American Literature, Mosaic,* and *American Book Review.* He is also the author of *Edward Dahlberg* in the Twayne United States Authors Series, and his own poetry has appeared in a number of little magazines.

William Sullivan is currently professor of English and coordinator of American Studies at Keene State College, University System of New Hampshire. His research, presentations, and writings focus on modern, contemporary pooetry and the ideological shifts in American culture.